RESEARCH
IN
PHILOSOPHY

RESEARCH IN PHILOSOPHY

By
D.D. CHATURVEDI
M.A. (Psy.), M.Lib.I.Sc.

ANMOL PUBLICATIONS PVT. LTD.
NEW DELHI - 110 002 (INDIA)

ANMOL PUBLICATIONS PVT. LTD.
4374/4B, Ansari Road, Daryaganj
New Delhi - 110 002

Research in Philosophy

First Edition, 1999
ISBN 81-261-0208-X

PRINTED IN INDIA

Published by J.L. Kumar for Anmol Publications Pvt. Ltd., New Delhi - 110 002 and Printed at Mehra Offset Press, Delhi.

Dedicated to My Eleder Brother
Acharya Shri Lakshmi Dutt Chaturvedi
with respect

CONTENTS

INTRODUCTION

Academic Researches are being carried out in all the disciplines by the scholars in India even before the independence. With the emergence of University Grants Commission in fifties the research work got much impetus and the number of Ph.Ds rose alarmingly. In the process of doing so a few scholars choose the topics of their research on which the work had already been done, resulting in repeatition and loss of time, labour and money not only of the researchers but of the nation as the whole. This prompted me to collect, compile and publish the classified list of the titles on which research works have already been done.

The present publication "The Research in Philosophy" is my seventh such classified list and the first in humanities. The titles included in this publication are from the very beginning to the end of 1997. All possible efforts have been made to collect and compile the maximum number of titles got from different sources but it may not be proper to claim that all the titles have been included in this publication. The titles left out may be listed in the second edition, if reported.

The titles listed here in this book have been placed under the Subject Headings currently known. The theses submitted in other than the English language have been identified with the first letter of the languages in bracket before the name of the University in the entries. Few Ph.Ds and D.Litt. degrees in the subject of philosophy have been submitted in Department of Sanskrit. In such a case the letter(s) in bracket have been added after the names of the Institutions.

The theses submitted in the Department of Sanskrit and included in this book were received in transliterated forms. Hence there may be some mistakes. It is unavoidable. Hope the readers will not mind it.

An alphabetical list of the scholars with the entry numbers are given in the end of the book to enable the research workers to locate the entries easily. An abbreviation of the names of the universities and the Institution are also given along with the abbreviation of the languages.

I am grateful to the persons, Institutions and the agencies for rendering me help in the process of collection of the informations. My special thanks goes to the Library, MMH College, Ghaziabad and its employees for extending their cooperation in completing this work. I express my gratitude to my son Shri Dhirendra and my wife and others for their support and help from time to time. The teachers and research workers of subject Philosophy will welcome this publication.

I express my special thanks to Mr. J.L. Kumar and his team at M/S. Anmol Publications (Private) Ltd. for bringing out this book in short time.

D.D. Chaturvedi

1

PHILOSOPHICAL CONCEPTS

1. Agrawal, Gitika
Rastriya ekata mein darshan tatha dharma ka yogdan (H).
Rohilkhand (Hist.), 1993.

2. Alexander, Charls P.
A few problems in psychotherapy and human emotions: An exploration.
NEHU, 1995.

3 Baksi, Kalipada
Philosophy and analysis.
Calcutta, 1976.

4. Balachandran, Jaya
State and philosophy of human resource development: The Indian reality.
Osmania, 1996.

5. Bansal, Krishna
The problem of description in philosophy with particular reference to Wittgestein and Husserl.
Delhi, 1982.

6. Bhagwat, Shailja
Cognitive discrepancy and attitude change.
Jabalpur, 1997.

7. Bhattacharya, Kalidas
An enquiry into the Fundamentals of Philosophy.
Calcutta, 1946.

8. Bhattacharya, Mridula
Falsity and reality: An Advaita approach.
Burdwan, 1997.

9. Bilthare, Anurag
Adhunik Bharatiya chintan mein ashubh kee samasya (H).
Saugar, 1993.

10. Chaudhari, Anil Kumar
The nature and purpose of evolution of Bergson and Sri Aurobindo.
Allabahad, 1982.

11. Chaudhary, Prabasjiban
Foundation of philosophy of science.
Calcutta 1951.

12. Datta, S.
The problem of relation in contemporary philosophy.
Allahabad, 1940.

13. Daya Krishna
The nature of philosophy,
Delhi, 1953.

14. Deka, Paru
Therapeutic conception of philosophy with special reference to John Wisdom.
BHU, 1979.

15. Devaraja, N.K.
Philosophy of Culture (D. Litt.).
Lucknow, 1956.

16. Elkis, D.
The concept of Omega point with philosophy of Pierre

Teilhard De Chardin.
Kerala, 1981.

17. Farnando, Joseph Edison
A critique of Thomas Kuhnis thesis of inconmensurability.
Poona, 1982.

18. Francis, B.
Interdependence and interpenetration philosophical thought and revelation.
Calicut, 1994.

19. Freeman, Joseph Benedict.
Science cause and god (D. Litt.).
Madras, 1944.

20. Ghosh, Dipika
Some modern criticism of sense dalum theory of perception.
Calcutta, 1969.

21. Gyory, R.A.
The emergence of being through Indian and Greek thought.
Bombay, 1976.

22. Maitra, Sisir Kumar
The neo-romantic movement in the contemporary philosophy.
Calcutta, 1919.

23. Mallick, Arindan
The methodology social science: A phenomenological approach.
NBU, 1985.

24. Methew, E.J. Joseph
Alternative perspective: Indian and western problems in their comparison.
Karnataka, 1991.

25. Nathan, Parimala
St. John of the cross and Mahikka vacagar: Some aspects of their mystical time.
Madras, 1985.

26. Pethe, Sadanand
Psychological foundations of philosophy.
Shivaji, 1986.

27. Rai, Surendra Nath
Ashinsa aur karuna: Samaj darshan kee prasangikata mein (H).
Durgawati, 1994.

28. Raju, P.T.
Thought and reality: Hegeliavism and Advaita.
Calcutta, 1935.

29. Ramanna, P.
The welfare of the disabled in Karnataka: A philosophical and socio-political analysis.
Banglore, 1997.

30. Ramanayya, Guntupalli Rakyalakshmi
The nature of proper names.
Nagpur, 1994.

31. Rao, C. Subramanyeswar
Jean-Paul Sartre: Conception of nothingness.
Osmania, 1967.

32. Rao, T. Venketa Seshagiri
New light on fundamental problems including nature and functions of Arts.
Madras, 1930.

33. Ray, Phanibhusan
Culture of harmony.
Calcutta, 1943.

34. Ray Chaudhuri, Sanat Kumar
A study of freedom: Metaphysical and scientific point of view.
Calcutta, 1961

35. Roy, Krishna
The Cartesian Cogito: A fresh approach to subjectivity in the light of some contemporary development.
Jadavpur, 1978.

36. Sahu, Dibaka
The concept o. stice: A critical study.
Berhampur, 1987.

37. Sampath, R.
The philosophy of Ernst Cassirer.
Madras, 1981.

38. Saryu Prasad
Philosophy of modern science with special reference to Einstein and Heisenberg.
Ranchi, 1976.

39. Sengupta, Kalyan Kumar
Language and philosophy.
Calcutta, 1965.

40. Singh, Kalpana Randhir
Kalingwood ka samajdarshan: Ek vivechanatmak adhyayan (H).
Indore, 1978.

41. Singh, Paras Nath
Asan evam shareerik tatha manashik rog nivaran (H).
BHU, 1994.

42. Singh, S.A.
Gautam and Aristotle: A comparative and critical study.
Bombay, 1985.

43. Sobrinho, B.J.C.N.
Scientific realism and consciousness: An application of the philosophy of science.
IIT, Bombay, 1979.

44. Sreenivasan, M.R.
The concept of justice, legal, moral, social and political.
Madras, 1987.

45. Surendra Kumar
Darshan ka swaroop (H).
Magadh, 1976.

46. Thapak, Rajani
Marxvad punjivad evam niskatma manavvad ka samikshatmak adhyayan (H).
BHU, 1994.

2

METAPHYSICS

47. Abdul Latif
An approach to the problem of the infinite.
Poona, 1987.

48. Agrawal, Ramaraghunath
The ultimate reality in human experience.
Poona, 1984.

49. Bagchi, Amalendu
Asthetics in modern psychology.
Calcutta, 1951.

50. Bandyopadhyay, Archana
Models of Meta Philosophy.
Calcutta, 1975.

51. Bandyopadhyay, Ranjana
The nature of truth.
Jadavpur, 1979.

52. Barathwal, Harish Chander
Bharatiya tatwagyan aur adhunik vigyan: Tulanatmak adhyayan (H).
Agra, 1977.

53. Barlingay, Surendra S.
The problem of change.
Nagpur, 1957.

54. Barua, Chandra Prabha
Modern Indian aesthetic thought.
Gauhati, 1991.

55. Barua, Girish Chandra
A critical study of the Vedañtic concept of ultimate reality with special reference to S. Radhakrishnan.
Gauhati, 1985.

56. Beray Evelyn
A comparative study of the metaphysics of Sankara Vijnanvadi Buddhism and Burkley.
Lucknow, 1957.

57. Bhagya Leela, R.
Studies in the philosophy of change.
Venkateswara, 1977.

58. Bhakt Dass
Brahmtatwa shugatatvyoh sameekshanam (S).
Sampurnanand, 1993.

59. Bhandari, Vidya
Tathata ka darshanik adhyayan (H).
Ravi Shankar, 1987.

60. Bharat Prasad
Nature of truth: A critical study.
Patna, 1979.

61. Bhattacharya, Harisatya
Reals on the Jain metaphysics.
Calcutta, 1947.

62. Bhattacharya, Janaki Ballabh
Negation.
Calcutta, 1948.

63. Bhattacharya, Prabhakar
Value orientation and modern society.
Burdwan, 1995.

64. Bhyrappa, Santesivara Lingannaieh
Truth and beauty: A study in the correlation between the epistemic and the aesthetic.
Baroda, 1963.

65. Brij Kishore Prasad
The idealistic metaphysics of F.H. Bradley.
Patna, 1970.

66. Chacko, K.C.
Metaphysical implications of Gandhian thought.
Calicut, 1982.

67. Chakraborti, Jitendra Kumar
Resurrection of metaphysics.
Calcutta, 1937.

68. Chakraborti, Kshitij Chandra
Vision reality of swarupanudhava.
Calcutta, 1966.

69. Chakraborti, Nivedita
A study of some fundamental ontological concept with special reference to time.
NBU, 1994.

70. Chakraborti, Sudhir Chandra
Satyapratistha vada.
Vishwa Bharati, 1975.

71. Chanda, Nina
Social authority and personal freedom.
Delhi, 1992.

72. Chatterjee, Anuradha
Good and evil.
Vishwa Bharati, 1979.

73. Chaubey, Awadhesh Kumar
Adhyatma vigyanyoh Sanshleshanatmakam adhgyanam (S).
Sampurnanand, 1993.

74. Chaudhuri, Nomita
Theory of universal: An Indian approach.
Burdwan, 1989.

75. Das, Adhar Chandra
Negative fact, negation and truth.
Calcutta, 1940.

76. Das, Dipty Moya
Gandhi's doctrines of truth and non-violence: A critical study.
NEHU, 1986.

77. Dash, Kailash Chandra
Knowledge of self and other mind.
Poona, 1993.

78. Datta, Manjula Parruck
A phenomenological study of Abraham Meslows concept of self actualisation with special reference to Rabindra Nath Tagore.
Vishwa Bharati, 1993.

79. Datta, Namita Cod
Concept of finite God: A critical survey.
Calcutta, 1980.

80. Dewashi, Mahadev
Some logio-epistemin problems regarding casual asymmetry with special reference to G.H. Von Wright.
Hyderabad, 1992.

81. Diverkar, Paramanand
Contribution of neotheism to ontology.
Bombay, 1965.

82. Dolas, Chitra Madhavrao
Problems of universals.
Nagpur, 1995.

83. Dravid, Raja Ram
The problem of universal in Indian philosophy.
BHU, 1958.

84. Dubey, Shri Prakash
Treatment of appearance in Sankara and Bradley.
BHU, 1967.

85. Garola, M.P.
Reinvestigation of matter spirit relationship in the light of recent discoveries.
Rohilkhand, 1983.

86. Ghosh, Manjulika
Formative knowledge and truth.
NBU, 1989.

87. Ghosh, Preeti Ranjan
Aesthetic experience and artistic intention.
Delhi, 1991.

88. Ghosh, Sanjib Kumar
Rehabilitation of metaphysics.
Ravindra Bharati, 1975.

89. Ghosh, Sukhamay
Concept of truth.
Jadavpur, 1974.

90. Goswami, Kumud Ranjan
Kant's metaphysical exposition of the concept of place: An exagetical and critical study.
Calcutta, 1989.

91. Gupta, Dikshit
Descriptive metaphysics: Its scope and prospects.
Calcutta, 1978.

92. Gupta, Ranjana
Theories of truth in Western philosophy.
Jodhpur, 1980.

93. Herbert, G.S.
A study of the metaphysics of time.
Venkateswara, 1967.

94. Janedhan, K.B.
A critical study of tribals aesthetic approach to reality.
Poona, 1983.

95. Jauhari, Prakash Narayan
Expressionism in contemporary astheties.
Allahabad, 1963.

96. Jha, Srikant
A critical study of Bertrand Russell's metaphysics.
Patna, 1979.

97. Jhanji, Rekha
A study in recent theories of aesthetics meaning.
Panjab, 1971.

98. Joshi, M.V.
Metaphysics of individuation (D. Litt.).
BHU, 1938.

99. Kamala Kumari
The motion of truth in Buddhism and pragamatism: A comparative study.
Bihar, 1989.

100. Kavimandan, Bhaskar Janardhan
Critical study of tribals aesthetics approach to reality.
Poona, 1983.

101. Krishnamachari, C.T.
On some spatial representation and other significance for the problems of recognition.
Madras, 1951.

102. Kunkolienher, Kamala Devi
Perspective on mind and consciousness: A critical evaluation.
Goa, 1993.

103. Lawande, Ganesh Narayan
The problem of universals.
Bombay, 1941.

104. Lobzang, Tsewang
Madhyamikcs conception of truth and error with reference to Acharya Tsang Khopa.
BHU, 1989.

105. Mahapatra, Himanshu Sekhar Das
Metaphysies of knowledge: A critical study in Indian philosophy with special reference to Buddhism, Nyaya and Advaita Vedant.
Kurukshetra, 1992.

106. Mathur, Raj
Bharatiya darshan mein mokshya ka swaroop (H).
Jodhpur, 1978.

107. Mehta, Usha Rani
A study of Kants metaphysics of experience.
Jabalpur, 1971.

108. Mercy, Halen
The metaphilosophy of Meritz Lazarus: A critical exposition.
Hyderabad, 1968.

109. Mishra, Madhuri
Problem of evil with special reference to Sri Aurobindo.
Bihar, 1982.

110. Mitra, Surana
Good, evil and beyond in Indian philosophy.
Calcutta, 141.

110a. Mitra, Malati
The absolute and appearance.
Calcutta, 1955.

111. Mukherjee, R.N.
Aesthetic Theory
BHU, 1956.

112. Mukhopadhyay, Satindra Kumar
The university of the world and the ego.
Calcutta, 1941.

113. Nag, Triplikana
Science, language and metaphysics: An enquiry into a reorientation of metaphysics in the light of contemporary philosophy of science.
Vishwa Bharati, 1972.

114. Nagendra
A critical study of metaphysics of Swami Chandradhar.
Meerut, 1973.

115. Nair, Sujatha M.G.
The mind brain identity theory: A critical study.
Calicut, 1986.

116. Nishabala
Goodness as process, necessity and significance: A study in Gandhian philosophy.
Delhi, 1992.

117. Nighoshar, Yogini Govindrao
Universals and particulars: An essay on contextual analysis.
Baroda, 1977.

118. Pal, Bibaddhanjan
Sattavad: Theory of reality.
Calcutta, 1990.

119. Panda, Ganesh Prasad
The concept of time in Indian grammatical tradition.
Poona, 1992.

120. Pandey, K.C.
Comparative aesthetics (D. Litt.)
Lucknow, 1948.

121. Pandey, Krantiprabha Purushottam
Critical examination of Kants aesthetics with reference to beautiful.
Poona, 1979.

122. Pandey, Rajendra Prasad
Problem of Fact.
Saugar, 1961.

123. Pandey, Satya
Samuel Alexender ke darshan ka alochanatmak adhyayan (H).
Allahabad, 1990.

124. Pant, Uma
Philosophy of PF Strawsan in the context of analytical movement in UK.
BHU, 1982.

125. Patel, V.K.
The theory of relation in contemporary logic and metaphysics.
Gujarat, 1986.

126. Pillai, A.S. Narayana
The psychology of aesthetics response.
Madras, 1951.

127. Purohit, Mahadishwar Anjali
The concept of change.
Bombay, 1993.

128. Rai, Shailendra Kumar
Mahatma Gandhi ke darshan mein satya kee avadharana (H).
BHU, 1993.

129. Rajendra Prasad
Vivekanand aur Gandhi ke paripekshya mein manav evam jagat ka swaroop (H).
BHU, 1994.

130. Ramaiha, G. Saudara
Native of destiny of soul in Indian philosophy.
Andhra, 1978.

131. Ramlal, James
The problem of being in Sankara and Heidegger.
Poona, 1971.

132. Rao, G.N.
A critical enquiry into meaning of life.
Bombay, 1991.

133. Rao, Y. Sundara
The world around us: A study in metaphysics.
Madras, 1927.

134. Ray, Kabita
The problem of historical objectivity: A historical and critical approach.
Calcutta, 1989.

135. Richard, Ramosh, P.
The dipolarity of the absolute whiteadian cosmology: A critical evaluation.
Delhi, 1991.

136. Rizvi, S.M.A.
Metaphysical concept of Dr. Iqbal.
Bihar, 1997.

137. Roy Chaudhury, Meenakshi
Method of metaphysics.
Jadavpur, 1972.

138. Roy, Manashi
A analysis of truth relation.
Nagpur, 1980.

139. Roy, Samarendra K.
Language and reality: A study in the metaphysics of Wittgensteins tractatus.
NEHU, 1985.

140. Sahai, Pooranima
Kant tatha Hussarl:
Ek tulanatmak adhyayan (H).
Gorakhpur, 1990.

141. Sahu, Bhaskar Chand
The problem of other mind.
Durgawati, 1993.

142. Salshingikar, Prasanna Kumar
Indian mysticism.
Durgawati, 1994.

143. Sanuillah Mir
Metaphilosophy of John Wisdom.
AMU, 1986.

144. Sarkar, Tushar Kanti
The conception of space time in the philosophy of Samuel Alexander.
Calcutta, 1967.

145. Saxena, Rakesh
A comparative study of ontology and epistemology of Spinoza and Marx-Engels.
JNU, 1994.

146. Saxena, Sushil Kumar
Metaphysics of Bradley.
Delhi, 1964.

147. Sengupta, Satyabhama
A critical examination of the ontological proof for the existence of God.
BHU, 1977.

148. Sen, Ramendra Kumar
Philosophical and physiological background of aesthetics enjoyment.
Calcutta, 1969.

149. Sen, Sanat Kumar
A study of metaphysics of Spinoza.
Calcutta, 1965.

150. Sen, Susanta Kumar
A study of universal.
Vishwa Bharati, 1966.

151. Sharma, Ghanasyam
The concept of man in Juche ideology: A critical study.
Rajasthan, 1993.

152. Sharma, Rameshwar Prasad
A critical and comprehensive study of the problem of evil.
Patna, 1973.

153. Sharma, Shamala Ramnath
Convergence of modern trends in aesthetic towards individualisation.
Bombay, 1962.

154. Shukla, Aditya
On universals.
Calcutta, 1985

155. Shukla, Bibbo Rani
Astik darshano mein moksh ke swaroop evam sadhanon ka alochanatmak aur tulanatmak adhyayan (S).
Gorakhpur, 1978.

156. Siddharsharama, D.P.
The metaphysics and mysticism of Sri Nagarjuna Shivayogi.
Bangalore, 1991.

157. Singh, Indu Prakash
An Advaitik appraisal of T.H. Greene's metaphysics.
Allahabad, 1958.

158. Singh, Nagendra
Prachin nyaya darshan Shaiva Siddhant darshan mein Atma: Ek tulanatmak evam Sameekshatmak vivechan (H).
BHU, 1993.

159. Singh, Mirbhai
The concept of reality in Sikh philosophy.
Panjabi, 1985.

160. Singh, Rajkumar Sanagaba
A study of the problem of other minds.
Manipur, 1996.

161. Singh, S. Syam Kishore
The nature of aesthetics experience: A comparative study of Kant and Abhinava Gupta.
Gauhati, 1989.

162. Sinha, Premi
A critical and reflective study of Kant's critique of theistic proofs.
Magadh, 1990.

163. Sinha, Shashi Bhusan Prasad
Some studies about metaphysics with special reference to some anti-metaphysical movement (D. Litt.).
Bihar, 1967.

164. Sinha, Vijay Kumar
Ontological argument for gods' existence.
Magadh, 1981.

165. Sreenivasulu, M.
Studies in the problems of the test of truth and error in Indian philosophy.
Venkateswara, 1990.

166. Srivastava, Arun Kumar
Problem of the space and time in contemporary philosophy of physical science.
BHU, 1989.

167. Srinivas, G.
Darsanesu monestatva: Paviseelanam.
Rastriya Sanskrit, 1993.

168. Srivastava, Harish Chandra
The metaphysical contribution of Santana to contemporary philosophy.
Allahabad, 1962.

169. Syed, Alam Khundmiri
Iqbal's concept of time: Its relation to contemporary western thought.
Osmania, 1989.

170. Tiwari, B.G.
Lenins theory of perception and his doctrine of absolute and relative truth.
Agra, 1948.

171. Tiwari, Ravi
A comparative study of Paul Tillich and Sankara with special reference to the concept of being.
Durgawati, 1985.

172. Tripathi, Gadhadhar
Bharatiya darshan mein anatmabad ka vikas: Boudh darshan ke vishesh sandarbh mein (S).
Kanpur, 1978.

173. Untoo, Gulam Mohammad
Metaphysics of Shaikh Ahmad Sirhimali.
AMU, 1982.

174. Valiaparampil, V. Thomas
Extentialist: The treatment of time in thought.
Delhi, 1984.

175. Verma, Ashok Kumar
Metaphysical foundation of Acharya Vinoba Bhave's thought (D. Litt.).
Patna, 1973.

176. Verma, Ashok Kumar
An evaluation of Sankar as critique of rival metaphysical systems.
BHU, 1972.

177. Verma, Ashok Kumar
The nature and function of moral judgement with special reference to two terms, good and right.
Bihar, 1971.

178. Verma, Samerendra Kumar
The nature and function of metaphysics.
Magadh, 1966.

179. Verma, V.K.
A study in the metaphysics of ideal language philosophy.
Jabalpur, 1979.

180. Vinod Kumar
The concept of space and time in the 20th century philosophy.
Kurukshetra, 1976.

181. Wahid Abdul Quaseem Fazal
A comprehensive study of the metaphysics and Aristotle and Ibn Rushd.
AMU, 1983.

182. Warhadpande, Nilkanth Raghunath
The problem of motion.
Nagpur, 1961.

3

EPISTEMOLOGY

183. Abdur Sattar
Humanism of Gandhi and MN Roy: A comparative study.
Venkateswara, 1989.

184. Acharya, Bhanu Shankar Nilkanth
Reconciliation of contradictory statements in the work regarding practical and applied astrology.
Bombay, 1952.

185. Agrawal, Murarilal
Traditional Indian concept of value in the context of contemporary scientific progress.
Allahabad, 1968.

186. Altekar, Eknath V.
The role of imagination in science.
Poona, 1991.

187. Amarjit Kaur
Concept of man in contemporary philosophy.
Punjabi, 1990.

188. Annammal, S.
Humenism in Bible (T).
Calicut, 1989.

189. Arora, Rajat Kumar
A study in contemporary Indian aestheties with special reference to Tagore and Aurobindo.
Delhi, 1965.

190. Arora, Rekha,
The development of self from phenomenology to existentialism.
Delhi, 1990.

191. Ashok Kumar
The concept of man in Existentialism and Buddhism.
Lucknow, 1968.

192. Atreya, J.P.
The concept of mind and its function in ancient Indian thought.
Ranchi, 1909.

193. Bạbu Ram
Bharatiya aur Pashchatya darshanon mein antahakaran ka ek tulanatmak adhyayan (H).
Gurukul, 1989.

194. Bagchi, Kalyan Kumar
The spiritual psychology of Krishna Chandra Bhattacharya: A study of the Subject as freedom.
Calcutta, 1978.

195. Bajaj, Veena
A critical study of Gilbert Roleis concept of mind.
Delhi, 1989.

196. Bala Subramaniam, P.
Concept of presupposition: A study.
Madras, 1980.

197. Bali, Devraj
Contemporary Indian humanism with special reference to Sri Aurobindo.
Agra, 1970.

198. Bandyopadhyay, Amita
Problem of contrafactual conditionals,
Calcutta, 1981.

199. Bandyopadhyay, Sankari Prasad
Knowledge of self.
Calcutta, 1966.

200. Bandyopadhyay, Saradendu
Psychoanalytic view of mind (D. Litt.).
Calcutta, 1982.

201. Banerjee, Bijay Bhusan
Bharatiya darshano muktivada (B).
Calcutta, 1952.

202. Basu, Sunanda
Humanistic ideals in contemporary philosophy with reference to Sartre.
Burdwan, 1989.

203. Basu, Sutapa
Consciousness and being in the philosophy of Sri Aurobindo.
Burdwan, 1990.

204. Batra, Usha Rani
A critical study of the laws of cause and chance in philosophy and physics.
Kurukshetra, 1976.

205. Begam Bilkis Banu
Gilberts Syles philosophy of mind: An examination.
NEHU, 1986.

206. Bhan, Rajnath
Deterioration in interest as a function of insecure mental health during and after the period of certain academic specialisations.
Kurukshetra, 1971.

207. Bhandare, S.V.
Status of memory as Prama and Pramana in Indian epistemology.
Bombay, 1991.

208. Bharati, Baleshwar Prasad
Penarjanma vichar ke samaj sastriya adhar: Manusmriti ke alok mein.
Magadh, 1993.

209. Bhargava, Sriganesh
Development trends in prediction of life performance.
Gujarat (Psy), 1984.

210. Bhatt, G.P.
Epistemology of the Bhatta's School of Purva mimansa.
BHU, 1956.

211. Bhatt, P.R.
Concept and meaning: A criteriological analysis.
IIT, Kanpur, 1980.

212. Bhattacharya, Chandidas
Meaning and bearers of meaning.
Jadavpur, 1982.

213. Bhave, Shrikrishna Mahadev
A philosophy of mathematics with special reference to the mathematical reality and the mathematical activity.
Poona, 1985.

214. Bhawmik, Mira
Concept of freedom.
Jadavpur, 1991.

215. Bist, K.
Our knowledge of future: A comparative study in epistemology.
Delhi, 1990.

216. Biswas, Gautam
Understanding man: An orientation to philosophical anthropology with special reference to Martin Buber.
IIT, Kanpur, 1985.

217. Bosmia, I.J.
Nature of self in Sri Aurobindo's philosophy.
Saurashtra, 1984.

218. Brahma, C.P.
Theory of causation in Indian philosophy.
Agra, 1946.

219. Brijraj
Sant darshan aur Kabir ka rahasyavad (H).
BHU, 1988.

220. Chakraborti, A.
Mind body dualism: A philosophical investigation.
NEHU, 1989.

221. Chakraborti, Dilip Kumar
The concept of self in psychoanalytic schools with special reference to Jung.
Gauhati, 1977.

222. Chakraborti, Satinath
A philosophico-sociological study of cognitive life.
Calcutta, 1979.

223. Chakraborti, Sibapada
Analysis and philosophy.
Ravindra Bharati, 1977.

224. Chandra Sekhara, H.L.
Nature of reality and the individual self—according to Annamocharya.
Mysore, 1986.

225. Chaturvedi, Ila
Humanistic tendencies in Twentieth Century Indian thought.
Patna, 1970.

226. Chaturvedi, Ramadhar
Chandra Shrangonnati.
Sampurnanand, 1966.

227. Chatterjee, Anjana
Studies in the theories of probability
Ravindra Bharati, 1983.

228. Chatterjee, Margaret
Our knowledge of other selves.
Delhi, 1961.

229. Chattopadhyay, Ganga Shankar
Ends and means.
Calcutta, 1980.

230. Chattopadhyay, Rama
Personal memory: An analysis of its meaning and logic.
Calcutta, 1983.

231. Chaudhuri, Anita
The concept of humanism in Vivekanand.
Gorakhpur, 1987.

232. Chaudhuri, Maha Sweta
Epistemology with or without a knowing mind, a reappraisal of Poppers theory of knowledge.
Jadavpur, 1988.

233. Chaudhuri, Mohammed Ashraf Ali
The true way to purify soul in the Gita by the side of Koran.
Ravindra Bharati, 1989.

234. Chaudhuri, Nirja Kant
Image worship is Ancient India.
Bihar, 1965.

235. Chaudhuri, Santimay
The concept of Prana with special reference to Nyaya Vaishesika mimansa and Buddhist system.
Vishwa Bharati, 1988.

236. Chennakesavam, Saraswati
Concept of mind in Indian philosophy.
Madras, 1957.

237. Chetani, Joseph
The future of man according to the psychic evolutions of Teithard De Chordin and Aurobindo Ghosh.
Indore, 1976.

238. Chopra, Iqbal Narayan
A study of upmana in Indian epistemology.
Kurukshetra, 1981.

239. Clety, Charles-Lawis Winaklemans
The world of persons.
Poona, 1967.

240. Daniel, Ezra Mercellus
Nietzsche on values.
Poona, 1984.

241. Daniel, Shadrock Cheliaraj
Some central problems in Humes philosophy.
NEHU, 1981

242. Das, Aditi
Human existence as freedom from Sartrean perspectives.
Calcutta, 1990.

243. Das, Bimala
A comparative study of the concept of causality in Buddhism and David Hume.
Gauhati, 1982.

244. Das, Gopeswar
The concept of knowledge and philosophies of Descartes, Locks and Hume.
Jadavpur, 1983.

245. Das, Keya
Self in empiricism.
Calicut, 1976.

246. Das, Rasbihari
The self and the ideal.
Calcutta, 1930.

247. Datta, Aruna
The concept of cause.
Calcutta, 1974.

248. De, Nagendra Kumar
The study of Burkleys epistemology with reference to the Yogachara School.
Ravindra Bharati, 1972.

249. De, Pranab Kumar
Role of sense and thought of knowledge.
Calcutta, 1973.

250. Degankar, Archana P.
Imagination, knowledge and action: A philosophical study.
Poona, 1981.

251. Deshpande, Madhukar Govind
Death: A religio-philosophical study: With reference to the problem of value.
Shivaji, 1973.

252. Dhar, Bandana
Some aspect of negation.
Vishwa Bharati, 1979.

253. Divakaran, R.
Epistemology of scientific progress; Kohn Poppen, Labatos and Fe yeraband, reexamined.
JNU, 1985.

254. Dominic, Charlsvas
God, world and soul according to the St. Thomas Aquines and Sri Madhavacharya: A comparative study.
Banglore, 1996.

255. Donald, J. Robert
Philosophical perspective of humanistic psychology.
Poona, 1979.

256. Dravid, Narayan Shastri
Bharatiya gyan shastra (H).
Nagpur, 1963.

257. Dubey, Asha
A critical study of Carnep's logical foundation of probability.
Rajasthan, 1983.

258. Dubey, Rita
Ramanuja theory of knowledge.
Burdwan, 1973.

259. Duraivelu, S.
A comparative study of mysticism in William Blake and Trimular. Madras, 1988.

260. Dwivedi, Bajarang
Bhaskaracharya Siddhant Sameeksha (H).
Sampurnanand, 1968.

261. Dwivedi, Krishna Chandra
Suryagrahana Vimarsh (S).
Sampurnanand, 1964.

262. Dwivedi, Rama Shanker
The development of the conception of Atma in Indian philosophy.
Allahabad, 1953.

263. Elanjmannil, John Chacko
An explanation of explanation.
Kerala (Edu), 1984).

264. Enric, Bece S. Cu
Saiva Tantra: A way of self-awareness.
BHU, 1982.

265. Fachow, W.
Comparative study of the pratimuksa on the basis of its Chinese, Tibetan Sanskrit and Pali versions.
Bombay, 1948.

266. Foster, Lervis A.
Matter, mind and knowledge: A comparative study.
Udaipur, 1971.

267. Gangadharan, P. Sakuntala
The doctrine of being and knowledge in the Advaita Vedanta Sankara presthantreye and prathma granthas.
Andhra, 1991.

268. Gautam, Satyapaul
A study of some problems of explanation of human actions.
Panjab, 1980.

269. George, N.V.
The doctrine of incarnation in Vaishnavism and Christianity: A critical and comparative study.
Gauhati, 1988.

270. Ghatak, Kankalata
Privacy of sansations: Problems of knowledge and ownership.
Burdwan, 1988.

271. Ghosh, Jolly
The problem of the synthetic: A priority.
Jadavpur, 1972.

272. Ghosh, Papia
Bertrand Russell kee gyan mimansa: Ek adhyayan (H).
Durgawati, 1991.

273. Ghosh Robin
A critical examination of rebirth and laws of karma as envisaged in Indian philosophy.
Patna, 1973.

274. Godkari, Visha Arvind
The concept of freedom and determination in modern thought.
Nagpur, 1981.

275. Gopalan, S.
The self and others in the philosophy of Jean Paul Sartre.
Madurai, 1988.

276. Gopinathan, K.
A critical of ordinary language philosophy of later Wittgestein with special reference to language game theory.
JNU, 1993.

277. Goswami, Shipra
A comparative study of the nature and destiny of man in Christianity and Shuddhadvaita.
Udaipur, 1982.

278. Guha, Abhay Kumar
Jivatma in the Brahma Sutras: A comparative study.
Calcutta, 1920.

279. Guha, Sathi
A study of some contemporary views of consciousness.
Burdwan, 1982.

280. Guha, Swapan Kumar
Intellect and emotion in Existantialism.
Ravindra Bharati, 1993.

281. Gupta, Madhu Bala
A study of personality with special reference to yoga and psychoanalysis.
Rohilkhand, 1990.

282. Gupta, Rameshwar Dayal
Introspection on concepts of soul as propounded in

Vedic literature.
Gurukula, 1987.

283. Gupta, Sharda
Validity of knowledge in Indian philosophy.
Kurukshetra, 1965.

284. Gupta, Suman
The problem of the knowledge of the material objects and the self.
Delhi, 1971.

285. Hajra, Madhumati
Bertrand Russell's theory of knowledge.
Calcutta, 1979.

286. Harh, Amal Kumar
The means of knowing a negative fact: A critical study of the theory of anupalabdhi in Indian philosophy.
NBU, 1995.

287. Harminder Kaur
Freedom with special reference to religious experiences and communication: A conceptual analysis.
Poona, 1986.

288. Hattori, Massaki
A study on Dignaga's epistemology.
Calcutta, 1962.

289. Hilde, Van Putten
Man's spiritual evolution and transformation: A comparative study of Paul and Sri Aurobindo.
Mysore (S), 1990.

290. Ingalalli, Rachappa Irappa
Sabda praman: An epistemological analysis.
Kernataka, 1982.

291. Innaiah, N.
Philosophical consequences of modern science with

special reference to the problem of determination.
Osmania, 1981.

292. Jain, Nirmala
A.J. Ayer's theory of knowledge.
Sukhadia, 1985.

293. Jalalul Haque
Bertrand Russell's philosophy of perception.
AMU, 1979.

294. Javadekar, Anant Ganesh
Axionoeties — Valuation theory of knowledge: An axiological study of knowledge in all its forms of science philosophy, Literature, History, morals, religion and arts (D. Litt.).
Bombay, 1965.

295. Jayashree, V.
The concept of man in modern Indian thought with special reference to Gandhi.
Madras, 1988.

296. Jethamalani, Shirley
Nietzzche's aestheties, moral picture of man.
Rajasthan, 1989.

297. Jha, Chandra Kishore
Bharatiya Jyotis ka vaigyanik vivechan (D. Litt.)
Darbhanga, 1985.

298. Jha, Chander Kishore
Grahaspostikaranam.
(S) Darbhanga, 1968.

299. Jha, Ganga Dutt
A study of Ryle's theory of mind.
Vishwa Bharati, 1966.

300. Jha, Lateshwar
Some problems concerning empirical knowledge.
Magadh, 1975.

301. Jha, Ram Sevak
Testimony as a means of knowledge in different schools of Indian philosophy (S).
Darbhanga, 1976.

302. Joshi, Gajanan, N.
The evolution of the concepts of Atman and Mokshya in the different systems of Indian philosophy.
Gujarat, 1954.

303. Joshi, Harisiddah Maganlal
The nature of mind: A philosophico-psychological study.
Baroda, 1966.

304. Joshi, Lalita
The concept of soul in Upanishad and early Buddhist literature.
Delhi, 1981.

305. Kagi, Naseem
Studies in Aristrotle's theory of science.
Rajasthan, 1993.

306. Kamat, Nirmala Ganesh
The concept of mind in Indian philosophy (S).
Poona, 1985.

307. Kanitkar, Balkrishna Moreshwar
The concept of soul in Indian philosophy.
Bombay, 1945.

308. Kawle, Sriniwas Raghunath
Nature and implication of value: A study in theory of value in light of contemporary trends in modern Western philosophy.
Poona, 1959.

309. Khalsa, Surjeet Kaur, G.S.
The nature of consciousness.
Poona, 1982.

310. Khan, Gopal Chandra
A critical examination of Huserl's philosophy of consciousness.
Burdwan, 1986.

311. Khanna, Suniti
Bharatiya darshan mein jeevan mukti (H).
Kurukshetra, 1970.

312. Kim, Hyoung Jun
Buddhist conception of anantman in the perspectives of early Upanishads.
Delhi, 1993.

313. Kishwar Ahmed
A study of the closed mind in relation to authoritarianism conservatism and rigidity and familial antecedent with in the Indian context.
Punjabi (Psy.), 1980.

314. Kulkarni, Prahlad
The concept of mind in Indian philosophy.
Poona, 1984.

315. Kulkarni, S.G.
Perception and scientific knowledge towards a realist epistemology.
IIT, Kanpur.

316. Kunte, Usha Yashwant
Idea of rebirth: A survey—through the mainstreams of Sanskrit literature.
Poona, 1964.

317. Lad, Ashok Kumar
A comparative study of the concept of liberation in Indian philosophy.
Jabalpur, 1968.

318. Lahiri, Anandi Kumar
The nature of knowledge.
Calcutta, 1967.

319. Lakshminarayana, S.
The concept of men in J. Krishna Murthy and Jean Paul Sartre: A comparative evolution.
Osmania, 1977.

320. Lal, B.K.
Man in contemporary Indian philosophy.
Patna, 1966.

321. Laldinani,
Meaning, truth and human action.
NEHU, 1991.

322. Lanka, Laxminarayan
Against fundamentalism, towards Quines naturalised epistemology.
Hyderabad, 1993.

323. Lab o-e Silva Z.S.
The problem of death: A philosophical analysis.
Bombay, 1987.

324. Madhu, T.V.
Knowledge and ideology: Towards a non-positivist of the epistemological scheme of Marxism.
Hyderabad, 1985.

325. Mahapatra, A.R.
The idea of the inexpressible: A philosophical analysis.
Poona, 1981.

326. Mahapatra, Sarat Chandra
Theory of perception in Indian philosophy: An analytical approach.
Sambhalpur, 1986.

327. Majumdar, Bani
Gandhi aur Dewey ke anusara gnana aur uske adhyayan kee avadharana.
Agra, 1989.

328. Majumdar, Ruchira
Proper names and some problems of reference.
Jadavpur, 1988.

329. Manaktala, Geeta
G.C. Moore's philosophy of language and perception.
Panjabi.

330. Manohar, R.M.
Existentialists conception of man: A critical study in the light of psycho-analytic and Marxist perspectives.
Poona, 1985.

331. Mathu Karstis, Suksmit
Comparative study of the concept of freedom in Buddhism, Jainism and Existentialism.
Bihar, 1983.

332. Mathur, Pratap Karan
Bertrand Russell's theory of knowledge.
Udaipur, 1973.

333. Mehta, Dharam Deo
Hindu astrology, its scientific and philosophical basis.
BHU, 1955.

334. Mehta, M.L.
Psychological interpratation of Karma.
BHU, 1955.

335. Marerk, P. Prayodh
A comparative study of the non-egological treatments of consciousness in Sartre's philosophy and early Buddhism.
Delhi, 1986.

336. Mishra, Anand
Manava-niyati. Acharya Shanker evam Jean Paul Sartre ke darshanon ke vishesh sandarbh mein (H).
BHU, 1994.

337. Mishra, Narmadeshwar Prasad
A critical exposition of G.E. Moore's epistemological views.
Patna, 1975.

338. Mishra, Ram Nandan
Some contemporary Indian-theories of knowledge with special reference to Radhakrishnan, Tagore and Sri Aurobindo.
Patna, 1974.

339. Mishra, Sabhajeet
Kartras concept of subjectivity and human freedom: A critical study.
Gorakhpur, 1976.

340. Mishra, Shashikala
A critical study of the freedom of Karma and rebirth in Indian philosophy.
Bihar, 1972.

341. Mohammed, Muslihud Din
The concept of freedom of will in Muslim thought.
Gauhati, 1976.

342. Mohanty, Chitralekha
A study of the relation between the two measures of meaning.
IIT, Kharagpur, 1976.

343. Moitra, Tapati
Analytic and synthetic.
Burdwan, 1987.

344. Mukherjee, Apda
The idealist theory of value.
Calcutta, 1960.

345. Mukherjee, Jayasree
Analyticity, synonymity and meaning.
NBU, 1996.

346. Mukhopadhyay, Amal Kumar
The nature of explanation in the physical sciences.
Jadavpur, 1982.

347. Mukhopadhyay, Deva Prasad
Some main existentialist approaches to man consciousness and freedom.
Calcutta, 1985.

348. Mukhopadhyay, T.
The Advaita conception of mind.
Utkal, 1977.

349. Mutsuddi, Sujata
Some problems concerning the nature of belief and knowledge.
Calcutta, 1992.

350. Nagarajan, K.
The concept of the mind of the Tamils.
Madras, 1985.

351. Nageswaran, Jyotsna
A comparative study of the concept of the person in Sankara and Sartre.
Madras, 1989.

352. Nair, P.R. Krishanan
The concept of self in the Upanishads and modern psychology.
Osmania, 1990.

353. Namesivayam, Chamu
On some aspects of determinism and freedom.
Madras, 1984.

354. Nanavati, K.C.
Freedom.
Bombay, 1974.

355. Narangsi, Suntham
The conception of Karma and rebirth in Theravada Buddhism..
BHU, 1969.

356. Narhari, H.G.
Karma and rebirth.
Madras, 1958.

357. Narasimhayya, P.
Knowledge and existence.
Madras, 1924.

358. Natarajan, Tara
The nature and structure of consciousness with special reference to Edmand Husserl in the light of Advaita Vedanta.
BHU, 1991.

359. Padmanabham, C.A.
The concept of casuality in Indian thought.
Kerala, 1974.

360. Padmavathy, K.
The concept of individual love in Ravindra Nath Tagore and Kalidas.
Osmania.

361. Pal, Supriya
A comparative study of the epistemological and Ontological doctrines of David Hume and A.J. Ayer.
JNU, 1996.

362. Palaniammal, P.
Tamilal sethaka ilakkiyangal (T).
Madurai, 1983.

363. Panchalaiah, S.
H.H. Prices theory of perception: A critique.
Venkateswara, 1993.

364. Pandey, Indu
A comparative study of the theories of knowledge in the philosophies of David Hume and Imma-nuel, Kant.
JNU, 1992.

365. Pandey, Madhuri
Yogvaisistha tatha divya jeewan: Shri Aurobindu krit mein chetna ke swaroop (H).
BHU, 1989.

366. Pandey, Muralidhar
Astrology and human destinity.
BHU, 1975.

367. Pandey, Ram Chandra
Chandra Joal Vimarsh (S).
Sampurnanand, 1969.

368. Pandey, Rita
Advait Vedant aur Kashmir Shaiva darshan mein atma ka swaroop: tulnatmak adhyayan (H).
BHU, 1986.

369. Pandey, Sriprakash
Chetna ka swaroop evam uske vividhayan Acharya Vasu Bandhu, Acharya Shankar evam Sri Aurobindu darshan ke sandarbh mein (H).
BHU, 1987.

370. Panigrahi, Shephali
Gandhi's philosophy of man.
NEHU, 1982.

371. Parekh, Soil Kaikhushroo
A study of the psychology of belief.
Bombay, 1954.

372. Pathak, H.D.
Rahasyavadna adhare Akhajis Sandarbh men (G).
Gujarat, 1987.

373. Pathak, Ram
Relationship between man and nature in Indian materialism.
Gorakhpur, 1986.

374. Patnaik, Tandra
James concept of meaning.
Utkal, 1982.

375. Poonia, Om Prakash
Mahatma Gandhi ka vyavaharik adarshwad (H).
Jodhpur, 1993.

376. Pophale, Shireen Gopal
A critical edition of samudrik tilaka of Duralabharaja with English translation and brief notes and an introduction.
Bombay, 1967.

377. Pramod Kumar
A comparative study of the theories of emancipation in different systems of Indian philosophy.
Agra, 1970.

378. Prasanna Kumar, S.
Passimism in Indian philosophy: A critical study.
Calicut, 1988.

379. Premlata,
Humanism in contemporary Indian philosophy.
Gorakhpur, 1987.

380. Rajkumari, T.D.
Contemporary trends in Indian and western thought: A comparative study with special reference to the concept of self.
Madras, 1970.

381. Rajendra, Prasad
Philosophical implications of Quantam physics.
Delhi, 1978.

382. Rakshit, Syam Sunder
Some problems concerning knowledge and belief.
Burdwan, 1978.

383. Rangaswami, J.
Metaphysics of self in Bhagawat Gita.
Annamalai, 1985.

384. Rao, Sujath Krishna
Problem classification, problem genesis and problem degination in the science.
Venkateswara, 1983.

385. Rao, S. Ramchandra
Critical enquiry into the impact of unconscious and ideology of Freud and Marx.
Osmania, 1990.

386. Ravishankar, M.
The place of value culture and personality relationship.
Madras, 1979.

387. Ray, Ratna
Imagination of modern philosophy: A study in Hume Kant, Ryle, Croce and Sartre.
Calcutta, 1982.

388. Reynolds, Altamont
The nature and destiny of man according to Shri Ramanuja and John Calvin.
BHU, 1967.

389. Rogonovic, Svetolik
A study of aesthetic theories in ancient Indian philosophy and its comparison with the Greek counterpart.
Delhi, 1969.

390. Rowe, Robert Lee
The concept of immortality by prominent Indian religious-thinkers in modern times: Ram Mohan Roy to the present.
Poona, 1974.

391. Roy, Pradeep Kumar
Studies in theory of value.
Poona, 1983.

392. Roy, Subhash Chand
Perceptual cognition: A philosophical study.
NBU, 1990.

393. Saha, Jyotsna
Meaningfulness and meaninglessness: Significance of distinction.
NBU, 1986.

394. Saha, Kaveri
Causuality in Nyaya, Sankhya and Aristotelean philosophy.
Ravindra Bharati, 1986.

395. Sahai, Indu Bala
The concept of mind: A psycho-philosophical study.
Bihar, 1990.

396. Sahu, Bhaskar Chand
The problem of other mind.
Durgawati, 1992.

397. Sajeda, Adeep
Philosophy of self in Sir Mohammad Iqbal and Jesiah Royee.
Osmania, 1981.

398. Samamar, Phramaha Som
The concept of human value in Hinduism and Buddhism: A comparative study.
Mysore, 1986.

399. Samanta, Sudhir Chandra
The problem of a priori knowledge: A critical survey.
Calcutta, 1978.

400. Samuel, Kariappa
The nature and destiny of individual soul in the philosophy of St. Thomas Aquinas and in theistic Vedanta.
Jabalpur, 1966.

401. Sarkar, Swapna
Some problems concerning the nature of human knowledge.
Calcutta, 1991.

402. Sarma, Ramesh Chandra
Consciousness and its functions in Sankhya yog.
Gauhati, 1983.

403. Satish, T.
Role of self in the philosophy of Wittgehstein.
Madras, 1979.

404. Satyanarain
A critical survey of causation in Indian philosophy.
Allahabad, 1982.

405. Sayeed, S.A.
Knowledge and reality towards a non-reductionistic view.
IIT, Kanpur, 1985.

406. Sen, Deobrata
Some problems concerning the nature of knowledge.
Calcutta, 1970.

407. Sen, Pranab Kumar
The notion of self as in Kant.
Calcutta, 1969.

408. Sen, Swapan Kumar
Development of aesthetic sensitivity among Indian students of secondary level through painting.
NBU, 1987.

409. Sengupta, Iva
The philosophical out took of Mahatma Gandhi.
Ravindra Bharati, 1992.

410. Shakya, Jaiprakash
Ravindra Nath Tagore evam Mahatma Gandhi ke manavavad ka tulnatmak adhyayan (H).
Awadesh, 1993.

411. Santa Nath
The Indian conception of value.
Panjab, 1973.

412. Sharma, Goswami Girdhari Lal
A critical study of the brihat parasara with special reference to Phalita Jyotisa.
Delhi, 1966.

413. Sharma, Gayatri
Gita Quran aur Bible mein manav swaroop aur unki niyati (H).
Ravishankar, 1990.

414. Sharma, H.L.
A critical and comparative study of Indian aestheties.
Agra, 1949.

415. Sharma, Lakshmi
Knowledge by upamana.
Delhi, 1989.

416. Sharma, Murari Lal
Grahganita mimansa (S).
Sampurnanand, 1964.

417. Sharma, Nilima
Nature and destiny of men in contemporary Indian philosophy.
BHU, 1966.

418. Sharma, Rajni Bala
Gandhi's world views and industrial civilisation: A paradigmatic construction to Gandhian order.
Rajasthan, 1993.

419. Sharma, Rama Shanker
A study of Samuel Alexender's theory of knowledge.
Lucknow, 1966.

420. Sharma, Surinder Mohan
Matter and mind: A reassessment in the light of modern scientific and philosophical researches.
Agra, 1971.

421. Sheikh, Adul Kasem
Some problems about universals.
Burdwan, 1986.

422. Shekhawat, Virendra K.
A philosophical study of the concept of matter in the light of recent physics.
Rajasthan, 1974.

423. Shukla. D.A.
Vedanga jyotish samaya mein Bharatiya khagolshashtra ni sthit (G).
Gujarat, 1964.

424. Shukla, Jagdish Prasad
The nature of mind.
Jabalpur, 1962.

425. Shukla, Jayendra Jata Shankar
The relation of epistemology with Ontology in contemporary philosophy.
Baroda, 1966.

426. Shukla, Kanak
Hume's theory of knowledge.
Lucknow.

427. Siddhanta, Aloka
Natural necessity and dispositional concepts in physical sciences.
Burdwan, 1989.

428. Siddiqui Abdul Latif Yousuf
An approach to the problem of the infinite.
Poona, 1987.

429. Singh, Arun Kumar
The concept of value in Sartre.
Gorakhpur, 1981.

430. Singh, Atantham Dorendra
Knowledge and belief in the context of contemporary philosophy.
Vishwa Bharati.

431. Singh, H.G.
Marxism and socialist humanist: A philosophical examination of some basic issues.
Poona, 1987.

432. Singh, Jay Bahadur
Sri Aurobindo darshan mein Bhagawati kripa evam manav swatantrata (H).
Gorakhpur, 1985.

433. Singh, Jayani Devi
The nature of destiny of soul in the philosophies and religions of the world.
Agra, 1964.

434. Singh, Kirpal
A study of the concept of alienation with special reference to Karl Marx, Erich Fromm and Jean Paul Sartre.
Kurukshetra, 1980.

435. Singh, Ram Deo Prasad
Concept of causality in Indian and Western philosophy in the light of modern physics. Magadh, 1980.

436. Singh, Rama Shankar
An examination of Prof. A.J. Agerts contribution to epistemology. Magadh, 1982.

437. Singh, Sadanand Prasad
A critical study of the problem of causality: Eastern and Western point of view.
Bihar, 1983.

438. Singh, Soyam Lokendrajit
The problem of freedom and necessity in human action.
Calcutta, 1983.

439. Singh, Upendra Narayan
Pratyabhigga darshan ke kuchh pramukh siddhant shoonyavad ke sandarbh mein (H).
BHU, 1986.

440. Somon, Prakash P.
Concept of critique: Perspectives and problems.
Poona, 1991.

441. Sreekala Devi, S.
Concept of man in the works of Dostiyevsky.
Calicut, 1992.

442. Srivastava, Jyotsna
Acharya, Shankar evam Husserl ke darshan mein chetna ke swaroop (H).
BHU, 1987.

443. Srivastava, Kalpana
Pt. Jawaharlal Nehru ka samagra manavvad, ek darshanik adhyayan (H).
BHU, 1993.

444. Srivastava, Ripusuden Prasad
The status and destiny of the individual in contemporary Indian idealism.
Bihar, 1967.

445. Subramanium, Vidya
A quest for authentic structure of human reality.
IIT, Bombay, 1983.

446. Sukla, Parai
A critical examination of Hume's philosophy of mind.
Burdwan, 1986.

447. Sundaran, C.
The concept of man in Gandhi and Scheweitzer: A comparative evolution.
Osmania, 1976.

448. Sunderorajan, K.R.
Doctrine of incarnation according to Hinduism and Christianity.
Madras, 1967.

449. Superna
Nature and destiny of man in philosophy of Sri Aurobindo.
BHU, 1992.

450. Surendra Kumar
Bharatiya Samaj mein mukti kee avadharana (H).
Magadh (Pol. Sc.), 1985.

451. Suresh Chandra
A study of Ayer's epistemology.
Vishwa Bharati, 1968.

452. Tariq Islam
Gilbert Ryles analysis of thinking.
AMU, 1991.

453. Tiwari, Dinesh Prasad
Bharatiya tatha pashchatya darshan mein Atma tatha parmatma Sambandhi vicharon ka tulnatmak adhyayan (H).
Kanpur (S), 1985.

454. Tiwari, Kapil Nath
The interest theory of value with special reference to Ralph Barton Parry.
BHU, 1969.

455. Tiwari, Nirmala
Kant's conception of autonomy of will.
Lucknow, 1979.

456. Tripathi, Brijendra Kumar
M.N. Roy tatha Jean Pal Sartre ke manavvad ka tulnatmak adhyayan (H).
Gorakhpur, 1990.

457. Tripathi, Chhotelal
An appraisal of Yogacharas theory of knowledge.
Allahabad, 1966.

458. Tripathi, Dhuni Ram
Prachya, Bharatiya rituvigyanam (S).
Sampurnanand, 1989.

459. Tripathi, Satya Narayan
Ayan chalan vimarsh (S).
BHU, 1953.

460. Ujjwal, Madhu
A study in Sartre's concept of freedom.
Jodhpur, 1993.

461. Vakil, Suresh I.
Nature of self in Swaminarayanisy.
Gujarat, 1984.

462. Valappil, Vijaya Kumari
The concept of freedom in the philosophy of Jean Sartre.
Calicut, 1987.

463. Vanlelmawia, K. Laldenga
Zoramthanga and the concept of freedom.
NEHU, 1992.

464. Varadachari, K.N.
The theory of knowledge in Sri Ramanuja philosophy.
Madras, 1931.

465. Vasupal, N.
Nature of Atma (soul) in Jain philosophy and comparative study with other philosophies.
Mysore, 1984.

466. Vedaparayana, G.
A comparative study of problem of freedom with special reference to Jean Paul Sartre and Jiddu Krishnamarthi.
Venkateswara, 1985.

467. Vedavalli, P.
Epistemology of visistadvaita with special with reference to Nyaya parisuddhi of Vedanta desika.
Madras, 1987.

468. Veena Kumari
Epistemology of Guru Nanak.
Gurunanak Dev, 1984.

469. Venkataraman, M.
The Humanism in Hume.
Madras, 1980.

470. Verma, A.N.
Concept of a priority judgement.
Ranchi, 1973.

471. Verma, Dayal Chand
The doctrine in the self in early Buddhism.
Panjab, 1976.

472. Verma, Renu
Concept of man in J. Krishnamurthi.
Gorakhpur, 1963.

473. Vidyawati
Dewey's theory of value.
Delhi, 1974.

474. Vijayaraghawan, Sujatha
The concept of man in the principal prose works of Swami Vivekanand, Ravindra Nath Tagore, and Sri Aurovindo.
IIT, Madras, 1986.

475. Vohra, Ashok Kumar
A study of mind with special reference to Wisttgenstein and Ryle.
Delhi, 1975.

476. Xavier, Joseph
The concept of self according to Sivagyana Baudhan of meikanda Beva in relation to the mystical experience of Saint Tirunavukhara Sar.
BHU, 1982.

477. Yadav, Kamala Prasad
The problem of moral freedom with special reference to Nicolai Hertmann.
BHU, 1989.

478. Yamashita, Koichi
Studies in formation of the analysis of mind in Patanjali Yoga philosophy and Buddhism.
Calcutta, 1990.

4

PARA PSYCHOLOGY

479. Atreya, Jagat Prakash
Philosophical implications of Para psychological discoveries (D. Litt.).
Ranchi, 1976.

480. Kasturi
Hindu view of survival and psychical research.
Rohilkhand, 1984.

481. Layek, S.
Analysis of dream in Indian philosophy.
Poona, 1988.

482. Mukhopadhyay, Srila
Problem of mind body relation.
Burdwan, 1980.

483. Ram Chander, P.
Relevance of predictive technique in future planing.
Osmania, 1992.

484. Shaḥ, Pranga R.
Tantra, its therapeutic aspect.
Gujarat, 1985.

485. Sharma, Hemnalini
Marnottar jeevan: Ek darshanik adhyayan (H).
Jiwaji, 1987.

486. Singh, Yogendra
The super-normal powers of man discovered by Para psychology.
Rohilkhand, 1983.

487. Sinha, Geeta
Dreaming.
NEHU, 1981.

488. Tabai, A.H. Taba
Alchemy of spiritual transformation.
Bombay, 1986.

5

PHILOSOPHICAL SYSTEMS

489. Abdul Rehman
A philosophical study of Sufi systems and their doctrines.
Waltair, 1997.

490. Abraham, E.M.
Hindu Christian and Kalalaistic mysticism with the special reference to Isakatha mundaka and kene the cloud of unknowing.
Bombay, 1991.

491. Agrawal, Prabha
A critical study of the Sautrantik and Vaibhashika realism.
Agra, 1971.

492. Angela, Vital Afonso
A study of methodological individualism.
Poona, 1982.

493. Athialy, Jasudas M.
Radical humanism M.N. Roy and Karls Marx: A critical study.
Poona, 1991.

494. Balasubramaniam, R.
A philosophy of modern mysticism with special

reference to Saint Ramalingam.
Annamalai, 1986.

495. Bandyopadhyay, Bidya
Schelling's system of transscendental idealism: A critical study.
Calcutta, 1970.

496. Bandyopadhyay, Swati
The concept of the unconsciousness.
Burdwan, 1975.

497. Basu, Mridul Kanti
Impact of positivism in Bengal.
Jadavpur, 1980.

498. Basu, Sandhya
Empirical knowledge: Its meeting and foundations.
Calcutta, 1972.

499. Basu, Sobharani
Some mysties and aspect of mysticism in modern India (D. Litt.).
Calcutta, 1948.

500. Baxi, Madhusudan Vishwnu Prasad
A contemporary antimentalism: A critical study.
Gujarat, 1981.

501. Bhanusree, B. Venketa Sakuntala
Contemporary humanism and early Buddhism: A comparative study.
Andhra, 1991.

502. Bhasin, Bhushan
The philosophy of pragmatism and its impact on modern social and ethical thinking.
Agra, 1965.

503. Bhatnagar, Rajendra Swaroop
Hegel in the light of existentialism.
Allahabad, 1959.

504. Bhattacharya, Bhakti
Different sub-schools of prativimbavad in Sankara monism. Gorakhpur, 1963.

505. Bhattacharya, Bhupendra Nath
Theism in Sankhya Systems.
Calcutta (S), 1977.

506. Bhattacharya, Bhaswati
Studies in absolute skepticism: Eastern and Western.
Jadavpur, 1979.

507. Bhattacharya, Bimalendu
Emparicism and the problem of meaning.
NBU, 1990.

508. Bhattacharya, Dipa
The existantialist notion of self.
Vishwa Bharati, 1964.

509. Bhattacharya, Dipali
Some theories of intution in Western philosophy.
Burdwan, 1983.

510. Bhattacharya, Champa
An enquiry into the nature and significance of the empiricist conception of language with special reference to modern empiricalists.
Vishwa Bharati, 1978.

511. Bhattacharya, Jyotirmay
Consciousness in existantialism.
Ravindra Bharati, 1982.

512. Bhattacharya, Pinaki Ranjan
The posivitist criterion of meaning.
Ravindra Bharati, 1973.

513. Bhattacharya, Susmita
A critical study of the concept of equality.
Poona, 1975.

514. Bhattacharya, Tuna
A critical study of phenomenology with special reference to modern development in psychology.
Burdwan, 1972.

515. Bhupendra, Nath
A study of mysticism in the religious philosophy of Ravindra Nath Tagore.
Magadh, 1990.

516. Bisht, Umeshwar Singh
The place of critique of judgement in Kant philosophy.
Allahabad, 1965.

517. Bose, Seema
The existantialist treatment of body with special reference to Sartre Mercel and Merleao Ponty.
Delhi, 1992.

518. Chacka, Valiaveet I.
The concept of Jiwanmurti in Shaiva Siddhanta.
BHU, 1975.

519. Chadha, Satish Chandra
Kant's theory of knowledge of the external world.
Meerut, 1973.

520. Chakraborti, Usharanjan
The problem of superman.
Calcutta, 1974.

521. Chandrakanta, Mohan
The native of reality in Buddhist realism: A comparative study.
Delhi, 1972.

522. Chakraborti, Prabhawati
Jean-Paul Sartre's philosophy of humanism: A critical survey.
Calcutta, 1982.

523. Chatterjee, Ashok Kumar
The yogachara idealism.
BHU, 1953.

524. Chattopadhyay, Gauri Prasad
Utilitarianism and its critiques.
Calcutta, 1983.

525. Chattopadhyay, Krishna,
An enquiry into the theory and practice of mysticism.
Ravindra Bharati, 1982.

526. Chattopadhyay, Manjusri
Mysticism and metaphysics: A philosophical study.
Calcutta, 1966.

527. Chaudhuri, Haridas
The philosophy of integral spirituality.
Calcutta, 1948.

528. Chaudhuri, Kamalesh Prasad Singh
A critical study of some modern Indian mystics.
BHU, 1965.

529. Chaudhuri, Nomiti
The concept of truth in existentilism.
Calcutta, 1971.

530. Chaurasia, Mahatma Prasad
Upanishad ka rahasyavad (H).
Kashi, 1993.

531. Christanandan, Thota
Humanistic trends in the philosophy of Mahatma Gandhi: A study.
1990.

532. Damle, Chhaya N.
Theories of reality.
IIT, Bombay, 1975.

533. Daniel, Dogata
Freedom of the will.
Vishwa Bharati, 1970.

534. Das, Devabrata
Bharatiya darshan jeevan mukti-o-Tahar darshanika paryalochana (H).
Jadavpur, 1991.

535. Das, Juthiks
Karl Jaspers and neo-dvaitism.
Gauhati, 1990.

536. Das, V.C. Narayana
An evaluation of the existentialist to a farm of Humanism.
Allahabad, 1979.

537. Dash, Kailash Chandra
Tetvaprabha balidrisha vabyarthviloknam.
Jagannath, 1991.

538. Date, Vinayak Hari
Anatomy of spiritual life.
Bombay, 1941.

539. Deenammal, Ontimetta
Ideology and education.
Andhra, 1977.

540. Deshpande, Balkrishna Yashwant
The concept of logical necessity in modern classical philosophies.
Nagpur, 1980.

541. Deswal, Raj Kumar
A critical study of some important concept of ideal person with special reference to Gita and Buddhism.
Kurukshetra, 1989.

542. Devendra, Kumar
Humanism and theism: A study in Gandhian philosophy.
BHU, 1990.

543. Dhruv, Sudha
Ethical humanism and Gita idealism.
IIT, Bombay, 1972.

544. D'souza, Gregory
Mystical experience on St. Teresa of Avila.
Mysore, 1979.

545. Eraiyl, Alphonse Louis
Humanism of Teithard De Chardin.
Kerala, 1986.

546. Farida Bi
Indian idealism: A critical study.
Rohilkhand, 1989.

547. Ghose, Rama
The concept of grace in Southern Shaivism.
BHU, 1973.

548. Goswami, Madhuri
A study of monism of the Previvarana school.
Jadhavpur, 1960.

549. Gupta, Kalyan Chandra
Monism: A critical survey. (D. Litt.).
Calcutta, 1960.

550. Gupta, Laxmi Shankar
Vyakarana darshan ke manyatayon ka anya astik Bharatiya darshan ke sath tulanatmak adhyayan (H).
Awadh, 1992.

551. Gupta, Shafali
Between skepticism and rationalism.
Jodhpur, 1970.

552. Gupta, Uma
Materialism in the Vedas.
Patna, 1967.

553. Girish Kumar, T.S.
Marxian concept of ideology. A critique of Antonia Gramsoi and louis Althusser.
NEHU, 1992.

554. Gurumurti, D.
Idealism and Theism.
Madras, 1934.

555. Himalayanath, D.
Existentialism and the future of mankind with special reference to Martin Heidegger.
Osmania, 1984.

556. Jain, Premlata
Shri Anand Ghan ka rahasyavadi darshan (H).
Awadh, 1985.

557. Jaiswal, Onkar Prasad
An introduction to subjective idealism.
Bihar, 1969.

558. Javadekar, Anant Ganesh
Approach to reality. Being a partly methodological and partly epistemological from an ethical point of view.
Bombay, 1952.

559. Joshi, Jayant Shanalji
Mysticism in mediaeval Gujarat poetry.
Gujarat, 1969.

560. Kambi, Veerabasavayya S.
Salasthalan virashaivism. A philosophical study.
Karnataka, 1975.

561. Karunakaran, S.
A critical study of the two level analysis of Plato

Shankaracharya and Kant.
Madras, 1982.

562. Kothari, M.M.
Modern evolutionism of the West and Parinamavada of Indian philosophies of evolutionism.
Rajasthan, 1961.

563. Lockwood, Michael Chipmen
Peirce and some questions concerning intution.
Madras, 1973.

564. Lahoti, Bhagwan Das
Nature of human predicament in the philosophy of Karl Jaspers.
Osmania, 1982.

565. Limaye, S.V.
Zen and mysticism: Its mysticism.
Bombay, 1984.

566. Meherunissa, Omar
The concept of transcendance in Karl Jaspers.
Osmania, 1988.

567. Mehtani, Shanta
Marx's materialism and contemporary materialism.
Rajasthan, 1982.

568. Mallik, Chitralekha
Bigyan vikhu and his philosophical attitude.
Jadavpur (S), 1967.

569. Malviya, Meera
A critical study of dedicate in Karl and Sankara.
Allahabad, 1974.

570. Masani, Behram
Some philosophical problems arising out of modern psychical researches.
Indore, 1978.

571. Mishra, G.N.
Dissolution of realism and idealism through individualisation.
Bombay, 1975.

572. Mishra, Ramashankar
Integral Monism of Sri Aurobindo.
BHU, 1952.

573. Mishra, S.D.
A critical comprehensive study of the different sub-schools of Abhasarada in Monism.
Gorakhpur, 1964.

574. Mitra, Manjushree
Humanism in contemporary Indian thinkers with special reference to Swami Vivekanand, Ravindra Nath Tagore, Aurobindo and Dr. Radhakrishnan.
Bihar, 1974.

575. Mitra, Uma
Humanism from Marxian perspective.
Calcutta, 1986.

576. Mittal, Kewal Kishore
Role of materialism in Indian thought.
Delhi, 1968.

577. Mohammad Kasim, U.
Utilitarian perspectives.
Madras, 1978.

578. Mukherjee, Bithika
The conception of categories in neo-realism.
Allahabad, 1956.

579. Mukherjee, M.D.
Recent trends in evolutionary philosophy.
Allahabad, 1950.

580. Mukhopadhyay, Adityanath
The concepts of monism and mysticism: A metaphysical essay with a short historical introduction.
Calcutta, 1969.

581. Mukhopadhyay, Anil Kumar
Consciousness in the philosophy of Whitehead.
Calcutta, 1975.

582. Murti J.R.V.
Madhyamik dialectic (D. Litt.).
BHU, 1948.

583. Namboodhari, K.P. Kesawan
The concept of apavarjan, in sankhya philosophy.
Kerala (S), 1976.

584. Naronha, M.D.F.M.
Towards a personalistic concept of person.
Bombay, 1986.

585. Narvekar, S.P.
An Ontological reappraisal of Indian realism.
Bombay, 1985.

586. Nawal Kishore
A comparative study of western utilitarianism and utilitarianism as arocated with Bhagwat Gita.
Bihar, 1974.

587. Nayar, P.K. Sasidharan
A study of the Sankhya karika with special reference to Sankeyatara Vasanta.
Madras (S), 1977.

588. Nasy, D.
Existentialistic trends in Neitgsche.
Kerala, 1980.

589. Padhi, Harprasad
Wittgenstein's philosophy of grammar: A reconstruction.
Hyderabad, 1992.

590. Pandey, Archana
Jain Bhasha darshan kee samasya (H).
BHU, 1992.

591. Pandey, Ghansyam
A critical examination of the principles of logical positivism.
Awadesh, 1974.

592. Pandey, Gorakh Prasad
And examination of concept of alienated in extentialism.
JNU, 1983.

593. Pundit, Girdharilal
Language and factual significance with special reference to logical empiricism.
Vishwa Bharati, 1972.

594. Parimalnathan,
St. John of the cross and Menkkavacager: Some aspects of there mystical lives.
Madras, 1984.

595. Pathak, Angelika
Institution as the mode of apprehending categorical structure.
Bombay, 1976.

596. Pathak, Diwakar
Hume and logical empiricism: A comparative study of the philosophy of David Hume and A.J. Ayer.
Bhagalpur, 1970.

597. Pathak, H.D.
Rahasyavad na adharo khajs sandarbh mein.
(G) Gujarat, 1987.

598. Peter, Mahanry, K.
A socio-spiritual approach to the problems of the disables.
Bharatidesam, 1990.

599. Phadnis, Hemlata Suryakant
Critical examination of Mills theory of utilitarianism.
Poona, 1977.

600. Phillip, Elizabeth
Mysticism personal and social expressions with illustration drawn from the works of St. Manikka Venger, and the St. Paul.
Madras, 1982.

601. Rajkumari
The study of basic propositions in logical positivism.
Kurukshetra, 1974.

602. Raju, A. Srirama
Modern Indian humanism: A study with reference to the works of Raja Ram Mohan Roy, Swami Vivekanand, Ravindra Nath Tagore, S. Radhakrishanan and M.N. Roy.
Andhra, 1974.

603. Ramkrishnan, M.
The new humanism of M.N. Roy: A critical study.
Calicut, 1989.

604. Rao, K. Ramkrishna
Pragamatism and practical idealism.
Andhra, 1962.

605. Rashidul Alam
Bertrand Russell's logical atomism (D. Litt.)
Ravindra Bharati, 1986.

606. Rastogi, Navjeevan
The philosophy of Karma monism of Kashmir: An analytical study.
Lucknow, 1968.

607. Rathod, Rambhau Tukaram
Critical study of David Humes secpticism.
Poona, 1983.

608. Raychaudhari, Anil Kumar
The doctrine of maya and studies in the Indian concept of the self with an appendix on objectivity. (D. Litt.).
Calcutta, 1951.

609. Ray, Manjushree
A critical examination of nomination.
Calcutta, 1970.

610. Ray, Pabitra, Kumar
Hume theory of passions: A study of Book II of the Treatise.
NBU, 1982.

611. Reyna, Ruth
Concept of maya in the frame of casual and prabalitistic interpretation of matter.
Poona, 1961.

612. Roy, Anjali
The development of mysticism in Bengal during the 18th and 19th centuries.
Allahabad, 1951

613. Roy, Subhas Ranjan
The realistic monism of Swami Vivekanand.
Bihar, 1963.

614. Saha, Smita
Ethics in perspective of Sartres existantialism.
Calcutta, 1984.

615. Salankhe, Anna Hari
A critical study of the Carvaka School of thought.
Shivaji (San), 1987.

616. Sambasiva Prasad, B.
The critique of philosophy of sense data.
Venkateswara, 1981.

617. Sanyal, Balai Kumar
Empiricism and society.
Ravindra Bharati, 1989.

618. Sanyal, Sandita
The concept of nothingness in Sartre's philosophical system.
Calcutta, 1973.

619. Saraswat, Uma
A critical study of utilitarianism with reference to Hume, Mill and Sidwick.
Rajasthan, 1976.

620. Sarkar, Sushil Kumar
A critique of phenomenology.
NBU, 1987.

621. Sarma, R. Nagarjuna
Reign of realism in Indian philosophy.
Madras, 1931.

622. Satapathy, D.
Towards a meta theory of innateness.
Poona, 1981.

623. Sen, Malabika
On the problem of revolution.
Delhi, 1981.

624. Sen Roy, Sutapa
An examination of some theories of subject and predicate.
Burdwan, 1985.

625. Seth, Indu Rani
Religion, sex age and altruism.
Lucknow (Psy), 1986.

626. Shaikh, Zuluikha
Mysticism of Jalal ud Din Rumi.
Karnataka, 1969.

627. Sharma, C.D.
Reign of dialectic in philosophy, Indian and Western (D. Litt.).
Allahabad, 1951.

628. Sharma, Dipti
The meaning and importance of subjectivity in the Kierkegaard's philosophy.
Allahabad, 1929.

629. Shesh, D.B.
Problem of individuality and its implications for modern idealism and Advaita Vedanta.
Agra, 1956.

630. Siddiqui, Mohammed Safiuddin
Al Ghazali and Islamic mysticism: A critical and historical approach.
Marathwada, 1968.

631. Sihari, Rama Kant Atma Ram
Contemporary existentialism: Its limitation.
Bombay, 1960.

632. Singh, Balkar
Sikh's mysticism: An analytical study in experience and expression.
Punjabi, 1984.

633. Singh, Bishwanath
A study in Sandhya materialism.
Bihar, 1965.

634. Singh, Chhetrapal
A critical examination of modern Western humanism.
Allahabad, 1965.

635. Singh, Hari
A study of existential philosophy in Paul Tillich.
Kurukshetra, 1981.

636. Singh, Jaojam Ghanshyam
Marxism and socialist humanism: A philosophical examination of some basic issues.
Poona, 1987.

637. Singh, Loitanathan Naobi
A critical study of scepticism and its role in modern philosophy.
Gauhati, 1991.

638. Singh, Mahendra
The metaphysical aspects of dialectical materialism.
Agra, 1959.

639. Singh, Mritunjaya Narayan
The concept of human person in existentialism.
Bihar, 1971.

640. Singh, Rajendra Kumar
Anekantvad aur pashchatya vyavaharikatavad: Ek tulnatmak adhyayan (H).
Magadh, 1981.

641. Singh, Ram Pratap
A creative monism of Sankara: The Vedanta of Sankara (D. Litt.).
BHU, 1944.

642. Singh, Vidyapati Prasad
A critical study of elements of existentism Indian philosophy with special reference to Carvaka Buddhism, and Jainism.
Bihar, 1985.

643. Sinha, Anant Prasad
Phenomenology of Martin Heidegger: A study with reference to Indian thought.
Agra, 1971.

644. Sinha, Arvind Kumar
The possibility of life after death: A reflective and critical analysis of claim and counter claims.
Magadh, 1991.

645. Sinha, Debabrata
Existentialist outlook in Indian thought.
Calcutta, 1958.

646. Sinha, Devendra Kumar
Moral judgement in British intuitionism.
Magadh, 1972.

647. Soni, Jayendra
The human prediament: A critique of some philosophical perspectives.
BHU, 1977.

648. Spyrou, Malliades, A.
Eudaemonistic trends in Indian philosophy.
BHU, 1970.

649. Srichandra
A critical study of G.E. Moore's realism.
Lucknow, 1966.

650. Srivastava, Chandra Prakash
Concept of subjectivity and freedom in Jaspers.
Gorakhpur, 1981.

651. Srivastava, Jagdish Sahai
Types of empiricism in philosophy: Western and Eastern.
BHU, 1964.

652. Srivastava, Ramesh Chandra
The absolute idealism of Krishna Chandra Bhattacharya.
Agra, 1962.

653. Srivastava, Smita
Concept of irrational and absurd in existentialism: Critical study.
Gorakhpur, 1992.

654. Suresh Prasad
Dhalukatha kee darshanik Sameeksha (H).
Magadh, 1981.

655. Tahir, A.F.M.
The mystical philosophy of Said Mohammed.
AMU, 1984.

656. Thakur, Keshavlal Ambalal
Mysticism in Gujarat.
Baroda, 1962.

657. Tilak, B. Balagangadhara
A critical examination of Jean-Paul Sartre's philosophy.
JNU, 1990.

658. Tiwari, Daljit Narayan
A study of the existential philosophy of Sorenker Kegara.
Bihar, 1972.

659. Tiwari, Usha
Man and his value in modern humanism.
Jabalpur, 1973.

660. Tongper, E. Richard
The idea of world view and understanding people.
NBHU, 1992.

661. Trigunayat, Kailash Narain
A critical analysis of the concept of the real Kants and Sankar.
Allahabad, 1990.

662. Trivedi, Bhavana Purushottam Das
An examination of the concept of change with special

reference to the philosophies of Bergson and Buddhism.
Poona, 1973.

663. Verma, Lakshmi
A critical study of the monistic tendencies in contemporary philosophy with special reference to British and Indian thought.
Allahabad, 1955.

664. Verma, Nenu Kumari
Passimism in Indian philosophy: A critical study.
Bihar, 1990.

665. Vinod Kumari
Basic structure of the constitution and supreme court judgement. A critical study in Indian constitutional jurisprudences.
Rajasthan, 1983.

666. Vyas, Manaklal
Spiritual experience: Its nature and realisation.
Jodhpur, 1974.

667. Wadhalkar, Mukund Laxman
Man in dialectical materialism: Marx-Engles.
Bombay, 1948.

668. Yadav, Mahesh Chander
Itihas prativad paksh aur vipaksha (H).
Rajasthan, 1985.

6

INDIAN PHILOSOPHY

669. Abdullah-al Mamun
Impact of an Indian thought.
Calcutta, 1976.

670. Acharyulu, K.V.S.P.B.
Vaikhan sajaina yogayo tulnatmak adhyayan.
BHU, 1992.

671. Advani, Mohini
Comparative study of Ravindranath Tagore and S. Radhakrishanan.
Rajasthan, 1969.

672. Agrawal, Manjula
Bharatiya darshan mein sambandh nirupan (H), (S).
Meerut, 1983.

673. Agrawal, Vandana
Shankaracharya evam Vallabhacharya ke tatva darshan ka tulnatmak adhyayan (H).
Ravishankar, 1989.

674. Ambastha, Radhe Syam
Social order according to Mahatma Gandhi and the contribution made to it by Vinoba and Jai Prakash Narayan.
Bihar, 1983.

675. Anand, Gita
Nad Bindu ka rehasya: Ek parisheelan (S).
Kanpur, 1976.

676. Anand Prakash
Yuvacharya Mahapragya ka darshan: Ek Anusheelan.
Dayanand (Aj.), 1993.

677. Anantharaj, A.
Siva ghana munivasin saive sidhdha vilekham (T).
Madurai, 1985.

678. Angiras, Ashutosh
A critical and comparative study of pratyabhigya and pratibha in trika system of Indian philosophy.
Panjab (San.), 1989.

679. Anlony Leo
Conflict resolution in Gandhi: Some aspects.
Kerala.

680. Antony, Prabhu Lancelot
The pathless approach: J. Krishnamurti's concept of methodology of psycho-social transformation: Their significance for the contemporary Indian scene.
Bombay, 1993.

681. Anuradha Kumar
Dr. Bhupendra Nath Duttaer matahado chinta others.
Jadavpur, 1992.

682. Aphale, Saneeli Jayant
Adhya Sankaracharya bhayashalichi vaishistha yai: Ek abhyas (M).
Nagpur, 1992.

683. Arbind Kumar
A critical study of Maharishi Raman's contribution to philosophy and religion.
Bihar, 1983.

684. Arora, Swatantra
Gandhi's approach to Hindu Muslim problem, 1915-1936: A critical study.
Panjab, 1976.

685. Arumugam, E.
The philosophy of Sri Satya Sai Baba.
Annamalai, 1987.

686. Arya Devi, T.
The concept of shabda as a pramanu in Nyaya Nyaya.
Calicut, 1992.

687. Arya, Praphull
Bharatiya darshan mein paramanuvada (H), (S).
Kurukshetra, 1985.

688. Bal, Saryu Ganesh
Study of the philosophy of Ekantha with special reference to his Bhagawata and the influence of Sankara's advaitism.
Poona, 1959.

689. Bandyopadhyay, Anukul Chand
Sarvastivada school and its literature.
Calcutta, 1945.

690. Bandyopadhyay, Pradyot Kumar
Abhihita nyayabad.
Calcutta, 1967.

691. Bandyopadhyay, Rama
Prama-o-praman sampandha Dharmakirti banklavya.
Jadavpur, 1971.

692. Bandhyopadhyay, Sankar Prasad
Bharatiya darshan sabdasya pramanata-tatva Samiksha (S).
Calcutta, 1977.

693. Banerjee, Santana
Rabindra Mathur savtta darshan (B).
Vishwa Bharati, 1972.

694. Banerjee, S.N.
Philosophy of practical human life as depicted in Panchtantra (S).
Kumaun, 1981.

695. Banik, Sapriya
Vishvanatha's analysis of the process of verbal testimony (S).
Jadavpur, 1988.

696. Bapat, L.S.
Dharamakirtas philosophy: A fresh study.
Poona 1985.

697. Bapal, S.S.
Vastu va Tiche Ghatak ya sambandhi Bhartiya tatwadnyanatil vichar (M), (S).
Poona, 1978.

698. Barnabas, Manorama
A study in the philosophy of social change the ideas of some liberal thinkers in nineteenth century, Maharashtra and their relevance to modernisation.
Poona, 1974.

699. Basu, Meeta
Philosophical contribution of thinkers of Indian renaissance, limited to the thinkers of Bengal from 1900-1920.
Baroda, 1995.

700. Bathla, Sunita
Humenistic trends in recent Indian thought.
BHU, 1977.

701. Bhadra, Ashis Kumar
A critical of the Kuvelayananda Karikas (S).
Jadavpur, 1984.

702. Bhanot, Pinki
Yogsutra aur vishndimag ka tulnatmak anusheelan (H).
Saugar, 1993.

703. Bharadwaj, Iswar Singh
Upanishadon mein Sanyasyog: Sameekshatmak adhyayan (H).
Gurukul, 1993.

704. Bharadwaj, R.
The philosophy of Tulsidas.
Agra, 1953.

705. Bhaskara, N.
Is India really free: Vinoba's diagnosis and prescriptions.
Bharatidasam, 1991.

706. Bhatnagar, Rajendra Swaroop
Dimensions of classical Sufi thought.
Allahabad, 1981.

707. Bhatnagar, Sarita
Vibhinna Bharatiya darshan sastron mein gyan ka swaroop aur siddhant (H), (S).
Rohilkhand, 1989.

708. Bhalwadekar, Sindhu Balkrishna
The upanishadic theory of value.
Baroda 1976.

709. Bhatt, Bhameshwar
Concept of culture according to Sri Aurobindo.
Osmania, 1967.

710. Bhattacharya, Abhay Chandra
Sri Aurobindo and Bergson.
BHU, 1950.

711. Bhattacharya, Bhaswati
The Nyaya Kusumanjali of Udayanacharya: An interpretative exposition.
Madras, 1976.

712. Bhattacharya, Bhupendra Ch.
Karma Karmayoga O. Srimad Bhagwat Gita.
Jadavpur, 1991.

713. Bhattacharya, Gaurinath
The philosophy of Bharathori (D. Litt.).
Calcutta, 1953.

714. Bhattacharya, Gopa
The nature and grades of consciousness in Sri Aurobindo's philosophy.
Burdwan, 1968.

715. Bhattacharya, Hareram
An aesthetic approach to Gaudiya, Vaishnavism (S).
Jadavpur, 1976.

716. Bhattacharya, Hirendranath
The concept of mind in Nyaya and Advaita Vedanta school of Indian philosophy: A comparative study.
NBU, 1992.

717. Bhattacharya, Hrishikesh
Shakty upasana vimarsh (D. Litt.) (S).
Darbhanga , 1982.

718. Bhattacharya, Jyoti Prasad
Pratyaksha Nyaya mata sameeksha.
Jadavpur, 1991.

719. Bhattacharya, Panchami
Spiritualistic humanism in twentieth century Indian

philosophy.
Gauhati, 1995.

720. Bhattacharya, Raghunath
An introduction to the philosophy of Tagore.
Ravindra Bharati, 1981.

721. Bhattacharya, Ravindra Nath
Viddhyarthav aditaiwa parisilanam (S).
Calcutta, 1978.

722. Bhattacharya, Shivani
Apadeviya Nyayaprakasa vimarsh vishwa.
Bharati, 1991.

723. Bhattacharya, Sikka
Bharatiya darshanar dristite pratyaksha gyan (B).
Calcutta, 1985.

724. Bhagru
A critical study of the Alwaru of Tamil vaishnavism with speical reference to satkopa and Andalkodai.
Agra, 1975.

725. Bhandwa, Shibhana Martandrao
Pramukh upanishadan teel jeevan mulyon che, chikilsuk vivechan (M).
Poona, 1997.

726. Bilthare, Anurag
Adhunik Bharatiya chintan mein ashubh ke samasya (H).
Saugar, 1992.

727. Bist, Umarao Singh
Theories of word and its meaning in Indian philosophy.

728. Biswas, Lakshmi
A comparative study of Tagore and Iqbal with speical reference to mankind, universe destiny and religion.
Bhagalpur, 1980.

729. Biswas, Lelarani
Concept of philosophy from stand point of Swarupananda.
Ravindra Bharati, 1990.

730. Bolia, Hemlata
A critical study of shabda pramana (S).
Udaipur, 1976.

731. Chakraborti, Jayanta Kumar
The problem of in determinate perception in Indian philosophy (San).
Jadavpur, 1987.

732. Chakraborti, N. Nath
Realism—phenomenalism controversy in Indian thought with speical reference to Nyaya Vaisesika and Buddhist school.
Vishwa Bharati, 1993.

733. Chakraborti, Sarbani
A critique of casuality with special reference to Nyaya Vaisesika mimansa and Buddhist theories.
Jadavpur, 1993.

734. Chakraborti, Satya Narain
A study of the Citramimansa of Appaya Dikshit (S).
Burdwan, 1982.

735. Chaturvedi, Shiv Kumar
An etymological treatment of the philosophical terms in the commentaries of Sankara.
Delhi, 1980.

736. Chakraborti, Surath Chandra
Concept of samadhi in Indian philosophy.
Calcutta, 1982.

737. Chaturvedi, Bansidhar
Shri Sankaracharya ka Strot sahitya: Ek adhyayan (S).
Agra, 1978.

738. Chaturvedi, Manjusha
Sarvapalli Radhakrishnan ke samaj darshan ka samikshatmak adhyayan (H).
Indore, 1978.

739. Chaturvedi, Sachidanand
Vairagya bhavana ke adhar per aubhoot Gita vivechak chhamani tatha vairagya shatroop ka darshanik evam tulnatmak adhyayan (H), (S).
Kanpur, 1985.

740. Chatterjee, Ratna
Prusastapad krit Padarth dharam Sangrah. Sameekshatmak adhyayan (S).
Darbhanga, 1981.

741. Chattopadhyay, Anupama
Critical study on Anupalabdhi as a pramana.
Ravindra Bharati, 1992.

742. Chattopadhyay, Santinath
Religion of men: A critical and comparative study on Ravindra Nath Tagore.
Calcutta, 1982.

743. Chattopadhyay, Tara
A critical examination of the theory of Svatah pramanaya.
Calcutta, 1969.

744. Chaubey, Chandrika
The philosophy of non-violence and the problem of war with speical reference to the teaching of Buddha, the Bhagwat Gita and Gandhi.
Bihar, 1977.

745. Chaube, Meena,
Dr. Radhakrishnan ke darshan mein tark aur aprakshanu bhuti vivad evam samadhan (H).
Jiwaji, 1982.

746. Chaube, Mukti
Pramukh Bharatiya darshanon mein sristi pralaya kee avadharana (H).
BHU, 1993.

747. Chaudhari, P. Ramakrishnaiah
A comparative study of the Gandhian concept of non-violence.
Venkateswara, 1982.

748. Chaudhuri, Reba
The religions philosophy of Dr. Radhakrishanan.
Bihar, 1964.

749. Chauhan, N. Singh
Sri Daya Dwivedi varachit Neeti Manjari: Ek Samalochanatmak adhyayan (S).
H.P., 1983.

750. Chauhan, Ravindra
Kashmir Shaiva darshan tatha Swami Vivekanand ke anusar mokshya (H).
BHU, 1993.

751. Chauhan, Usha,
Some aspects of the philosophy of Bharthahari (S).
Madras, 1985.

752. Chinchalkar, Laxaman Gopalrao
Concept of spiritual evolution in philosophy of Sri Aurobindo.
Nagpur, 1964.

753. Chingamani, M.A.
Relations in Nyaya vaishesika sankhya visista advaita and dwaita system.
Madras, 1984.

754. Chitranjan Dayal
Swami Dayanand ke Yajurveda bhasya mein Indra

evam Marut ke swarup: Ek sameekshatmak adhyayan (S).
Kurukshetra, 1988.

755. Darshan Devi
Ishwar jeeva aur prakriti: Dayanand darshan ke vistist sandarbh mein.
Punjab, 1991.

756. Das, Binoyanand
Philosophy of Shri Ramkrishna Paramhansa,
Bihar, 1969.

757. Das, Chandra Mohan
The philosophy of Ravindranath Tagore and the Upanishads.
Gauhati, 1982.

758. Das, Gopikrishna
Geetabitan: Ravindranath and human society.
Vishwa Bharati, 1989.

759. Das, Guru Prasad
The concept of highest good in the light of modern Indian thinkers.
Vishwa Bharati, 1983.

760. Das, Hari Pad
Synthetic spiritualism of Sri Rama Krishna through history and philosophical perspectives (Edu).
Gauhati, 1984.

761. Das, Maya
Saddarsana purusarthe vichar darshanon on purusarthe in six systems of philosophy.
Vishwa Bharati, 1984.

762. Das, M.S.S.
Jiwan mein yog aur yoga ka samanway: Atma vivechan (H), (S).
Ranchi, 1979.

763. Das, Ramakant
Neo Vedantic concept of maya with special reference to the philosophy of Swami Vivekanand, S. Radhakrishnan and R. Tagore.
Magadh, 1989.

763a. Das, Sunil Kumar
Shri Chaitanya aur Guru Nanak.
Ravindra Bharati, 1972.

764. Das, Tushar
Shri Ram Krishna ka samanvayavadi darshan: Ek samolochanatmak adhyayan (H).
Bhagalpur, 1981.

765. Dash, Usha Rani
Sankhya tattwa dipikaya: Sameekshatmak adhyayan.
Jagannath, 1993.

766. Datar, Indumati Dattatraya
Nagarjunas philosophy of casuality. Based on his worse Aku tobhaya and sunyata saptati restored in Sanskrit.
Bombay, 1949.

767. Datta, Gita
A critical study of Swami Vivekanand's philosophy of education.
Gauhati, 1993.

768. De, Surendra Kumar
The central contribution of Sri Aurobindo in the light of modern philosophy.
Allahabad, 1972.

769. Dekhana, R.A.
Bharud vangmayateel tattwagyan sent Ekanathacharya sandarbhat (M).
Poona, 1985.

770. Despande, Sharad Chand Shakhe Ram
A critical examination of Gaudapadas philosophy in

Markandeya Karikas.
Poona, 1976.

771. Devanathan, N.
The basis of Ramanujas Visist advaita in uphaya vedanta sankrit drivida vedanta (S).
Poona, 1980.

772. Devdas, Maline
The concept of personality in the philosophy of Sri Aurobindo and problem of human destinity.
Osmania, 1958.

773. Devidass, Narayannath
Vacaspalis advaita: A critical study.
Poona, 1992.

774. Devraj, P.I.
Neo Vedanticism of Swami Vivekanand: A critical study. 1993.

775. Dhereswari, S.
The concept of faith and religion in the philosophy of Radhakrishnan.
Osmania, 1909.

776. Dharam
The Narayaniyam: A philosophical study (S).
Delhi , 1983.

777. Dharambir
The social philosophy of M.N. Roy.
Meerut, 1975.

778. Dharampal
Sahridyanand ka sameekshatmak adhyayan (S).
Meerut, 1982.

779. Dhawan, Shiv
Relevance of Gandhi's social economic and political thought to the contemporary Indian situation.
Delhi, 1993.

780. Dhiman, Naresh Kumar
The contribution of Ganga Prasad Upadhyay to the exposition of Indian philosophy.
Punjab, 1992.

781. Dhir, Renu
Madhavacharya krit anuvyakhyayan ka vevechanatmak adhyayan (S).
Delhi, 1990.

782. Dikshit, Mandvi
Bharatiya darshan mein guna vimarsha (S).
Lucknow, 1990.

783. Dikshit, Piyush Kant
Sahacharyaniyam pancha kanvishanam.
Sampurnanand, 1990.

784. Dimple, Usha Ram Chandra
The worldly philosophy of saint Ram Das.
Durgawati, 1985.

785. Dimri, Bhagwati Prasad
Khyativada in orthodox system of Indian philosophy.
Delhi, 1979.

786. Dinesh Kumar
Samakaleen Bharatiya darshan ke paripekshya mein Sri Aurobindo ke nirpekshya tatva (H).
Gorakhpur, 1977.

787. Divetia, Suchita C.
Dristi srstivada in Indian philosophy (S).
Gujarat, 1986.

788. Doloi, Rajanikanta
Paramanu karanavade Sameeksha.
Calcutta, 1983.

789. Dubey, Anil Kumar
Bharatiya darshan mein Ishwar kee avadharana Nyaya

aur advaita vedanta ke vishesh sandarbh mein (H).
BHU, 1992.

790. Dubey, Manorama
Acharya Vinoba Bhave ka adhyatma darshan (H).
Gorakhpur, 1982.

791. Dubey, Prem Narayan
Social and religious thought of Mahatma Gandhi. Contemporary effect on society.
Saugar, 1971.

792. Dubey, Raghavendraji
Sri Krishnayamal tatrasya sameekshatmak Madhyayanam.
Sampurnanand, 1993.

793. Dubey, Satya Prakash
Yogatantra sahitya kaledidhya prashesthyam (S).
Sampurnanand, 1993,

794. Durrony, Khurram Shah
Mahatma Gandhi conception of religion with special reference to its bearing on society.
AMU, 1968.

795. Dutta, Deepti
Sankhya as presented in Devahuti Kapilas discourse and its development till Sankhya Karika.
Delhi, 1992.

796. Dwivedi, Pratibha Rani
Aastik darshanam mein manastatva: Ek Sameekshatmak evam tulnatmak adhyayan (H), (S).
Agra, 1981.

797. Dwivedi, Ram Rangoli
Maharaja Shivnath Singh ke darshanik siddhanton ka adhyayan (H).
Awadesh, 1980.

798. Dwivedi, Renu
Bharatiya darshan mein Karṇatavad Ek Sameekshatmak adhyayan (H).
BHU, 1993.

799. Ganeshi Lal
The philosophy of Bhagwan Das: A critical study and its significance to the contemporary culture.
Agra, 1989.

800. Gangadharan
Studies in gnanamritam.
Madurai, 1979.

801. Gangapadhyay, Mrinal Kanti
Vinitadeva's nyaya bindu — Tika, text reconstruction from tibetan into Sanskrit with English translation and annotations.
Calcutta, 1975.

802. Gangopadhyay, Paritima
A critical and comparative study of Jivadevata (Superman) in the philosophy of Ravindra Nath Tagore.
Ranchi, 1972.

803. Garg, Sushama
Kundkundacharya kee pramukh kritiyon mein darshanik dristi (S).
Jodhpur, 1978.

804. Gargi Devi
Sri Nimbarkacharya ke siddhant evam upasana pakshon ka etihasik adhyayan (H), (S).
Agra, 1982.

805. Ghosh, Jayasri
Vivekendev siksha on sikshatatwa.
Calcutta, 1989.

806. Ghosh, Dipak
Abhava-visayka Bharatiya darshanik siddhant.
Calcutta, 1982.

807. Gian Chand
Nature of matter and energy in Indian philosophy.
Agra, 1965.

808. Gill, Jaswinder Kaur
Guru Nanak's concepts of value.
Gurunanak Dev, 1978.

809. Giri, Gagan Deo
Shrimad Bhagwat Gita ke sankara bhasya ka samalochanatmak adhyayan (H).
Ranchi, 1976.

810. Godbale, Ranganath Sadashiv
Jnaneswara and Kabir : A study in the comparative philosophy.
Baroda, 1971.

811. Golakiya, Savjibai Arjunbhai
Philosophical contributions of J. Krishnamurti.
Baroda, 1982.

812. Gomathi, K.
A study of padartha sangraha and its commentary Madhava siddhantic seva by Padmanabh Suri.
Annamalai, 1993.

813. Gopal Krishnan, R.
Gandhiji and the west.
Annamalai, 1976.

814. Goswami, Ashok Kumar
A critical exposition of the Sudha khand of the Bhasa paricheda.
Gauhati, 1979.

815. Goswami, Dudhpuri
Praman: Ek parisheelan. Madhyakaleen dvaita veda aur advaitenadi Acharyon ke Bhasya evam darshon ke paripekshya mein (H).
Gurukul, 1992.

816. Goswami, Krishna
Concept of the individual self in Nyaya philosophy.
Calcutta, 1980.

817. Goswami, Malini
Latest critical edition and the critical exposition of the Vighanese Janmodays of Gouri Kant Dwiza (S).
Gauhati, 1988.

818. Gupta, Lalit Kishore
Umra sudharvadi, manavatavad mein nihit darshan vivechanatmak vivechan (H).
Bihar, 1984.

819. Gupta, Neelam
Shri Yeshovijay Suri Virachit Jain nyaya khandakhandya ka ek sameekshatmak adhyayan (H).
Kumaun, 1992.

820. Gupta, Pramila
Girvan Gira vaigyanik sahitya Bharatiya darshanon (S).
Rajasthan, 1988.

821. Gupta, Rashmı
Bharatiya darshan mein purush tatwa: Ek sameekshatmak adhyayan (H).
Panjab, 1992.

822. Gupta, Santosh
Gandhi ke anusar sadhyu sadhan, vichar.
Durgawati, 1986.

823. Gupta, Sarita
Problems of relations in Indian philosophy.
Delhi, 1978.

824. Gupta, Satya Pal
Psychopathology in Indian medicine Ayurveda with special reference to philosophical basis.
Agra, 1997.

825. Gupta, Shail
Samadhi in Indian philosophy.
AMU, 1977.

826. Gupta, Sharda
Brahmanand and his Advaita Martand (S).
Jammna , 1980.

827. Gupta, Siddartha
Bharatiya darshan cintayemon.
Vishwa Bharati, 1994.

828. Guru, Laxmi Shankar, Vishwanath
Philosophical ideas found in the principal Ayurvedic Text.
BHU, 1970.

829. Guru, Vimala
Humanistic elements in Indian thought.
Saugar, 1975.

830. Feys, Jean
The philosophy of evolution in Sri Aurobindo in Teil Hara De Chardin.
Ranchi, 1971.

831. Hari Prasad
Pramukha darshanika prathanon mein pratyaksta ka Swaroop.
Kurukshetra, 1993.

832. Hari Ram
Sri Manikantha krit nyaya ratnam ka samalochnatmak adhyayan (H).
Delhi, 1992.

833. Hedge, Venkateswaran Subray
Gandhi's philosophy of law.
Karnataka, 1977.

834. Iyav, Kesarkali Waterson
Approaches to personhood in Indian thought.
Poona, 1982.

835. Jadeja, Saharkunvarba U.
Critical study of the prosastopadabhasya (S).
Gujarat, 1981.

836. Jagdish Kaur
A socio-philosophical study of trends and tendencies of modern Indian society.
Rohilkhand, 1987.

837. Jaikrishna
Ashtonga yoga: Ek parisheelon (H).
BHU, 1993.

838. Jain, Deepaklata
The concept of soul Karma (Bondage) Moksha in Shuddhadvita and Jainism: A comparative study.
Sukhadia, 1988.

839. Jain, Kamala
Conception of Gita in various schools of Indian philosophy. Delhi, 1967.

840. Jain, Kiranbala
Syadved Manjari: Ek Sameekshatmak adhyayan (H), (S).
Kurukshetra, 1985.

841. Jain, Krishna
Shad darshanam mein sristhi aur laya kee dharma ka vikas (H).
Saugar.

842. Jain, Lalit Kumari Sadhvi
Bharatiya darshan mein parmanandvad: Jain darshan ke vishesh sandarbh mein.
Indore, 1977.

843. Jain, Nirmda
Pramaya Kamal Martand: Ek samikshatmak adhyayan (H), (S).
BHU, 1977.

844. Jain, Prudyumna Kumar
Metaphysical synthesis: Its nature and value as suggested by study of the philosophy of Kundkund.
Agra, 1983.

845. Jain, Prakash Chand
Jain sristi vidya evam pauranik srishti vidya ka vikasvad ke sandarbh mein tulnatmak adhyayan (H).
Jabalpur, 1971.

846. Jain, Saumal Kumar
A critical study of Sevarth siddhi of Acharya Pujyapad (S).
Kurukshetra, 1987.

847. Jamila Khatoon
The place of God, man and universe with philosophical system of Iqbal.
AMU, 1962.

848. Janki Devi
Aprokshaneebhuti aur Shankaracharya (H), (S).
Ranchi, 1986.

849. Jatav, Daya Ram
Evolution of contemporary Indian social philosophy (D. Litt.).
Agra, 1973.

850. Jatav, Daya Ram
A critical estimate of social philosophy of Dr. B.R. Ambedkar.
Agra, 1963.

851. Jayashree, M.A.
The concept of mind in Indian philosophy.
Banglore, 1993.

852. Jha, Baldeo
The Khandan of Byakte Vibek.
Darbhanga, 1979.

853. Jha, Kirtyanand
Vyatpattivadah, (S).
Darbhanga, 1981.

854. Jha, Nareshmohan
The philosophy of satyagrah: A study in Gandhi life.
Bhagalpur, 1980.

855. Jha, Parmanand
Pranav Brahma (D. Litt.) (S).
Darbhanga, 1984.

856. Jha, Ram Susheel
Mimansha dhikaruna Kaumudi: Ek parisheelan (H).
BHU, 1992.

857. Jha, Shashi Nath
M.M. Bharhnath krit proyoga pallavaha (D. Litt.).
Darbhanga, 1985.

858. Jha, Shatrushna
The impact of Upanishads on the metaphysical thought of Kabir.
Patna, 1976.

859. Jha, Syam Nandan
Kundkund evam Shankar ke darshanik pakshon ka tulnatmak adhyayan (H).
Vikram, 1976.

860. Jha, Sita Saran
Matantrasmeeksha poorva kanipata nodhyota kalv vachakatvanyantra vyasthapnam (S).
Darbhanga, 1986.

861. Jha, Sita Nath
A critical and comparative study of the Sivapurana with special reference to its philosophical background.
Bihar, 1971.

862. Jha, Uma Raman
Acharya Bhasarragyas: Ek adhyayan (S).
Darbhanga, 1981.

863. Joshi, L.V.
A critical study of the pratyaksha parichheda of the Nayabhusna of Bhasarvajna (S).
Gujarat , 1979.

864. Joshi, Kamda
Jain Semmat Druvyaswaroop vishleshan.
Kumaun, 1991.

865. Joshi, Madhukar Ramdos
Nathapantha che Telvagyan ani tyacha pracheen maratha samkaleen vichar vareel prabhav (M).
Nagpur, 1970.

866. Joshi, M.N.
Treatment of secular arts and science in some swara manosollasa (S).
Karnataka, 1985.

867. Joshi, M.N.
Amrithubhai: Ek chikitsak abhyas (M).
Bombay, 1986.

868. Joshi, P.V.
Pramanalaksana of Madhav with Jeyatirthas commentary: Translation and critical study.
Poona, 1988.

869. Joshi, Rajendra Kumar, V.
Towards a critical understanding of Sri Aurobindo's philosophy.
IIT, Bombay, 1991.

870. Joshi, S.A.
A study of lokyate: Critical evaluation.
Bombay, 1985.

871. Kale, Anjali Dinkar
Moral and political concepts underlying Panchtantra.
Poona, 1977.

872. Kalla, Asha
Swami Dayanand Sarswati ke samanvayavadi darshan (H).
Jodhpur, 1991.

873. Kamal, Shamla Ganesh
Mayavada of sankara: A critical and comparative study (S).
Poona , 1984.

874. Kamat, N.G.
Bharatiya Tattwagyonateel manabi sankalpana (S).
Poona , 19086.

875. Kamat, Prem Kumari
Mahabir aur Mahatma Gandhi ke darshanon mein chimsa kee avadharana: Ek tulnatmak adhyayan (H).
Mithila, 1986.

876. Kapoor, Ashish
Modern Indian philosophy thought in relation to our socio-political problem with special reference to Swami

Vivekanand, Ravindra Nath Tagore, Mahatma Gandhi and Sri Aurobindo.
Punjabi, 1996.

877. Kapoor, O.B.L.
Philosophy of Sri Chaitanya.
Allahabad, 1938.

878. Kapoor, Rajinderpal
Social philosophy of J. Krishnamurti.
Punjabi, 1995.

879. Kapoor, Veena
A comparative study of the commentaries of Kumarila Bhatta, and prahbdaron purva mimansa (S).
Panjab, 1979.

880. Karna, K.K.L.
Mahatma Gandhi's contribution to Hinduism.
Ranchi, 1970.

881. Karan Lakha
Critical and comparative study of relationship of Sankhya yoga and Vedanta (S).
Panjab, 1989.

882. Kaushal, Saroj
Vardarajacharya kee tarkik raksha ka samolochnatmak adhyayan.
Jodhpur, 1991.

883. Kaushik, Sanchita
Anubhuti prakash ka darshanik anusheelan (H).
Kashi, 1993.

884. Ketkar, B.G.
Nagarjuna: A fresh study.
Poona, 1986.

885. Khandelwal, Mamta
Ballabhacharya tatha Aurobindo kee darshanik

vichardharayan: Ek tulnatmak adhyayan (H).
Devi Ahilya, 1995.

886. Khandelwal, Usha
Adhunik manyataon ka vaigyanik pratipadan. Pt. Sri Ramsharma Acharya ke samanvayatmak dristikon ke sandarbh mein (H).
Durgawati, 1993.

887. Khanna, Sujata
The problem of suffering with special reference to Schopenhaver and Indian thought.
Delhi, 1970.

888. Khare, Pradeep Kumar
Madhu Sudan Saraswati ke darshanik siddhanton ka sameekshatmak Anusheelan (H).
Durgawati, 1991.

889. Khosla, Sneh
The nature of pramanya.
Delhi, 1988.

890. Kinghadekar, Shree Kala Anil
Nadkar Vedanta ke paripekshya mein Vedanta, Sangyavati ka anusheelan (H).
BHU, 1993.

891. Kochar, Manjula
Shrimad Bhagwat Gita kee samkaleen vyakhya, Tilak, Gandhi va Aurobindo ke vishesh sandarbh mein (H).
Indore, 1997.

892. Kotecha, M.D.
Shri Raman Maharshi: A philosophical study.
Gujarat, 1978.

893. Krishan, Gopal
Social thought in Ravindranath Tagore.
Meerut, 1971.

894. Krishna Devi
Tripura Bahasya: A philosophical study (S).
Kurukshetra, 1983.

895. Krishnamurthi, Radha
Sivatattvaratnakara: A cultural study (H), (S).
Poona, 1985.

896. Krishnamurthi, R.
A study of the Istasiddhi of Vinyllatmen in the light of the commentary of the state siddhi vivarana by Anubhutiswa (S).
Madras, 1983.

897. Krishna Nandan Prasad
Prachin Bharatiya vangmaya ka alok mein Tulsi Kavya ka sanskritic evam darshanik vivachary (H).
Ranchi, 1975.

898. Krishna Prasad Deo
Elements of mysticism in contemporary Indian philosophy with special reference to Ramkrishna Paramhansa and Ravindra Nath Tagore.
Bihar, 1972.

899. Kshatriya, Trilokinath
Baudhik achar mimansa ke samalochanatmak adhyayan (H).
Ravishankar, 1992.

900. Kaijpors, F.H.J.
The role of experience in Gandhian philosophy.
Poona, 1975.

901. Kulkarni, Sunanda Gunadapant
The critical and philosophical study of the Chatur stuti of Shri Bhashya Shri Ramanujacharya (S).
Shivaji, 1982.

902. Kundu, Arunesh Chandra
Sankaracharya bakyasudha granthor talparyang vishleshan (H).
Jodhpur, 1991.

903. Kundu, Yashodhara
Hindu marriage institution: A philosophical study.
Poona, 1978.

904. Lalitha, K.
Saiva nayanmers and Siva saranas: A comparative study of philosophical and religious perspective.
Mysore, 1981.

905. Lalith Kumari, P.P.
Theories of categories in Indian philosophy.
Andhra, 1980.

906. Leelamani, C.
A critical study of Agappa Dikshits Citra mimansa.
Calicut, 1991.

907. Lederle, M.R.
Philosophical trends in modern Maharashtra.
Poona, 1964.

908. Lenaerta, Henri
A study of the pratyabhigna philosophy of Kashmir.
BHU, 1971.

909. Lohani, Jaya
Bharatiya darshan shastron ke anusar shod swarup evam pad padarth vivechan (H), (S).
Kumaun, 1988.

910. Loundo, R.P.D.C.L.
The role and function of reasoning: Tarka in Sankaracharya Vedant.
Bombay, 1992.

911. Machhi, Dineshbhai Punabhai
Shri Vidyaranya rachit Panchadashi: Ek adhyayan (H).
Patel, 1993.

912. Madhu Sudan Prasad
The philosophy of Ram Mohan Roy.
Patna, 1966.

913. Maharanjan, M.
A study on tradition and modernity in Gandhian thought.
Madras, 1989.

914. Mahashobde, Sangeeta
Swami Vivekanand aur Shri M.N. Roy ke manavatavadi vicharon ka tulnatmak evam sameekshatmak adhyayan (H).
Burktulla, 1993.

915. Maheshwari, Hazarilal
The philosophy of Swami Ram Tirtha.
Agra, 1950.

916. Maheswari, Snehlata
Bharatiya darshan mein Avyuwin siddhant (H), (S).
Meerut, 1983.

917. Mahnashelly
Sri Aurobindo's concept of human unity and its relevance to modern times.
Durgawati, 1992.

918. Malik, Neela
The concept of abhava.
Delhi, 1990.

919. Mallik, Kalyani
History and the philosophical doctrine and the produce of Nath school of Yogis.
Calcutta, 1946.

920. Mandal, Lila
The conception of self in Indian philosophy: An approach from the Neo-Vedantic stand points.
Calcutta, 1970.

921. Manduli, Ram Dayal
Samkaleen Bharatiya darshan ko shernanand ka yogdan (H).

922. Manmodkar, D.N.
Varkari sampradaya: Tatvagyan va sadyakaleen auchitya varkari sampradayache, ailihasic samalochan, tatwa dnyapar adhisthyag ani vartaman kalatil mahatva (M).
Poona, 1978.

923. Mantri, Laxmikant Bhaskar
A critical study of Mahatma Gandhis doctrine of satya and Ahinsa: A philosophical analysis and assessment.
Poona, 1972.

924. Manual, Florence
Saint Taya monavar: A study in religious experiences.
Madras, 1974.

925. Magilamani, A.B.
The Hindu Christian concept of non-violence.
Osmania, 1973.

926. Mathai, M.P.
Gandhi's world view.
Gandhi, 1993.

927. Meena Rani
A critical study of Jimutava henas Dayabhaga in the context of Dayabhagapra dodhini of Sri Krshotarkalankara (S).
Panjab, 1982.

928. Mehta, Sobhalaxmi
Krishnanand ka alochnatmak adhyayan (S).
Jabalpur, 1981.

929. Meshram, R.B.
Bharatiya darshan sastra mahanubhava tatvo gyanay sathan (S).
Nagpur, 1972.

930. Mishra, Asha
Sankhya sutra evam Sankhya karika ka tulnatmak evam vivechanatmak adhyayan, vivid vyakhyo karon ke adhar per (H), (S).
Kanpur, 1979.

931. Mishra, Brajendra
Parjanyha vidha sameeksha (D. Litt.).
Darbhanga, 1982.

932. Mishra, Chandra Narayan
The problem of neo-science in Indian philosophy.
Bhagalpur, 1952.

933. Mishra, Deepak Kumar
A critical study of nyayadarshan.
Jagannath, 1996.

934. Mishra, Harendra Kumar
Bharatiya darshan mein kal tatva kee avadharana (H).
BHU, 1993.

935. Mishra, Haridaya Narayan
Dharmik anubhavan ka manovaigyanic adhyayan. Sri Ramkrishna ka jivan tatha dharmic anubhavon ke prasang mein (H).
Agra, 1968.

936. Mishra, Jai Govind
Studies in the philosophy of Asanga (S).
Gorakhpur, 1980.

937. Mishra, Kedar Nath
Goswami Vithalnath krit vidwan mondav ke ek sameekshatmak adhyayan (H).
BHU, 1988.

938. Mishra, Laxman Prasad
The philosophy and religion of Sri Ram Tirath and Vivekanand: A study on the new Vedantism.
Saugar, 1968.

939. Mishra, Laxmikant
Swami Vivekanand evam Sri Aurobindo ke darshanik vichar: Ek tulnatmak adhyayan (H).
Kanpur, 1974.

940. Mishra, Mamata
Bhatta Praman mimansa ka ek sameekshatmak adhyayan: Mimansa shlok vartik ke vishesh sandarbh mein (H).
BHU, 1992.

941. Mishra, Mahabir
Narsahasank charita syam Sangopangsmolchatmak matihasikam chandyoya -nam.
Sampurnanand, 1978.

942. Mishra, Nagendra
Acharya Amrik Chandra Suri krit samaya sar teeka ka darshnik anusheelan (H).
BHU, 1989.

943. Mishra, Namonorayan
Naamarth vimorsham.
Sampurnanand, 1990.

944. Mishra, Parmanand
The concept of nirodha in Indian psychology.
BHU, 1953.

945. Mishra, Ram Kumar
Vigyan Bhikchu krit yogvarti kasys vishistama-dhyanam (S).
BHU, 1982.

946. Mishra, Ramesh Chandra
Bhaıatiya darshan mein pretvad (H).
Rohilkhand, 1984.

947. Mishra, Satyabade
Reality as value in Sri Aurobindo.
Utkal, 1962.

948. Mishra, Savitri
The impact of western thought in contemporary Indian thinking.
Agra, 1969.

949. Mishra, Usha
Vibhakatyarth vimarsh (S).
Agra, 1978.

950. Mithilesh Kumar
A literary and philosophical study of Utpaladeva Shivastrotas.
Allahabad, 1978.

951. Mitra, Jyotir
The study of philosophical material in Charaka and susruta.
Agra, 1966.

952. Mitra, Jayanti
Shankaracharger Atyoboth granther bishleshnatmak sameeksha.
Jadavpur, 1993.

953. Moghe, Sandhya
Tilak evam Vinoba ke Gita vyakhyon ka tulnatmak

adhyayan (H).
Saugar, 1986.

954. Mohammed Rafeeque
A comparative study of the philosophy of Sri Aurobindo and Dr. Iqbal.
AMU, 1969.

955. Mohanta, Dilip Kumar
Scepticism in Indian philosophy.
Vishwa Bharati, 1969.

956. Mridula, Ram Prakash
Bharatiya darshan mein bhautikvadi vichardharaon ke vikas mein samkaleen Bharatiya darshanikon ka yogdan ka samalochanatmak adhyayan (H).
Rajasthan, 1993.

957. Mukherjee, Chitra
Shri Chaitanya samprdaya ka darshanik swaroop (H).
Jodhpur, 1980.

958. Mukherjee, Sakumar
Relationship between God and the absolute in the philosophy of Radhakrishnan.
Nagpur, 1964.

959. Mukhopadhyay, Devabrata
Asaucorinirnayah.
Jadavpur, 1992.

960. Mukhopadhyay, Rudrani
Bharatiya darshane sakshir swroop (S).
Ravindra Bharati, 1986.

961. Munot, Santosh
Bharatiya darshan mein vastuvad (H).
Jodhpur, 1983.

962. Muralidharan, V.R.
Manamayadaya: A critical study.
Calicut, 1993.

963. Murty, D.V.S.R.C.
Darsonoshu sabda pramanyavicharah (S).
Andhra, 1985.

964. Musaraf, Hossain
Swami Vivekanands philosophy of education: A psychometaphysical approach.
Calcutta, 1973.

965. Muthulakshmi, K.
Malputhur Narayana Bhatta as a philosopher.
Kerala, 1993.

966. Muthappan, P.L.
A critical study on the work of Arulnondisivachariyer (T).
Madras, 1987.

967. Nag, Shobha
A critical survey of the philosophy of Sri Aurobindo and Kashmiri Saivism.
Jabalpur, 1973.

968. Namboothiri K. Narayana
The methodology of Sankara.
Delhi, 1980.

969. Namdeo, Gauri Shankar
Swami Vivekanand vichar darshan aur adhunik punuruthan mein unka yogdan (H).
Saugar, 1984.

970. Narayana, V.S.
Philosophy of Ravindra Nath Tagore.
Allahabad, 1946.

971. Narayan, J.
The conception of absolute in Sri Aurobindo and Alfred Narth Whitehead.
Ranchi, 1969

972. Narayanan, K.
The philosophy of Sivavakkiar.
Madras, 1991

973. Narayanan, T.S.R.
A critical study of theoretical differences in the schools of Bhatta and Prabhachara with reference with reference to pramanas.
Rastriya Sanskrit, 1993.

974. Natarajan, K.
A interpretation of the jivan mukthiviveka of vidyaranya.
Madras, 1991

975. Nautiyal, Mamta
Shankar ke abhasvat tatha Nagarjun ke Shunyavad ka tulanatmak adhyayan (H).
Garhwal, 1987.

976. Nawal, Surinder Kumar
A study of Sri Aurobindo's concept of the human unity.
Kurukshetra, 1981.

977. Neena Kumari
Vivarane prameya sangraha: A study (S).
Panjab, 1985.

978. Nene, Somnath
Bhatta Chintamani, Tarkapad: Ek sameekshatmak adhyayan (H), (S).
BHU, 1975.

979. Nigam, Satyabrat
Contribution of Swami Vivekanand in modern renaissance in Indian philosophy and culture.
Agra, 1968.

980. Nigam, Shobha
Adhyatm Ramayana: Ek darshanik adhyayan (H).
Ravishankar, 1981.

981. Nirmala Devi, D.
Concept of nature in Indian thought.
Calcutta, 1984.

982. Nirotma
Maharishi pranit granth sangraha evam pravachan: Ek sameekshatmak adhyayan (H).
Panjab, 1992.

983. Ojha, Ram Prabha
Shandilya bhakti sutras ke swapna shwar bhasya ka darshanik adhyayan (H), (S).
BHU, 1983.

984. Omena, S.
The philosophy of Sree Narayan Guru.
Kerala, 1980.

985. Onkaranand
Shaiva Siddhant: Ek samalochnatmak adhyayan (H).
Meerut, 1976.

986. Om Prakash
Namartha vicara.
Kurukshetra (S), 1990.

987. Padmaju, K.
Philosophy of Shri Chattambi Swamikal.
Calicut, 1988.

988. Pal Nitai, Chandra
Priti Sandarbha of Sir Siva Goswami.
Agra, 1980.

989. Panda, Gajendra Kumar
NRU Simhashrami Saraswati virachit vedant tatva viveka granthsya adhyayan.
Rastriya Sanskrit, 1993.

990. Pandey, Ashutosh
Shwetash wataropnishad ka darshanik anusheelan (H).
BHU, 1989.

991. Pandey Bhrigunath
Eleavali vidyadhar krit ka ek sameekshatmak evam tulnatmak adhyayan (S).
BHU, 1977.

992. Pandey, Chandraswer
The problem of god in Indian philosophy with special reference to Nyaya, yoga and vedant.
Bihar, 1985.

993. Pandey, Girija Shankar
Nagarjuna kee shanyuta kee avadharana (H).
Durgawati, 1985.

994. Pandey, K.
Bramha darshan per naitik mulyon ka prabhav (H).
Rohilkhand, 1993.

995. Pandey, Laxmikant
Prasthanatriyi kee vyakhyon ke vishesh sandarbh mein Radhakrishnan ke Vedant ke pratidristi (H).
BHU, 1977.

996. Pandey, N.
Manmaya prakashaka: Ek adhyayan (H), (S).
Kumaun, 1984.

997. Pandey, Priyamvada
Tatparya ka shestriya nirupan (S).
Gorakhpur, 1988.

998. Pandey, Priyamvada Kumari
Bharatiya darshan visheshkar nyaya mimansa evam vyakaran kee dristi se shabda artha evam unke sambandh kee sameeksha (H).
BHU, 1983.

999. Pandey, Raghunath
A critical study of Acharya Bhavadeka Prajne Pradeepa (D. Litt.).
AMU, 1983.

1000. Pandey, Ram Awatar
Prachyupesh chatgobhaya darshdristhtya jeewan swroop vimarshah.
Sampurnanand, 1993.

1001. Pandey, Ram Chandra Sharma
The problem of meaning in Indian philosophy.
BHU, 1957.

1002. Pandey, Ram Das
Astitvavad mein tarka evam pratibhavon ka sthan (H).
Kanpur, 1983.

1003. Pandey, Rashmi
Bharatiya darshan mein parmenu (S).
Panjab, 1987.

1004. Pandey, Ravindra Nath
Bharatiya darshan mein anishwerbad.
Kashi, 1993.

1005. Pandey, Rewati Raman
Concept of nature in Indian philosophy.
Allahabad, 1969.

1006. Pandey, Sri Ram
Vidhitikaropagyvicha ranameto chanam.
Sampurnanand, 1978.

1007. Pandey, Surendra Kumar
Bharatiya darshan mein Karma siddhant (H).
BHU, 1993.

1008. Pandey, Vijay Shree
A critical study of Mahatma Gandhi's philosophy of religion.
Allahabad, 1974.

1009. Pandya, Malshankar Maganlal
The philosophical basis of Ayurveda.
Gujarat, 1969.

1010. Pang, Chun Lun
Indian thought: A reinterpretation according to the numinous experience.
BHU, 1961.

1011. Pani, Binita
The influence of Indian scriptures on Sri Aurobindo's philosophy of life divine.
Utkal, 1991.

1012. Pant, Chandra Lekha
Sankhyatatva kaumudi yuktidipika ka tulnatmak adhyayan (H).
BHU, 1979.

1013. Paranjape, Sucheta Madhav
A critical study of Jaiminiya sraute literature.
Tilak, 1992.

1014. Patel, Shantilal Manganlal
Philosophy of Srimad Rajchandra.
Baroda, 1966.

1015. Pathak, Chintamani
Shri Aurobindo's interpretation of Indian religious thought and his contribution to it.
BHU, 1968.

1016. Pathak, Mundernath
Psychological basis of Buddhist ethics: A study of Theravada Buddhism.
Ranchi, 1976.

1017. Pathak, M.M.
Critical edition of the Viveda-Candra of Miraru Mishra (S).
Bombay, 1989.

1018. Pathak, Rajendra Prasad
Urihattrayee ka darshanik adhyayan (H).
Rohilkhand; 1986.

1019. Pathak, Sachidanand
Bharatiya darshan mein Jagat ka swaroop (H), (S).
Allahabad, 1978.

1020. Pathak, Sarvanand
Charavakmet kee darshanik bhumika (H).
Bhagalpur, 1963.

1021. Pathya, Arun Madhukar
Framework of Nagarjuns philosophy.
Poona, 1982.

1022. Pati, Nilakantha
A critical edition of tattva muktavali (C).
Utkal, 1984.

1023. Pandiyal, Pushpa Sharan
Bharatiya darshanon mein karmavad: Ek tulnatmak adhyayan.
Gurukul, 1993.

1024. Paul, K. Purushottam
Philosophy of Dayanand Saraswati.
Andhra, 1989.

1025. Pillai, R. Kalappa
Sivneri prakasam.
Annamalai, 1982.

1026. Pillai, T. Unni Krishanan
Repudiation of the samkhya and yog by Sankara.
Madras, 1991.

1027. Prabhakar, M.
An examination into ethico-philosophical implications of Yoga.
Osmania, 1992.

1028. Prajapati, Karan
Sanskrit vangyamaya ko Madhavacharya kee den.
Gorakhpur, 1988.

1029. Prasad, Kavita
Anupalabdhi: Ek Sameekshatmak vishleshan (H).
Magadh, 1987.

1030. Pramila Kumari, V.
The concept of reality in Vedanta.
Kerala, 1993.

1031. Pratima, Devi
Amitgat shravakacher ka sameekshatmak adhyayan (H).
Rohilkhand, 1993.

1032. Prema Kumari, Amma A.
Brahmatattwa prakashika: A study (S).
Kerala, 1990.

1033. Pujari Bandana
An enquiry into the problems of God and absolute with special reference to Sankara and Rashdoll.
Gauhati, 1995.

1034. Puri, Rashmi Sudha
Mahatma Gandhi on war and peace.
Panjab, 1980.

1035. Purkayastha, Brijabihari
A critical evolution of anti-theistic in Indian philosophy.
Calcutta, 1981.

1036. Purkayastha, Sujata
The philosophy of Sarvajnatmanum.
Gauhati, 1988.

1037. Purohit, Abha
Samkaleen Bharatiya darshanon mein Nyaya Vedant, Swami Vivekanand, Ravindra Nath Tagore, Dr. S. Radhakrishnan ke sandarbh mein (H).
Jodhpur, 1993.

1038. Puthanathara, Anupdev Micheal
Sri Aurobindo: A synthesis of tradition and modernity.
BHU, 1974.

1039. Radhakrishnan, C.V.
Social and political philosophy of Rajaji.
Madras, 1981.

1040. Rai, Akhilesh Kumar
Mahatma Gandhi ka dharma aur darshan (H).
BHU, 1901.

1041. Rai, Narmadeshwar
Bharatiya astik derhnik vangmaya mein trigun swarup evam manav jeevan mein uski upyogita (H), (S).
Kanpur, 1987.

1042. Raina, Chaman Lal
Sri Aurobindo tatha Iqbal ke darshan ka tulnatmak adhyayan (H).
Kashmir, 1988.

1043. Raizada, Tripta
Social philosophy of Dr. Annie Besant.
Rohilkhand, 1982.

1044. Rajamohan, C.
Social concern in Indian philosophy: A study.
Calcutta, 1983.

1045. Rajani, Kalangi Remi
The ideal of human Unity: A critical study of Sri Aurobindo's philosophy.
Andhra, 1990.

1046. Rajeshwari, Kanjumma A.C.
Vivekanand's letters: A study.
Kerala, 1979.

1047. Rajgopalan M.
The philosophy of Nammelvev with special reference to Thiraraimohi.
Madras, 1983.

1048. Rajpal, Anita
Raghunath Siromani krita padarth attvani rupanam: Ek Adhyayan.
Delhi, 1991.

1049. Ramashish Prasad
A critical and comparative study of intellect and intuition in the conception of Radhakrishnan and Sri Aurobindo.
Ranchi, 1973.

1050. Ramaswami, Subashini
A critical study of J. Krishnnamurti's philosophy.
Annamalai, 1983.

1051. Ram Chandra Deo
Mandan Mishra ke vidhiviveka ka sameekshatmak adhyayan (H), (S).
BHU, 1977.

1052. Ram Chandran, T.P.
The Indian philosophy of beauty: Part one: perspective. Part two: specific concepts.
Madras, 1980.

1053. Ram Chandran, B.
Ends and means in Gandhi and Marx.
Osmania, 1993.

1054. Ranga Char, S.
The philosophy of Pancharattas.
Mysore, 1969.

1055. Ranganath, S.
Contribution of vacaspathi Mishra, to Indian philosophy (S).
Banglore, 1990.

1056. Rao, Bhagwati
Pratyak aur prack (H).
Rajasthan, 1971.

1057. Rao, G.S.S. Sriniwas
Modern Vedanta with reference to the work of Raja Ram Mohan Roy, Swami Vivekanand and Swami Ram Tirtha.
Andhra, 1970.

1058. Rao, M. Narsimha
The concept of Prana in Indian philosophy with special reference to Upanishads and Patanjali Yoga.
Shivaji, 1986.

1059. Rao, M.S. Kumaraswami
The value system in Indian tradition and its relevance to contemporary Indian society.
Madras, 1992.

1060. Rao, Sriniwas
Theories of perceptional error in Indian philosophy: A dialectical reconstruction.
Mysore, 1987.

1061. Rao, Srinivas
Analysis of matter in orthodox Schools of Indian philosophy.
Andhra, 1993.

1062. Rao, S.D.A. Joga
Interaction between science and Indian philosophy: A critical study with special reference to Caraka Samhita.
Andhra, 1982.

1063. Rao, V. Katumba
Tarka Sastra Andharanam yoga danam.
Rastriya Sanskrit, 1993.

1064. Rastogi, Pratima
Vigyan Bhikshu, ka Sankhya yoga tatha Vedant ka den (H), (S).
Jodhpur, 1979.

1065. Rathod, S.B.
J. Krishnamurthi: the man and his mission.
Bombay, 1986.

1066. Rathunam, Ram Kumar
The concept of Dukha in Indian philosophy with special reference to early Buddhism.
Venkateswara, 1991.

1067. Rautela, Vijaylaxmi
Bharatiya darshan mein antahkarana ka swaroop (H), (S).
Delhi, 1989.

1068. Rawal, M.M.
The Gita's philosophy of man management.
Gujarat, 1989.

1069. Rawal, Ram Narayan
Vadic evam anpnisha, darshan: Ek tulnatmak adhyayan. Maharishi Dayanand ke paripekshya mein (H).
Gurukul, 1988.

1070. Rebeiro, Meluyn Joseph
A critical study of the thought of Dr. Bhagwan Das.
BHU, 1974.

1071. Reddy, D. Krishna
Vemana and Sankara: A comparative study.
Venkateswara, 1976

1072. Reddy, K. Vasudeva
The concept of welfare state with reference to India with special reference to ancient Indian texts.
Venkateswara, 1979.

1073. Reddy, P. Sita Ram
Gandhi's philosophy of Sarvodaya.
Osmania, 1974.

1074. Reddy, Rajeev Karan
Social reconstruction in the philosophy of Jai Prakash Narayan: A critical study.
Osmania, 1996.

1075. Reddy, V. Madhu Sudan
The concept of evolution in the philosophy of Sri Aurobindo and the problem of human destiny.
Osmania, 1958.

1076. Reddy, V. Manmohan
Interpretation of the Vadaswamy Dayanandand Sri Aurobindo.
Osmania, 1972.

1077. Reddy, R. Venkat
Significance of suffering in the philosophy of Gandhi.
Osmania, 1978.

1078. Reddy, V. Anand
The concept of physical transformation in Sri Aurobindo's philosophy.
Madras, 1989.

1079. Reddy, V. Narayan Karan
The concept of man in Tagore and Radha Krishanan.
Osmania, 1968.

1080. Rekha Rani
Mokshakar Gupta krita tarka Bhasa: Ek sameekshatmak adhyayan (H).
Kurukshetra, 1993.

1081. Roop Kishan
Sri Ramkrishna ke darshan mein maya.
Agra, 1982.

1082. Roy, Gitali
The comparative study of the philosophy of Sri Aurobindo and Sri Ravindra Nath Tagore.
Bihar, 1971.

1083. Roy, Gauri
The bondage and liberation of the Jira according to Sri Chaitanya.
Agra, 1973.

1084. Roy, Nilay
Some philosophical problems concerning man and society in Ancient Indian philosophy.
Calcutta, 1983.

1085. Roy, Permanand
Prachya evam pashchatya achar darshan kee pristibhoomi mein Mahatma Gandhi ke achar darshan ka tulnatmak evam sameekshatmak adhyayan (H).
Bihar, 1978.

1086. Roy, Ram Balak
Moral philosophy of Mahatma Gandhi.
Bihar, 1977.

1087. Sadashivaiah, R.S.
A critical study of Siddhanta Sikhamani of Sivayogi Sivacharya.
Banglore, 1991.

1088. Sadhu, Brahmanand
Sri Sankaracharya and Sri Aurobindo: A critical and comparative study.
Gujarat, 1982.

1089. Sah, Renu
Acharyavigyan Bhikshu krit yogasar sangraha ka sameekshatmak adhyayan (H), (S).
Kumaun, 1987.

1090. Saini, Krishna Chand
A critical study of J. Krishnamurthi's philosophy of education.
Kurukshetra, 1993.

1091. Saini, Mangat Ram
Vedic padarth vigyan evam ship vidya aur Maharishi Dayanand.
Ajmer, 1993.

1092. Sam, Christopher C.
Compassion in Indian philosophy with special reference to St. Ramlinga.
Annamalai, 1993.

1093. Samanta, Srikanta
System of Indian philosophy on the concept of Nirikalpak, pratyaksa: A critical study.
Burdwan, 1996.

1094. Sampoorna, C.
The theories of perception in Indian philosophy: An evolution.
Venkateswara, 1971.

1095. Sangavai, Vijay V.
Purushartha: Ek chikistsak abhyas.
Poona, 1991.

1096. Sannellappean Var, S.L.
Kannada Sahityadalli yogado vivechana.
Karnataka, 1992.

1097. Sant Kumari
Sri Vedantdeshik ke sahitya kritiyon ka samalochnatmak adhyayan (S).
Agra, 1978.

1098. Santa Kumari
Swami Dayanand ka anuvartividavanon ka upanishad

vyakhya karya (H).
Panjab, 1992.

1099. Santis, Stefanoce
Mans relationship with nature: Some Indian philosophical perspective.
BHU, 1993.

1100. Sanyal, Manyurisri
Srikanthe conception of absolute
Burdwan.

1101. Sanyal, Syamali
The concept of Swalakshana and Samanyulaksana: A critical evaluation.
NBU, 1990.

1102. Sarkar, Aditi
The development of concept of Maya and Avidya with special reference to the concept of Vivavtea: An interpretation of Sankara's philosophy (D. Litt.).
Patna, 1981.

1103. Sarma, C.V.S. Subramanya
Ajnana dhwanta condebhasharya patha sameekshatmak samadanam.
Rashtriya Sanskrit, 1990.

1104. Sarma, Rajendra Nath
A critical exposition of the vaggartha metrka of the prakarana penoka (S).
Gauhati, 1984.

1105. Sarmah, Hiran
An analytical study of the gunas of the sankhya system.
Gauhati, 1992.

1106. Saroja, G.V.
A study of Tilak's Gita Rahasya in the light of Sankara's commentary on the Bhagwat Gita.
Madras, 1975.

1107. Satyanarayana, Chintapati
Venkshadri Buddha kruta tarka Bhasha pravesika vyakahyayah tarka sankhgayam partha sameekshatmakam, samdanam.
Rashtriya Sanskrit, 1993.

1108. Satya Narayana, Suryaderarg
Philosophical foundation of radical humanism: A study of M.N. Roy.
Andheri, 1980.

1109. Satyanarayana, Y. Venketa
Marx and Gandhi: A comparative study of social philosophies.
Andheri, 1981.

1110. Saraswati, Swami Pragyanand
Shri Chitsukhmani krit Naishkarmya sidahitika bhavtatva prakashakyah. Sampadanam.
BHU, 1993.

1111. Severimuthu, Dominus Arulsamy
Siddhantic Astakam of Umapathi Sivacoryer: A study.
Madras, 1984.

1112. Saxena, Alok
Radhakrishnan ke darshan mein anrikshanumati ka sthan: Ek sameekshatmak adhyayan (H).
Agra, 1980.

1113. Saxena, Bimala
The problem of error with special reference to Indian philosophy.
Delhi, 1975.

1114. Saxena, Pratibha
A study of karma theory in the orthodox system of Indian philosophy (S).
Allahabad, 1976.

1115. Saxena, Sudha
Sri Aurobindo ka samajik rajnitik evam Sanskritik darshan (H).
Lucknow, 1986.

1116. Sekhar, P.
Gleanning from the Sribhasya.
Madras, 1993.

1117. Sen, Brinda
Akanbsa: Its role in generating verbal knowledge.
Jadavpur, 1991.

1118. Sen, Debika
Concept of man in contemporary Indian philosophy with special reference to Swami Vivekanand Sri Aurobindo, Sri Ravindranath Tagore and Mahatma Gandhi.
Burdwan, 1983.

1119. Sen, Devipriya
The concept of divine love in Indian thought with special reference to Bengal Vaishnavism.
BHU, 1975.

1120. Sen, Roma
A critical study of Gandhian philosophy.
Patna, 1975.

1121. Sengupta, Dipa
Mahavidyanumana as pramana (S).
Ravindra Bharati, 1987.

1122. Sensharma, Devbrata
Man and his destiny according to the Trika philosophy of Kashmir,
BHU, 1958.

1123. Sethi, Kiran
Astitvavad mein satta ka swaroop (H).
Jabalpur, 1976.

1124. Shab, Nila S.
Sri Shantanand manikrit adharm satsangi jeevan vivechanatmak adhyayan.
Gujarat, 1985.

1125. Shah, Jitendra Babulal
Dwadeshar, Nayachakra ka darshanik adhyayan (H).
BHU, 1993.

1126. Shah, S.M.
The dialectic of two forte standpoint and reality in Indian philosophy, Kundkunda, Nagarjuna, Gaudopada and Sankara.
Poona, 1980.

1127. Shahi, Tribhuwan Prasad
A critical and comparative study of Buddha Vivekanand and Vinoba with special reference to their contribution in the realm of moral and social philosophy.
Bihar, 1982.

1128. Shankar Prasad, Uma
Shrimad Bhagwat Puran pratipadityaga swarupana Sah Patanjal yoga darshanasya tulnatmak adhyayan.
Rashtriya Sanskrit, 1992.

1129. M. Sonmugham
Saiva Siddhanta and the social philosophy of St. Ramalingam.
Madras, 1978.

1130. Shems M.
Suffism and Saiva siddhant in Tamilnadu with special reference to poet Mohammed Musthan Sahab.
Annamalai, 1977.

1131. Sharma, Anil Kumar
Mandukykarika: Ek sameekshatmak adhyayan.
H.P., 1991.

1232. Sharma, Archana
Bradley evam Sri Aurobindo darshan mein Jagat kee satta (H).
Agra, 1982.

1133. Sharma, Deepak
M.M. Anand Krishanan Shastrikrita advaita tattva shuddhi ka samolachnatmak adhyayan.
Delhi, 1991.

1134. Sharma, Dharmanand
Comparative and critical analysis of the philosophy of Gandapada and Shankara Charya (S).
Panjab, 1983.

1135. Sharma, Dwijendra Prakash
The concept of God in the Bhagwat Gita and neo Vedantic thinkers: A comparative study.
Rohilkhand, 1995.

1136. Sharma, Indra Deo
Sri Aurobindos Savitri. A study in perception. A Jungian interpretation.
H.P. 1992.

1137. Sharma, Indu Mala
Ahimsa: A comparative study in Buddha and Gandhian thought.
Delhi, 1984.

1138. Sharma, Jaikishan
A study of stavachintamani and its place in Kashmir's Saiva darshan (S).
Jammu, 1979.

1139. Sharma, Mohan Lal
Comparative study of Patanjali's yoga darshanom and Vasu Gupta Siva Sutram.
Jammu, 1991.

1140. Sharma, Nandlal
Bharatiya darshanesu pratipaditanam sristhetha ki layanam tulnatmak vivechana.
Rastriya Sanskrit, 1992.

1141. Sharma, Om Dutt
Swami Dayanand Dwara vedon kee Yatharthvadi vyakhya kee darshanik sameeksha (H).
Meerut, 1989.

1142. Sharma, Purushottam Dutt
A study of the Siddhanta Bindu of Madhusudan Saraswati (S).
Punjab, 1983.

1143. Sharma, Preeti
Abhipraya prakashika: Ek adhyayan.
Delhi, 1992.

1144. Sharma, Rajendra Singh
Samkaleen Bharatiya darshon mein huye anusandhanon ke prakash mein Shankar Mayavad ka alochanatmak adhyayan (H).
Rohilkhand, 1984.

1145. Sharma, Rajeev
Mahatma Gandhi chintan per vibhinna darshan evam vicharakon ka prabhav (H).
Rohilkhand, 1989.

1146. Sharma, Ratni
Samkaleen Bharatiya darshanikon kee dristi mein Bharatiya Sanskriti ka swaroop: Mahatma Gandhi, Sri Aurobindo. Dr. Radha Krishnon ke vishesh Sandarbh mein (H).
Durgawati, 1993.

1147. Sharma, Raj Kumari
Maharishi Dayanand ke paripekshya main Mahabharat

mein nirdisht dharnaun darshanon ka samakaleen adhyayan (S).
Gurukul, 1986.

1148. Sharma, Ram Nath
The philosophy of Sri Aurobindo: A critical study.
Rajasthan 1970.

1149. Sharma, Ram Nath
The social philosophy of Sri Aurobindo (D. Litt.).
Meerut, 1974.

1150. Sharma Ranjan Kumar
Vidnag praneet Nyayaprakash kee Haribhatra Srikant vritti ka sameekshatmak adhyayan Mool evam vritti ka sampadan anubhav tatha tippan sahit (H).
BHU, 1993.

1151. Sharma, Shakti Dhar
Upanishadon aur Gita mein yog tatva Patanjal yog darshan ke paripekshya mein (H).
Punjab, 1992.

1152. Sharma, Sharada
Bhatta Chintamani ke tarkapade ka adhyayan.
Delhi, 1985.

1153. Sharma, Shardanand
Vishisthe dvaitasdwetavedyo: Vishist vishyayana samikshatmak tulnatmak adhyayanam (S).
Darbhanga, 1998.

1154. Sharma, Soma
Vyayogas in Sankrit (S).
Delhi, 1980.

1155. Sharma, Suneeta
Madhusudan Saraswati virachit Anarat mandakini: Sampadan evam sameeksha.
Rajasthan, 1991.

1156. Shan, Sanpson C.
Confucious and Tagore (D. Litt.).
BHU, 1947.

1157. Shanta Kumar, B.R.
Advaita as transformative metaphysics.
Pondicherry, 1992.

1158. Sheshiprabha Devi
A comparative study of the commentaries on Sankara Bhasya catup sutras.
BHU, 1977.

1159. Shashiprabha
Sri Aurobindo's ethical philosophy and its relevance in modern times.
Rohilkhand, 1995.

1160. Shastri, R.L. Narasimha
Patenjatam Maha-Bhesyam Loukika nyayah: A study (S).
Andheri, 1988.

1161. Shivarudrappa, A.L.
Religion and ethics of Mahatma Gandhi: Shiraraprappu, A.L. A philosophical study.
Mysore, 1972.

1162. Shiv Shankar
Budh, Jain aur yoga darshan mein Panchsheel swaroop vivechan (H).
Magadh, 1992.

1163. Shringhy, Ravindra Kumar
Philosophy of J. Krishnamurthy: A systematic and critical study.
BHU, 1973.

1164. Shuhpurkar, Joyti
Jaiprakash Narayan ka samaj darshan: Ek

Sameekshatmak vivechan (H).
Vikram, 1993.

1165. Shukla, Baliram
Anumana Pramana (S).
Delhi, 1993.

1166. Shukla, Indrajeet
Gorakshnath siddhantana darsh mikam sanbritikanch mulyankan.
Sampurnanand, 1993.

1167. Shukla, Maya
Santi Parva mein darshanik vichar (H).
BHU, 1992.

1168. Shukla, Ravi Shankar
Srimad Bhagwat Gitaya Madhu Sudan neeteekeyah samkshyao gatshya sameekshatmak adhyayan.
BHU, 1993.

1169. Shukla, Sangeeta
Paramhansa yoganand ka Bharatiya darshan mein yogdan: Ek tulnatmak sameekshatmak adhyayan (H).
Bihar, 1992.

1170. Sil, Brijendra Nath
Mechanical physical and chemical theories of the ancient Hindus.
Calcutta, 1960.

1171. Siksha Das
S. Radhakrishanan and J. Krishnamurthy: A comparative study.
Bihar, 1990.

1172. Singh, Arun Kumar
Pratyabhigya evam yogachar vigyanvad darshanon mein chinta ka swaroop (H).
BHU, 1987.

1173. Singh, Bijaypal
A critical study of the philosophy of Gorakh Nath (S).
Garhwal, 1987.

1174. Singh, Birendra
Madhyamik darshan kal parikasha paddhati (H).
BHU, 1992.

1175. Singh, Chandrabhan Prasad
Rahul Sankrityayan ka itihas dristi.
JNU, 1986.

1176. Singh, Darshan
Gandhivad ko Vinoba kee den (H).
Bhagalpur, 1993.

1177. Singh, Durgvijay
Baudh darshan evam Advaita Vedant mein pratyaksya vichar: Nyaya bindu evam Vedant peribhasha ke sandarbh mein (H).
BHU, 1992.

1178. Singh, Gauri Shankar
Acharya Hem Chandra dwara Nyaya evam. Baudha darshan ke vishesh sandarbh mein (H).
BHU, 1993.

1179. Singh, Jai
A critical study of shabda pramana in Indian philosophy.
Kurukshetra, 1986.

1180. Singh, Jagbir
Utpaldeo ka Kashmir Shaiva darshan ko yogdan (H), (S).
Jammu, 1986.

1181. Singh, Karan
Dayanandiya vangmai mein shuddarshan vishayak sandarbhon ka alochnatmak adhyayan (H), (S).
Pubjab, 1990.

1182. Singh, Laxmishwar Prasad
Bharatiya darshanon mein kantatwa evem Jain parampera: Vishisthatya mayan prajay charya gat uska" vishasate (H).
Bihar, 1982.

1183. Singh, Madhuria
Karma punarjanma aur mokshya: Hindu evam Baudh darshano ka tulnatmak adhyayan (H).
BHU, 1994.

1184. Singh, Narendra
A critical examination of Sankaracharya's doctrine of maya in contemporary Indian philosophy.
Allahabad, 1979.

1185. Singh, Nathuni
Sri Aurobindo evam Ballabhacharya ke darshanon mein prem tatva ka tulnatmak evam sameekshatmak adhyayan.
Jadavpur, 1993.

1186. Singh, Padmakar
Argument for and against the existence of God orthodox and unorthodox school of Indian thought.
Magadh, 1977.

1187. Singh, Pawan Kumar
Kashmir Shaiva darshan evam Advait Vedant mein dharma ka tulnatmak adhyayan (H).
BHU, 1994.

1188. Singh, Pramod Kumar
Valmiki ka darshanik dristikon (H).
Rohilkhand, 1995.

1189. Singh, Pratibha
Chitra mimansa ka sastriya adhyayan (H).
Awadh, 1993.

1190. Singh, Prem
Concept of Jeeva in Indian philosophy (S).
Kurukshetra, 1981.

1191. Singh, R.K.
Plato aur Shankar ke anusar puran tatwa: Ek tulnatmak sameeksha (H).
Agra, 1980.

1192. Singh Radhesyam
Prachin nyaya darshon tatha Saiva Siddhant darshan main Ishwar: Ek tulanatmak evam sameekshatmak adhyayan (H).
BHU, 1992.

1193. Singh, Ragav Pratap
Gandhi kee naitik vichardharaon ka alochanatmak adhyayan (H).
Awadhesh, 1975.

1194. Singh, Rajpal
Arya samaj ke pramukh vidwanon kee Bharatiya Shiddarshan ko den (H).
Panjab, 1985.

1195. Singh, Ram
Mahabharat mein Vedant ka anusheelan (H), (S).
Kanpur, 1980.

1196. Singh, Rameshwar Prasad
The social philosophy of Swami Vivekanand.
Bihar, 1972.

1197. Singh, Ranvijay
Vivekanand aur Tagore ke chintan mein manusya ka swaroop aur uska lakshya (H).
Kashi, 1993.

1198. Singh, Surjit
A comparative study of the concept of avidya in Indian

thought with special reference to orthodox system of Indian philosophy.
Punjabi, 1991.

1199. Sinha, Avanindra Kumar
The dramatic art of Sri Aurobindo.
Bihar, 1974.

1200. Sinha, Harendra Prasad
The comparative and critical study of Tagore and Radhakrishnana conception of religion.
Patna, 1975.

1201. Sinha, G. Pratap
Arthapatti: A critical and comparative study of the views of purva mimansa, Advaita Vedant and Nyaya vaishesik system.
Venkateswara, 1990.

1202. Sinha, Kali Prasad
The concept of the absolute in Indian philosophy (S).
Burdwan, 1983.

1203. Sinha, Laxman Prasad
Mahatma Gandhi ke satya evam Ahinsa sambandhi vichar: Ek alochanatmak adhyayan (H).
Ranchi, 1973.

1204. Sinha, Manjulika
Ravindra nather soundarya tatwa (B),
Vishwa Bharati, 1975.

1205. Sinha, M.K.
The conception of world and its destiny in Sri Aurobindo's philosophy.
Ranchi, 1980.

1206. Sinha, Neelima
Gyan ke swarup ke sambandh mein Bharatiya aur sam samayik pashyatya kamon ka tulnatmak, adhyayan (H).
Magadh, 1984.

1207. Sinha, Raniroopmati
Samkaleen Bharatiya darshon mein ashubh kee samasya: Ek tulnatmak evam sameekshatmak adhyayan (H).
Magadh, 1989.

1208. Sinha, Umeshwar Prasad
Contemporary Indian social philosophy with special reference to Mahatma Gandhi, Vivekanand and Jaya Prakash.
Magadh, 1973.

1209. Singh, Surendra Nath
A critical study of socio-ethical and religious aspects of the philosophy of sarvodaya Bihar, 1978.

1210. Sitaram Charyalu, Vedela Venkata
A critical evaluation of Vedic and non-Vedic darsanas (S).
Andhra, 1988.

1211. Sivasubrameni, P.A.
The philosophy of St. Ramalingam with special reference to its basic concepts.
Madras 1973.

1212. Soni, Raja Ram
Hindi ka chhayavadi kavya: Ek darshanik unusheelan (H).
Durgawati, 1988.

1213. Soni, Uma
Mahamohapaddhyay, Anand Charan Tark chadamoni: Vyaktitwa; evam krititva (H), (S).
Saugar, 1984.

1214. Sridharan, N.R.
Gangadhereeya hetwabhasa samanyu niruktha vyakhagansya Raghunath purva the krithasya nyayarat nasya patha. Sameekshatmak sampadanam.
Rastriya Sanskrit, 1993.

1215. Sriniwas, Kunchopadi
A critical evaluation of A.J. Ayers philosophy.
JNU, 1983.

1216. Srivaishnav, Siyaramdas
Bhagvannam Kaumudh vyakhyanam tatra mimansa-nyayanam vivechanam.
BHU, 1994.

1217. Srivastava, Anand Kumar
Mahishiya Bhasya aur Tribhashyratna ka alochanatmak tatha tulnatmak adhyayan (H).
BHU, 1977.

1218. Srivastava, Arbind Kumar
The conception of God and is relation with the finite self in Tagores philosophy.
Ranchi, 1972.

1219. Srivastava, Arti
A critical study of Sankshepa sariraka (S).
Allahabad, 1978.

1220. Srivastava, Arti
Swami Vivekanand ke darshan mein vishwa dharma kee awadharana (H).
Durgawati, 1996.

1221. Srivastava, Ganesh Narayan
Vivekanand darshan mein adhyatmik evam dharmanishpakhata shiksha (H).
BHU, 1992.

1222. Srivastava, Krishna Kumar
The ethical theory of Mahatma Gandhi: Its sources application and value.
Agra, 1968.

1223. Srivastava, Pratap Narayan
Corporate philosophy in India since 1913.
Rajasthan, 1989.

1224. Srivastava, Prem Chandra
Parvamimansa aur Nyaya darshan mein praman (H).
BHU, 1993.

1225. Srivastava, Ram Kumar Das
Jung and Indian thought.
BHU, 1964.

1226. Srivastava, Sandhya
The concept of spiritual transformation of man in Sri Aurobindo's philosophy.
Allahabad, 1979.

1227. Srivastava, Surendra Kumar
The philosophy of nischaldesa.
BHU, 1970.

1228. Srivastava, Tripurari Babu
Acharya Shankar krit upanishad Kavyon ka sameekshatmak adhyayan (H).
Saugar, 1991.

1229. Srivastava, Umesh Kumar
Syadvad evam Stunyavad: Ek tulanatmak adhyayan (H).
BHU, 1994.

1230. Srivastava, Uma
Geeta ke prakash mein patanjali yog ka alochanatmak adhyayan (H).
Gorakhpur, 1991.

1231. Subrthinam, S.P.
A study of the Kiranagama with special reference to Jnanapada (T).
Madras, 1982.

1232. Subharayudu, K.B.
Jeev brahambhad Satyavasat yatavvimarsh,
BHU, 1988.

1233. Subramaniam, S.P.
A study of Saiva siddhanta and allien school with special reference to siddhi.
Annamalai, 1985.

1234. Sukhada
Pramalochan nyara, advaita vedas aur purva mimansa, ke paripekshya mein (S).
Gurukula.

1235. Sulekha, A.K.
Nature and destiny of man in the philosophy of Sri Aurobindo.
Kerala, 1991.

1236. Sumitra Kumari
Moral philosophy of the Gita and its important western parallels.
Kurukshetra, 1995.

1237. Surendra Kumar
Bharatiya samaj mein mukti kee avadharna (Hist.) (H).
Magadh , 1985.

1238. Surendra Kumar
Pandit Akhilanand evam Acharya Madhavrat dwara pranit Dayand Digvijay Mahakavyon ke adhar per Swami Dayanand ke vyakhitva evam darshan ka vishleshanatmak adhyayan (H).
Panjab, 1993.

1239. Surendra Kumar
Bharatiya darshan mein ahinsa tatva ka tarkik evam manovaigyanik vishleshan.
Gurukula, 1990.

1240. Sushma
Satyam Shivam Sundaram: Ek darshanik paripekshya mein (H).
Rohilkhand, 1993.

1241. Suther, Rohtas Kumar
A critical study of socio-ethical values of Ram Charit Manas.
Kurukshetra, 1993.

1242. Suryanarayana, A.
Theism in vishistadvata: A critical study with special reference to Sri Ramanuja.
Venkateswara, 1992.

1243. Suther, Ganeshi Lal
Bhasavajna ke nyaya sara ka samalochnatmak adhyayan (H).
Jodhpur, 1979.

1244. Swaran Prabha
The concept of salvation and Rishi Dayanand (S).
Kurukshetra, 1983.

1245. Syad Murtaza Hasan
The construction of Indian philosophy in the light of Swami Vivekanands interpretion of Indian philosophy.
Patna, 1979.

1246. Tabassum, Hameed
Swami Vivekanands contribution to Advaita Vedant.
Banglore, 1995.

1247. Tare, M. Martendrao
The problem of determinism and freedom in Indian philosophy.
Lucknow, 1989.

1248. Tasadduq Husain
Philosophy of Shah Waliallah.
AMU, 1976.

1249 Tatacharya, N.R.S.
Srigopallatdeshik virachitya svabhichir sa manu yoniraletilip naya: Sameekshya sampadanam.
BHU, 1999.

1250. Thakkar. D.P.
Sophistic mysticism in Gujarat literature.
Gujarat, 1975.

1251. Thorat, Suresh K.
Mansik sanpratyayon sambandhi adhunik darshanik vishleshan ka samolochnatmak adhyayan (H).
Nagpur, 1988.

1252. Tikekar, Indu Balkrishna
The philosophy of sarvodaya.
BHU, 1966.

1253. Thakur, Ambalal Dalsukh Ram
Reconstruction of Sankar likhit smriti with a critical study (S).
Baroda, 1981.

1254. Tiwari, Bharat Kumar
Samkaleen Bharatiya chintan mein Vivekanandji kee den (H). Saugar, 1985.

1255. Tiwari, Krishna Kant
Sabdadwaita shaivedwaitayo tulanatmak medhya yanam.
Sampurnanand, 1993.

1256. Tiwari, Manju
The conception of God in Vaishnav system.
BHU, 1976.

1257. Tiwari, Prabha
Bharatiya samkaleen pramukh shiksha darshanik sarva Shri Tagore, Aurobindo, Dayanand evam Gandhi ke shiksha darshan ka tulanatmak adhyayan (H).
Rohilkhand, 1995.

1258. Tiwari, Shiv Murti
Sarvapally Radhakrishnan's view of the nature of science, philosophy and religion.
Delhi, 1997.

1259. Tiwari, Sriniwas
Naiskaram siddhi ka ek alochanatmak adhyayan (S).
Allahabad, 1981.

1260. Tangpev, E. Richard
The idea of a world view and understanding people.
NEHU, 1993.

1261. Tripathi, Aruna
Acharya Maitreyanath kee kritiyon ka darshanik adhyayan (H).
Gorakhpur, 1992.

1262. Tripathi, B.
Bharatiya darshan mein jeeva ka swaroop: Ek samalochanatmak adhyayan (H).
Gorakhpur, 1992.

1263. Tripathi, Dharmanarayan
Sri Mahatripur Sundari ke vishesh sandarbh mein shakti tatva evam upasana (H).
Jiwaji, 1988.

1264. Tripathi, Kamala Kant
Bharatiya darshan mein kyativad (H).
BHU, 1993.

1265. Tripathi, Kamala Kant
Lochan siddhant sameeksha.
Sampurnanand, 1990.

1266. Tripathi, Kanti, Swaroop
Chandkoshikam: Ek samalochnatmak adhyayan (H), (S).
Agra, 1979.

1267. Tripathi, Rameswar Prasad
Bhartiharika darshan: Bramhakanda ke alok mein.
BHU, 1977.

1268. Tripathi, Sudheracharya
A critique of the theory of rebirth in Indian philosophy (S).
Allahabad, 1976.

1269. Tripathi, Vashistha Narayan
Bondage and its analysis in Indian philosophy.
Allahabad, 1971.

1270. Tripathi, Vishal Prasad
The concept of Kashmiri shaivism and Vedenta (S).
Delhi, 1980 .

1271. Tripathi, Yamuna Ram
Vidhivivekasya sameekshatmak makmadyayanam.
Sampurnanand, 1990.

1272. Trivedi, R.J.
A critical study of Sri Sankaracharya's philosophical doctrine as depicted in his prakarnagranthas (S).
Saurashtra, 1984.

1273. Trivedi, Sumati Chhalishankar
Bharatiya darshan paramparoma Sukhme sharir no khyal (G), (S).
Gujarat, 1980.

1274. Udaseen, Karsey Maharana
Siddhanta tatwa namak Vedant prakasan ka sameekshatmak adhyayan (H).
BHU, 1993.

1275. Unikrishanan P.V.
The philosophy of Mata raja Guru: A critical study.
Calicut, 1988.

1976. Upadhyay, Adhinath Neminath
An essay on Kundkunda, his date pravachan a sara and other works with English translation of Prava Chanasava. 2. Sri yogindudevas penematma prakasa

and yogasava. 3. Pamkasuttam. 4. Varanagacharita (D. Litt.).
Bombay, 1939.

1277. Upadhyaya, Shivcharan Prasad
Mahashashusya sapta meshtma dhyayarth prayogonam sandh atwatanvaryukhan purassara mupatabd koshanus anusilanam.
Sampurnanand, 1994.

1278. Uttam Chandra,
Mahabharat, mein sankhya aur yoga ka swaroop (H), (S).
Kurukshetra, 1990.

1279. Vagehi, Amritashu, Shekher
A new approach to the philosophy of Swami Vivekanand with special reference to his political philosophy (S).
Darbhanga, 1980.

1280. Vageesh Kumar
Bharatiya darshanon mein antarnihit samasyayen (H), (S).
Garhwal, 1983.

1281. Vaghmare, N.J.
Pali vangamaya mein karma siddhant tulanatmak adhyayan (S).
Rani Durgawati, 1983.

1282. Vaisya, Veerayan Chandra
The concept of liberation in the Gita and the Sankhya yoga: A critical and comparative study.
Gauhati, 1993.

1283. Varakhedkar, Anand Teertha
Concept of pramana in Indian logic with special reference to Gangopadhyay Tattva Chintamani (S).
Osmania, 1981.

1284. Vasavada, A.U.
Radhakrishnan and modern thought (D. Litt).
BHU, 1944.

1285. Vayyapure, R.
Philosophy of Santhalinga swamigat, Tamil philosophy (T).
Madras, 1983.

1286. Ved Prakash
Shad darshanon mein pramen mimansa: Ek adhyayan (H).
Dayanand Ajmer, 1993.

1287. Ved Prakash
Adhunik yug ko Maharshi Dayanand kee darshnik den. (H).
Agra, 1963.

1288. Veena, Kumari
Josiah Roce and Sarvapally Radha Krishnan
A critical and comparative study in cultural synthesis of East and West.
Ranchi, 1972.

1289. Veerbala
Shudh darshano ke srishri vichar ka sameekshatmak evam tulnatmak adhyayan (S).
Meerut, 1979.

1290. Venkataraman, K.
The philosophy of Nagarjuna with special reference to the maha prajnaparamita sastra (D. Litt.).
Vishwa Bharati, 1960.

1291. Venketesh, S.
Vivekanand darshana ondu adhyayana.
Mysore, 1992.

1292. Verma, Dayal S.
Mahatma Gandhi's social philosophy in relation to those of Nietzsehe and Marx.
Agra, 1963.

1293. Verma, Madhuri
Swami Vivekanand's contribution to the religion.
Ranchi, 1974.

1294. Verma, Mamta
Aurobind darshan kee mool manyotoyar aur Hindi sahitya mein unki abhivyakti.
Rohilkhand, 1992.

1295. Verma, Mithilesh Kumar
Some aspect of the social philosophy of M.N. Roy.
Magadh, 1982.

1296. Verma, Pushpa
A historical and cultural study of saddhar mapundarika sutra.
Delhi, 1993.

1297. Verma, Rajeshwar Prasad
Radhakrishanan's philosophy and religion.
AMU, 1973.

1298. Verma, Sharda
Bhatta Chintamani ke tarkpada ka dahyayan (S).
Delhi, 1985.

1299. Verma, Surendra
Metaphysical foundation of Mahatma Gandhi thought.
Vikram, 1966.

1300. Vidya
A psycho-ethical analysis of Satyagrah in Buddha's and Gandhian thought.
Delhi, 1985.

1301. Vimala, K.
Philosophy of Tirumuler with special reference to thirty verses called updesham with Tirumendiram.
Madras, 1981.

1302. Virendra Pal
Upanishad evam Plato ke unsart manava: Ek tulnatmak adhyayan (H).
Agra, 1980.

1303. Vishwaswari, Ammak
Philosophy of Udayan (S).
Kerala, 1984.

1304. Vrinte, Joseph
Personality structure in Sri Aurobindo's integral psychology and in the Mastow's psychology.
Rohilkhand 1995.

1305. Vyas, Kuman Lal
Sri Aurobindo darshan aur uska pant aur sunderam per prabhav.
Osmania, 1986.

1306. Wali, Kaushalya
The conception of Ahinsa in Indian thought according to Sanskrit sources, Vadic, Jain and Buddhistic.
Allahabad, 1960.

1307. Walsan, Iankesaradi
Approaches to personhood in Indian thought.
Poona, 1983.

1308. Yadav, Dharma Raj Singh
A study of Gandhian as a philosophy of value.
Allahabad, 1966.

1309. Yadav, Harish Chandra
Sri Vallabhachavya krit sarva nir naya prakaran ka ek samalochnatmak adhyayan (H).
BHU, 1989.

1310. Yadav, Jagadish Ram
The philosophical background of Sri Ram Krishnas Teaching.
Agra, 1973.

1311. Yadav, Pratibha
Naishediya charit srishti vaigyanik adhyayan Pt. Madhu Sudan Ojha kė darshvad rashasya ke sandarbh mein.
Dayanand Ajmer, 1992.

1312. Yadav, Ramadhyan Prasad
A critical study of the concept of avidya with reference to Buddhism and Vedanta.
Magadh, 1985.

1313. Yadav, Suresh Singh
Gandhi evam Ambedkar ke samaj darshan: Ek tulnatmak adhyayan (H).
BHU, 1994.

1314. Yagnik N.K.
Sant maiji aur sant Drulabh Ramji vaniyaon ka tulanatmak adhyayan.
Gujarat, 1988.

1315. Yamanato Kazuhiko
Navyanyaya theory of Peksate.
Poona, 1992.

SANKHYA

1316. Agrawal, Sunil Kumar
Sankhya aur yoga darshan mein atma vichar (H).
BHU, 1989.

1317. Basu, Swapna Dinda
A critical and comparative study of the theories of creation, dissolution and salvation in the Sankhya

System of philosophy.
Calcutta, 1980.

1318. Bhattacharya, Bhupendra Nath
Sankhya theory of evolution and its influence on later works.
Calcutta, 1965.

1319. Chaitanya, Brahmachari Shiv
Sankhya yog puranetihasha shu shristhi vimarsh. (S),
BHU, 1971.

1320. Chattopadhyay, Latika
Self in Sankhya Philosophy.
Vishwa Bharati, 1961.

1321. Chattopadhyay, Nikhilas
Tantrasastri vaisnavas assusastra ka Sankhya sastruyu prabhivanirusyali (S).
Calcutta, 1985.

1322. Chattopadhyoy, Pratima
Sankhya elements in vadic and pauranik thought (S).
Calcutta, 1982.

1323. Chaturvedi, Urmila
Sankhya darshan ke vigyan Bhktshu krit vyakhya ka ek sameekshatmak adhyayan (H).
BHU, 1973.

1324. Chaudhary, Manju
Sankhya O vednater samanvaye vaigyan vikshurabaden paryalochana (B).
Vishwa Bharati, 1977.

1325. Das, Kalicharan
The concept of personality in Sankhya Yoga and Gita.
Gauhati, 1966.

1326. Giri, Archana
Sankhya karika kee mathuravritti ka annvad (H), (S).
Gorakhpur, 1988.

1327. Gupta, A.S.
Evolution of Sankhya school of thought.
Lucknow, 199.

1328. Harish Chandra
Sankhya aur advaita Vedant mein Karanta siddhant (H).
BHU, 1992.

1329. Jha, Shrikrishan
Sankhya darshan kee shresthata.
Darbhanga (S), 1977.

1330. Jhaveri, Indukala N.
The Sankhya yoga and the Jain theories of parinama.
Gujarat, 1953.

1331. Jashi, Ganga Dutt
Shreemad Bhagwat Gita sankhyayog tatva vimarsh (S).
BHU, 1971.

1332. Joshi, Kaumudi Rajni Kant
Sankhya yoga mein gur siddhant (H).
Gujarat, 1977.

1333. Kale, M.P.
Sankhya yoga and Ayurveda.
Poona, 1985.

1334. Kergha, Chintamani Trayanbak
Sankhya of the Bhagwat Gita and the system of Isvarakrishna.
Poona, 1959.

1335. Kaushal, Shakti Bala
Sankhya darshan kee shastriya sameeksha. Sanskrit Jain granthon ke adhar per (H), (S).
Rohilkhand, 1987.

1336. Maratha, Nanda Kumar Ardyut
The theistic Sankhya.
Bombay, 1988.

1337. Mishra, Chandra Shekhar
Agyat katrik sankhya granth yuktidipika ka adhyayan (H), (S).
Gorakhpur, 1988.

1338. Mishra, Hari Govind
Shrimad Bhagwat mein Sankhya darshan kee Sameeksha (H).
BHU, 1989.

1339. Mishra, Sunita
Sankhya aur Vedant mein jeewan mukti vichar (H).
BHU, 1993.

1340. Mishra, Vandana
Sankhya darshan evam Buadh darshan ka tulanatmak adhyayan (H). Gorakhpur, 1992.

1341. Nakada, Maomichi
Early Sankhya philosophy with special reference is Chinese and Tibetan sources.
Delhi, 1967.

1342. Neelam
Sankhya yog ka shaiv darshan per prabhav: Ek sameekshatmak adhyayan (H).
Rohilkhand, 1989.

1343. Ojha, Vimalesh
Muktideepika ke vishesh sandarbh mein Sankhya karika kee teekayon ka sameekshatmak adhyayan (H), (S).
Rajasthan, 1985.

1344. Pancholi, Badrinarayan
Srimad Bhagwati yam sankhyan (S).
Sampurnand, 1969.

1345. Panday, Jaya
Avipiryat Vigyan Bhikshu virachit sankhya pravachan bhasya ka sameekshatmak adhyayan (H), (S).
Kumaun, 1988.

1346. Pandey, Ram Suresh
A comprehensive study of Sankhya philosophy in the Mahabharat and Puran.
Gorakhpur, 1963.

1347. Phirangi
A comparative study of the ancient commentaries of Sankhyakririka. Sankhyakririka kee prachin takaon ka tulnatmak adhyayan (H), (S).
Gorakhpur, 1990.

1348. Pujari, Anuridha Mukund
Vijnanabhikshu krut Sankhya shashrache Samarthan (M), (S).
Poona, 1983.

1349. Rao, K.B. Ramkrishna
Theism of Sankhya on the Ayurveda.
Calcutta, 1964.

1350. Samajdar, Madhavi
An introduction to the Sankhya (S).
Calcutta, 1980.

1351. Satyawati
Sankhya darshan ka dwandatmak naitikvadi vishleshan (H), (S).
Meerut, 1984.

1352. Seema Rani
Concept of Sankhya in principal Puranas (S).
Kurukshetra, 1990.

1353. Sharma, Dayanand
Sankhya shastras aur charak samhita: Ek darshanik

tulnatmak adhyayan.
Gurukula, 1987.

1354. Sharma, Premlata
Sankhya darshan mein manusya kee avadharana (H).
Rajasthan, 1985.

1355. Shiv Kumar

A study of the Sankhya thought as found in the Brahmanical system of Indian philosophy (S).
Poona, 1978.

1356. Shukla, Laxmi
Sankhya aur yog ka manas shastriya chinta evam adhunik manovaigyanik vichardhara (H).
Vikram, 1968.

1357. Singh, Poonam
Sankhya siddhanton ka sameekshatmak adhyayan (H).
BHU, 1985.

1358. Sinha, Shrilekha
A critical study of Vachaspati Sankhya tatva Kumudini in the light of India's philosophical system.
Patna, 1978.

1359. Srinivasan, Gummaraju
Reinterpratation of Sankhya: Critical personalism.
Mysore, 1962.

1360. Srivastava, Lallen Prasad
Sankhya yog evam Ayurveda ke paripekshya mein Panch Mahabhut ka swaroop (H).
BHU, 1969.

1361. Srivastava, Nirupama
A comparative and critical study of the dualigtic philosophies of Descartes and Sankhya.
Kanpur, 1975.

1362. Srivastava, Nisha
Sankhya darshan mein achara mimansa (H), (S).
Delhi, 1979.

1363. Tripathi, Rakesh Kumar
Charak samhita mein Sankhya darshan ka tatwa (H).
BHU, 1990.

1364. Tripathi, Vishwambher Nath
Sankhya darshan mein varnit tattwon kee anya darshanon se tulnatmak sameeksha (H), (S).
Gorakhpur, 1982.

1365. Vij, Sushema
Critical and comparative study of the different schools of Sankhya.
Punjab, 1982.

1366. Vimala Kumari
Sankhya darshan ke aitihasik vikas aur uske nastik per prabhav (H).
BHU, 1993.

1367. Yadav, Narendra Nath
Sankhya yoga darshan main Ishwarvad (H).
BHU, 1979.

1368. Yogendra, Jayadeva
Sankhya yoga in the moksha,
Bombay, 1955.

MIMANSA

1369. Bhatnagar, Mala
Sanskrit sahitya per mimansa darshan ka prabhav (S).
Rohilkhand, 1982.

1370. Bhattacharya, Lakshmi Narayan
Poorva mimansar dristite vakya mahavakya tatparta nirupanerapay sameeksha (S).
Burdwan, 1991.

1371. Chakraborti, Lalita
Mimansa darshan O vyayp aishegik darshanammata pratyakshabimansha.
Vishwa Bharati, 1992.

1372. Chaturvedi, Dharmadutt
Dhatvarth mimansa (S).
BHU, 1987.

1373. Chintamani, T.R.
A history of purvamimansa literature.
Madras, 1932

1374. Devasthalli, Govind Vinayak
Mimansa: the vakya shastra of ancient Indian based on the mimansa sutra of Jamini and Sabarasvamins bhasya thereon.
Bombay, 1946.

1375. Dubey, Nanhaku Ram
Davya swaroop mimansa (D. Litt.) (S).
Ranchi, 1977.

1376. Gachter, Othmev
A study of language as the core of hermaneutical experience with special reference to sabara Bhasya.
BHU, 1977.

1377. Gautam, Bhurnesh
Astika darsanam mein pratipadita mimansa, siddhant (S).
Delhi, 1988.

1378. Gokhale, Vivek Narayan
Mardekrachi Saundarya mimansa.
Nagpur, 1990.

1379. Gupta, Peeyush Rani
Vedant aur Jain darshan mein tatva mimansa (S).
BHU, 1990.

1380. Indra Devi
Mimansa nyaya prakash: A study (S).
1979.

1381. Jha, Ganganath
The Prabhakar school of purva mimansa (D. Litt.).
Allahabad, 1909.

1382. Joshi, A.R.
Mimansa in medhalithi with reference to his commentary on the Manusmriti (S).
Bombay, 1983.

1383. Kishore Das
Bharatiya darshaneshu mukti mimansa (S).
Sampurnand, 1968.

1384. Mishra, Gopal Chandra
Mimansa sastrasya dharma sastre prabhava (S).
BHU, 1969.

1385. Mishra, Jagat Narain
Shanker evam Ramanuj ke darshan mein gyan mimansa evam tatsambandh vivechan (H).
Kanpur, 1985.

1386. Mogha, Shantiram Ganesh
Mimansa in the Bhagavanta Bhaskara of Nilakanta.
Bombay, 1967.

1387. Musalgaonkar, Gajanan
Mimansa darshan ka tulnatmak itihas (H).
Agra, 1965.

1388. Musalgoanker, Raju
Mimansa darshan mein gyan mimansa: Tantra siddhanta Ratnavali ke paripriksha mein (H).
BHU, 1994.

1389. Nigam, Vinita
Kamarita Bhatta krita tantravartika ka smritipada (H) (S).
Delhi, 1978.

1390. Pandey, Kapildeo
Mimansanyoga prakasa: A critical study.
BHU, 1967.

1391. Pandey, Mithilesh
Shaliknath kee kritiyon ka samekshatmak adhyayan (H), (S).
Gorakhpur, 1986.

1392. Pandey, Ram Byas
Kashika parisheelan (S).
Gorakhpur, 1978.

1393. Pandit, Purushottam
Bhagwat dharmon kee tattva mimansa.
Nagpur, 1996.

1394. Panse V.P.
A reconstruction of third school of purva mimansa (S).
Poona, 1986.

1395. Parashav, Kanhaiyalal
Vadik vangmai pappunia mimansa (S).
Punjab, 1987.

1396. Pratibha Rani
Vadik samhitaon mein mimansa.
Delhi, 1986.

1397. Ramamurthy, K.
Appayya Diksitas Gita mimansa: A study (S).
Venkateswara, 1982.

1398. Ramulu, Ayagna
A study of the vartikam of Kumarila Bhatt with special reference to his criteria of Sabaros view (S).
Osmania, 1989.

1399. Ray, Rina
Prabhakar mimansa darshan proman (B).
Vishwa Bharati, 1978.

1400. Sana, Prabhakar Shankar
Mimansa rules in practice as observed in the Mitakshera on Yajnavalkya smriti.
Bombay, 1954.

1401. Sharma, Kiran
Gyan mimansa Sankhya, nyaya, Jain aur Baudha darshan ke pariprekshya mein (H).
Gurukul, 1993.

1402. Sharma, Madan Lal
Mimansa darshanika samalochanatmak itihas (H).
Rajasthan, 1959.

1403. Sharma, Om
Jain Baudha aur nyaya darshanon mein gyan mimansa: Ek tulnatmak adhyayan (S).
Gurukul, 1987.

1404. Shastri, Pasupati
Introduction to the Purva mimansa.
Calcutta, 1924.

1405. Samayajula, Ramilla Rama
Mimansa, sastra artha vadavicarapa (S).
Andhra, 1988.

1406. Taneja, Anil Kumari
Bharatiya naitik chintan tatva mimansa kee prasthbhoomi mein (H).
Rajasthan, 1976.

1407. Tiwari, Nagender
Mimansa darshan mein shabda praman (H).
BHU, 1993.

1408. Tripathi, Surender Kumar
Mimansa darshan mein prabhakar sampradaya.
Bundelkhand, 1987.

1409. Tripathi, Vandana
Prabhakar mimansa darshana parman vimarsh (S).
Saugar, 1987.

1410. Upadhyay, Vachaspati
A critical study of the theory of self validity of knowledge in mimansa philosophy.
Calcutta, 1967.

1411. Yadav, Lalita Devi
Bharatiya darshan mein nirishwar bad vishesh roop se charvak. Baudh, Jain tatha mimansa darshan ke prasang mein (H).
Patna 1979.

1412. Yadav, Vijaylaxmi
Mahatma Gandhi and Sri aurobindo kee mulya mimansayon ka tulnatmak adhyayan (H).
Agra, 1985.

NYAYA

1413. Acharya, Renuka
Nyaya o Vedanta mata sabdetative sameeksha (S).
Vishwa Bharati, 1987.

1414. Adhikari, Nandini
Nyaya vaisesika darshan kee pransan vishleshan prakriya (H), (S).
Ranchi, 1980.

1415. Aggarwal, Karana
Brahmanad saraswati virachit nyaya Ratnavali tika sahit siddhant Bihduka samalochanatmak adhyayan.
BHU, 1979.

1416. Atmanand Paramhans
Vadic darshanashu gyanvishayakam vichiranam pargalochanam (S).
Sampurnanand, 1969.

1417. Bajpai, Rekha
Nyaya vaisesika darsana mein abhava padartha ka nirupan (H), (S).
Lucknow, 1986.

1418. Bear, Sumit Kumar
An enquiry into world and meaning according to nyaya philosophy.
Madras, 1973.

1419. Bhaduri, Sadanand
Some problems of nyaya vaisheshika metaphysics.
Calcutta, 1942.

1420. Bharadwaj, Ramesh Chandra
A study of nyaya Ratnawali (S).
Delhi, 1985.

1421. Bhatt, Siddheshwar Rameshwarji
A study of Ramanujas system in comparison with Panchratna school and Alvars.
Baroda, 1966.

1422. Bhattacharya, Aruna
Communication in nyaya philosophy (S).
Ravindra Bharati, 1978.

1423. Bhattacharya, Gauri
Nyaya darshan aravarga.
Calcutta, 1992.

1424. Bhattacharya, Gopika Mohan
The problem of God in Nyavashe shika philosophy.
Calcutta, 1960.

1425. Bhattacharya, Joy
Nyaya theory of jeeva.
Jadavpur, 1989.

1426. Bhatacharya, Manjusree
Problems of casuality in nyaya and Sankhya philosophy.
Burdwan, 1980.

1427. Bhattacharya, Pramath Nath
Vaiseshika dharma tatva sameeksha (H), (S).
Burdwan, 1979.

1428. Bhattacharya, Tarashankar
The nature of vypati according to nyaya (D. Litt.).
Calcutta, 1948.

1429. Bhowmik, Krishna
Nyaya vaisesika darshana adristvad.
Jadavpur, 1991.

1430. Bishwas, Bijan
The nyaya theory of perception: An epistemological study.
Calcutta, 1983.

1431. Brahmachari, Madhava Chaitanya
Sabda saktih (S).
Sampurnanand, 1965.

1432. Chakraborthy, Arun Kumar
Nyaya darshan barnita vichar (S).
Jadavpur, 1987.

1433. Chaman Ram
Proofs of existance of God in nyaya and yoga system: A comparative and reflective study.
Magadh, 1989.

1434. Chattapadhyay, Satish Chandra
A critical and comparative study of the Nyaya theory of knowledge.
Calcutta, 1938.

1435. Chaturvedi, Daya Shankar
Uddyotkar kee nyaya vertika: Ek adhyayan (H).
Lucknow, 1964.

1436. Chaturvedi, Markandeswari
Darshanantra pakshya tarkikapavar guaijhishtayam.
Sampurnanand, 1979.

1437. Chaturvedi, Shanti
Nyaya darshan mein karmavad ke siddhant. Tulnatmak evam alochanatmak adhyayan (H).
BHU, 1972.

1438. Chinchara, Mongla Ram Chandra
Vadanyaya: A glimps of nyaya and Buddhist controversy.
Poona, 1982.

1439. Datta, Sujata
Naya theory of Stomism: A critical and comparative study.
Gurunanak Deo, 1978.

1440. Desarkar, Bharati
Pandit MS nyaya charya since dead (S).
Calcutta, 1987.

1441. Dwivedi, shankar Dayal
Jayant Bhatt krit nyaya manjari ka shadd khand: Ek alochanatmak adhyayan (S).
Allahabad, 1981.

1442. Gangopadhyay, Shivaram
Sri Siddhart krit nyaya kaumidi sameekhanam.
BHU, 1989.

1443. Ghosh, Raghunath
Vyapti and the means of its knowledge according to the nyaya system of philosophy.
Calcutta, 1982.

1444. Ghosh, Rekha
Studies in the contribution of Gopala nyaya pancanama as a digestevriter.
Calcutta, 1977.

1445. Giri, Maneswaranand
Comparative study of promanas of prachya nyaya and Buddha nyaya.
Bihar, 1970.

1446. Goswami, Biswanarayan
The concept of samavaya in the nyaya vaishesika philosophy. (D. Litt.) (S).
Burdwan, 1981.

1447. Harish Kumar
The nyaya doctrine of inference: A comparative and critical study.
BHU, 1979.

1448. Harish Narayan
Evolution of nyaya vaisheshika categoriology.
Lucknow, 1967.

1449. Joshi, Hem Chandra
A study of udayanas nyaya kusumanjali.
Lucknow, 1967.

1450. Karmakar, Bakul
Nyaya mate sabdarth tattva sameeksha.
Vishwa Bharati, 1992.

1451. Kumar, Shashi Prabha
Vaisheshika darshan mein padarth nirupan (H), (S).
Delhi, 1983.

1452. Lalita, R.
Nyaya Ratnamala ka samikshatmak parisheelan (H), (S).
BHU, 1977.

1453. Laxmi Devi
Nyaya pravesh sutram: Ek sameekshatmak adhyayan (H).
Kurukshetra, 1991.

1454. Madhu, Kumari
Nyaya parishuddhi: Ek alochanatmak adhyayan (H), (S).
Banasthali, 1988.

1455. Maiti, Prasad Kumar
Nyaya concept of self (D. Litt.)
Calcutta, 1967.

1456. Mandal, Pradyot Kumar
The status of perceived object: A study of some aspects of prachin nyaya and navya nyaya theories of perception vis-a-vis. Sabdika and Baudh theories.
Vishwa Bharati, 1986.

1457. Mandal, Kusum
Udayanacharya krit nyaya Kusumanjali ka sameekshatmak adhyayan (H), (S).
Jodhpur, 1980.

1458. Mehta Shashi Bala
Sabda pramana in nyaya philosophy (S).
Kurukshetra, 1981.

1459. Mishra, Arjun
The treatment of universals in nyaya vaisheshika philosophy.
Lucknow, 1959.

1460. Mishra, A.
Nyaya concept of cause and effect relationship with special reference to Bhavandas Karantavichara (S).
Poona, 1988.

1461. Mishra, Godavarisha
A critical edition of Anubhuti prakash of Sri Vidyaranya with an introduction and appendices (S).
Madras, 1986.

1462. Mishra, Mudita
Nyagachatur granthika kee praman mimansa ka sameekshatmak adhyayan (H).
BHU, 1993.

1463. Mishra, Pravesh
Padarth Dharm sangrah mein dravya ka swaroop. Sridhara charya krit nyaya Kaumudi ke adhar per (H), Gorakhpur, 1989.

1464. Mishra, Sabita
Navyanyage anumiti (D. Litt.) (B).
Calcutta, 1965.

1465. Mishra, Satya Narayan
Sridhar virachit nyaya kundali: Ek adhyayan (S).
Lucknow, 1976.

1466. Mishra Surendra Mohan
Anuman Pariceheda of nyayabha sana: A study (S).
Kurukshetra, 1988.

1467. Mishra, Srinarayan
Vaishishika darshan: Ek adhyayan (H).
Bihar, 1971.

1468. Mishra, Umesh
The conception of matter according to nyaya vaishesika (D. Litt.).
Allahabad, 1932.

1469. Miyasaka, Yaka
The concept of avaechedakatva in Nyaya nyaya (S).
Poona, 1981.

1470. Mukherjee, Saswati
Nyaya vaishesita O mimansa darshanabhab.
Vishwa Bharati, 1992.

1471. Mukhopadhyay, Debaranjan
Sakti philosophy and shake literature.
Jadavpur, 1963.

1472. Narayanan, N.R. Soumaya
A comparative study of nyaya Siddhant and vaishasika

darshan on padarths.
Rastriya Sanskrit, 1993.

1473. Narayanan, T.K.
Nyaya sar of Bhasavajna: A critical study (S).
Kerala, 1982.

1974. Narendra Kumar
Nyaya vaishasika mein pramog tattva swaroop (S).
Meerut, 1986.

1475. Nirmal Rani
Concept of Chala and Jati in nyaya system (S).
Kurukshetra, 1987.

1476. Pahari, Devabrata
Nyaya mater praman O pramatattva vyuvathapan purvak khondan.
Jadavpur, 1993.

1477. Pandey, Kaushal Kumar
Bhasarvajna krit nyayasar: Ek adhyayan (S).
Lucknow, 1986.

1478. Pandey, Kamala
Nyayavartri ka tatparya parisuddhi (S).
BHU, 1977.

1479. Pandey, Prabha
Nyayasar: Ek samalochnatmak adhyayan (H), (S).
Kumaun, 1986.

1480. Pandey, Raghavendra
Majar Helvabhasas: A formal analysis with reference to nyaya and Buddhist.
BHU, 1981.

1481. Pandey, Vindehyeshwar
Jeewatma swaroop vimersh (S).
Sampurnanand, 1969.

1482. Pandey, Vindhyavasini
Nyaya siddhant manjari: Ek adhyayan (S).
Delhi, 1987.

1483. Patnayak, Pyare Mohan
Nyaya paribhashaya samalochanatmak sampadanon.
Jagannath.

1484. Patra, Brundaban
The rationale of indeterminate perception in navya nyaya (S).
Poona, 1990.

1485. Purnima, B. Singh
Sayadhadh siddhi va darshanic adhyayan (H), (S).
Rohilkhand, 1981.

1486. Rashurathna Charya, S.V.
Nyayashastrakatpramanama mimansashastra drishtya parisheelanan.
Sampurnanand, 1959.

1487. Ramarah, C.
A study of the nyaya vaishasika theory of causation,
Venkateswara, 1971.

1488. Rao, A.R. Panduranga
Nyaya vivarana of Madhava: A study.
Madras, 1997.

1489. Sab, Deepa
Nyaya Manjari: Ek samalochanatmak adhyayan anuman ke sandarbh mein (S).
Kumaun, 1986.

1490. Saha, Biswaroop
Nyayamate subdartha sambandhya sameeksha (S).
Jadavpur, 1987.

1491. Sain, Sarojbala
Nyaya darshana aur arthavijenama (S).
Delhi, 1989.

1492. Sain, Siddheswar
Navya nyaya aloukik sannikarsa (S).
Ravindra Bharati, 1981.

1493. Sarkar, Jatil Chandra
The nyaya vaishesika theism: A logical approved to the problem.
Calcutta, 1958.

1494. Sarma, D. Prabhakara
Nyaya vaishesikah atma tattva sameekshanam.
Andhra, 1991.

1495. Sen, Bishwa Nath
Concept of parts and whole: An examination of the nyaya vaishesika view.
Calcutta, 1974.

1496. Sangue, Hukamchand Parshwanath
Vaishesha vashyak bhasya ka darshanik adhyayan (H).
BHU, 1977.

1497. Shankar Sadan
Baudh nyaya mein pratyaksh parman: Ek sameeksha (H).
Bhagalpur, 1985.

1498. Sharma, Hari Dutt
Realism logic and metaphysics of nyaya vaishesika (S).
Punjab, 1983.

1499. Sharma, Kamala
Epistemology of nyaya philosophy.
Jadavpur, 1982.

1500. Sharma, Punita
Concept of santence analysis in nyaya philosophy (S).
Delhi, 1987.

1501. Sharma, Ratna Dutta
Nyaya and paratha numanu.
Jadavpur, 1988.

1502. Shastri, D.N.
The nyaya vaishasika realism and its conflict with the Buddhist epistemology: Dignaga School (D. Litt.)
Agra, 1959.

1503. Singh, Badri Prasad
Nyayamata shabdobodh vimersh (D. Litt.) (S).
Sampurnanand, 1909.

1504. Singh, Tej
Knad (vaishesika darshan) evam arusti ke anusar padarth vichar. Tulanatmak va sameekshatmak adhyayan (H).
Agra, 1980.

1505. Sri Sanghasena
A study of critical edition of the sfutartha Srishaneeara sargeahatika.
Calcutta, 1968.

1506. Sushama
Concept of Jagat in nyaya vaishasika (S).
Kurukshetra, 1980.

1507. Swarnakar, Urmila
Sivadityakrit saptepadarth ka ek sameekshatmak adhyayan (H), (S).
BHU, 1977.

1508. Tiwari, Heeraman
A study of nyaya parisuddhi of Vedanta— desika (S).
Delhi, 1989.

1509. Tiwari, Ranjana
Origin and development of vad in prachin nyaya (S).
Allahabad, 1976.

1510. Tiwari, Saraswati Devi
Apadevkrit mimansa nyaya prakost alochnatmak adhyayan (H).

1511. Tripathi, Yogendra Kumar
Nyaya sutra evam charaksanghita kee sambandhi samagri ke darshanik evam vaigyanik adhyayan (H).
Jabalpur, 1980.

1512. Upadhyay, Devadutta Sharma
Tatvoa parishudhi.
BHU, 1966.

1513. Veeraiah, M.
A comparative study of vaishesika system and aristolles orgenon with special reference to inference.
Venkateswara, 1969.

1514. Vijaylaxmi
Psychological material, in nyaya and vaishesika system.
Agra, 1960.

1515. Vyas, Ramashankar
Vaishesika sutra chandranandavritti: A study.
BHU, 1979.

1516. Wada, T.
The concept of invariable concomitance in navya nyaya (S).
Poona, 1988.

1517. Yadav, Manraj
Contribution of Sridharacharya, the author of nyaya Kundali vaishesika.
Allahabad, 1969.

YOGA

1518. Acharya, Mandini
Yogavashistha evam Baudh darshan ka tulanatmak

adhyayan (H), (S).
Ravishankar, 1983.

1519. Adhikari, Krishna Gopal
The conception of liberation in the Patanjali yoga system.
Calcutta, 1992.

1520. Agnihotri, Balram Sadashiv
The investigation of yoga. Its origin and development in vadic literature from samhitas to yoga parishads.
Bombay, 1948.

1521. Agrawal, Kanwarlal
Yoga as a science of psychical integration.
Delhi, 1956.

1522. Agrawal, Meera
Patanjali yoga sutra aur yoga vaishist ke yog ka tulanatmak adhyayan (H).
Rohilkhand, 1984.

1523. Anand, Aruna
Contribution of the principle Jainacharyas to yoga philosophy (S).
Delhi, 1988.

1524. Atreya, B.L.
The philosophy of yoga vasistha (D. Litt.).
BHU, 1948.

1525. Atreya, Shanti Prakash
Yoga as a system for physical mental and spiritual health.
BHU, 1963.

1526. Bade, Indubhusan Vaman
Yoga ayurved and hypnosis: Comparative study of the philosophy and therapy.
Bombay, 1987.

1527. Batra, Arjun Dass
A philosophical study of the yoga sutra of patanjali.
Poona 1974.

1528. Bezharaha, Dipaly
Nature and form of consciousness in yoga and modern psychoanalytical school.
Gauhati, 1980.

1529. Bhalla, Krishna
Patanjali yoga tatha Sri Aurobindo yog ke tulanatmak adhyayan (H).
Rani Durgwati, 1982.

1530. Bhanot, Pinki
Yogsutra, aur vishuddhi marg ka tulanatmak anusheelan (H).
Saugar, 1993.

1531. Bhattacharya, Siddheswar
Yog darshan: Ek gambhir adhyayan (H).
Bihar, 1972.

1532. Brahma, Nalinikant
Philosophy of Hindu sadhana.
Calcutta, 1931.

1533. Chaturvedi, Mukul
Ashatanga yog mein praniyon ka pralaya: Ek adhyayan (H).
Agra, 1989.

1534. Das, Saraju
A study of the patanjali yoga darshan in the light of modern psychology (S).
Gauhati, 1982.

1535. Dasgupta, Surendra Nath
The yoga philosophy in relation to other Indian system of thought.
Calcutta, 1992.

1536. Dash, Subhash Chandra
The concept of yograradhi in Indian philosophy with special reference to Gangesas tattva chintaman (S).
Poona, 1990.

1537. Dubey, Sachhidanan
Yog vashistha mein mukti ka swaroop evam sadhan (H), (S) .
Rani Durgawati, 1983.

1538. Godse, V.S.
A critical study of the system of new philosophical concepts in the yoga sutras of patanjali with special reference to its dualigtic/nondualigtic character.
Poona, 1929.

1539. Gupta, Ramesh Chandra
Hathyog mein sharirik evam adhyatmik paksh: Darshanik vishleshan.
Agra, 1971.

1540. Hanuman Prasad
A comparative study of madhyamika sunya vada and yogacara vijananvada (S).
Gorakhpur, 1986.

1541. Jain, Balchand
Burkley's subjectivism and the yoga vashistha.
Saugar, 1966.

1542. Jain, Rama
Contribution of Nagesh to yoga philosophy (S).
Delhi, 1987.

1543. Jaiprakash Narain
Acharya Harishandra ke yog granthon ke alochnatmak adhyayan (H), (S).
Magadh, 1982.

1544. Joshi, Kailash Chandra
Yoga vashistha ka samalochanatmak adhyayan (H).
Kumaun, 1993.

1545. Joshi, K.S.
Human ideal in yoga philosophy: A estimation of the yoga technique of personalities development.
Saugar, 1964.

1546. Kanjilal Priti
Concept of mind in Sankhya yoga system: A analytical study.
Lucknow, 1960.

1547. Kaul, Hirday Kumar
A study of yoga theory and practice with special reference to Punjab.
Punjab, 1989.

1548. Khera, Rajkumar
Rediscovery of kundalini yoga.
Kurukshetra, 1984.

1549. Lalitha, V.
The concept of anubhavadvaita to the Yogesura of Appayosrya (S).
Madras, 1986.

1550. Mahajan, Suraksha S.
Patanjati yogsutra samadipad vivechandndmak adhyayan (S).
Gujarat, 1987.

1551. Maheswari, Archana
The Gita synthesis of yoga in the light of Sri Aurobindo.
BHU, 1987.

1552. Malviya, Ramji
Yogatantra drishtuya mantra matrikya tatwa vicharsha.
Sampurnanand, 1978.

1553. Miravite G.F.
The conception of chitta in yog with special reference to the yoga sutra.
Vishwa Bharati, 1956.

1554. Mitra, Sumita
Studies on the philosophical concept in yoga bhasya.
Calcutta, 1984.

1555. Mokasha, M.G.
Psycho-physical and philosophical basis of patanjali yoga: A study.
Bombay, 1986.

1556. Nair, K. Ravindran
Concept of samadhi: A comparative study of yoga zen Budhism christian and sufi mysticism.
Saugar, 1980.

1557. Naresh Kumar
A study of yoga from Sanskrit sources, and its theropeutic evaluation in the light of Ayurved (D. Litt.).
Agra, 1978.

1558. Nigam, Braj Bihari
The four yogas and the perfection of personality.
Agra, 1960.

1559. Pandey, Rajkumar
Bharatiya yoga parampara ke vividh pakshon ka tulanatmak parisheelan (H).
Gorakhpur, 1986.

1560. Pandey, Rakesh Kumar
Nathyog aur upanishad yog ka tulanatmak adhyayan (H).
Gorakhpur, 1990.

1561. Patel, Paramanand
Hathyog, udgam, vikas aur vartman sambhavana ke

paripekshya mein Haathyog ke prakriyaon ka sambhavya sthan (H).
Saugar, 1990.

1562. Pawan Kumari
Tatva vaiserdi evam yoga vartika ka tulanatmak adhyayan (H).
Delhi, 1977.

1563. Prem Sagar
Sahaja marga system of yogic sadhana. Its contribution to contemporary renasissance in Indian philosophy.
Agra, 1971.

1564. Raj, Aswani Kumar
Comparative studies in Jaina yoga.
Bihar, 1971.

1565. Rajendran, S.
The concept of integral yoga according to Sri Aurobindo.
Annamalai, 1986.

1566. Rao, P. Sriniwas
A critical study of karma yoga with special reference to Bhagawat Gita.
Venkateswara, 1987.

1567. Reddy, D. Narsimha
A study of yogapada of Padma samhita in the light of Patanjali yoga darshana (S).
Venkateswara, 1988.

1568. Sachdeva, Indrapal
Yoga and psycho analysis with special reference to integration of personality.
Allahabad, 1965.

1569. Sah, Renu
Acharya Vigyan Bhikshu krit yagasar sangrah ka sameekshatmak adhyayan (H).
Kumaun, 1987.

1570. Sarala
A comparative study of the yogashastra work in Jainism and the Patanjali yoga darshan.
Agra, 1969.

1571. Sivana, Sushama
A comparative study of four mein yogas viz Gyana yoga, Bhaktiyog and Karmayog, Rajyoga.
Agra, 1980.

1572. Sharma, Satya Prakash
Yog ka udbhav aur vikas: Ek vivechnatmak adhyayan (H), (S).
Jiwaji, 1978.

1573. Sharma, Shashi
Upasana yoga vashistan targata Sanskrit pramukh moksopaya (S).
Jodhpur, 1980.

1574. Singh, Angad
Yoga sanna tasham yoganusari vargikaranam vishleshanam.
Rastriya Sanskrit, 1993.

1575. Singh, Anjuni Kumar
Sri Aurobindo ka poorna yog tatha anya yog sampradaya: Ek tulanatmak adhyayan.
Gorakhpur, 1981.

1576. Singh, Bhopal
Acharya Haribhadra Surikrit yog Bindu ka sameekshatmak adhyayan (S).
Kurukshetra, 1989.

1577. Singh, Hari Krishna
Yoga evam ayurvigyan (S).
BHU, 1987.

1578. Singh, Lattan Prasad
Tantra: Its mystics and scientific basic (D. Litt.)
Ranchi, 1972.

1579. Singhvi, Rajkumar
Patanjali yog sutra ka jain darshanik drishtikon se vivechnatmak adhyayan.
Jodhpur, 1991.

1580. Sinha, B.P.
Karmayoga siddhant (H).
Bihar, 1968.

1581. Srivastava, Avinath Kumar
A comparative study of samadhi (yoga) in some of the early Buddhist texts and Bhagwat Gita.
Magadh, 1981.

1582. Srivastava, G.M.L.
The yoga of Patanjali and the integral yoga of Sri Aurobindo.
Ravishankar, 1982.

1583. Sundaram, M.A.
A synthesis of yoga and Vedant: A comparative study of yoga sutra of Patanjali Shrimad Bhagwat Gita vashistha.
Calicut, 1994.

1584. Suri, Ashok Kumar
A critical study of the integral yoga of Sri Aurobindo and its educational implications.
Punjab, 1984.

1585. Sushil Kumar
Yoga darshan mein samadhi nirupana: Ek adhyayan yoga pradipika and yoga siddhant Chandrika ke paripekshya mein.
Dayanand, 1993.

1586. Tilak Chand
Patanjal yog aur Shri Aurobindo yoga.
BHU, 1977.

1587. Tripathi, Mithlesh Kumar
Yogabindu evam Patanjali yoga sutra mein yoga kee avadharana (H).
BHU, 1992.

1588. Tripathi, Ram Karan
Sankhya yog darshan mein bandh aur moksh (H).
Gorakhpur, 1978.

1589. Tripathi, Ramraksha
Yogasya tadanganacha tokikopoyog.
Sampurnanand, 1978.

1590. Tyagi, Jeetendra
Yog aur jiwan (H).
Gurukul, 1978.

1591. Upadhyaya, J.
Yoga and modern psychotheraphy.
BHU, 1965.

1592. Vasni, Ram Prakash
Patanjali mahabhasya navahink kee vyakhya mein kevet aur Shivranender ka tulanatmak adhyayan (H), (S).
Meerut, 1989.

1593. Vathsala, G.B.
A critical and comparative study of vyasa bhasya and Bhoj vriti on Patanjali yoga sutra (S).
Mysore, 1988.

1594. Vijay Pal
Yoga tatwa vaisharadi aur yoga vertik ka tulanatmak adhyayan (S).
Meerut, 1981.

1595. Yadav, B.S.
Acharya Hem Chandra krit yogshastra: Ek adhyayan (S).
Kumaun, 1986.

VEDANT

1596. Abhedanand
Sankrottara Advaita Vedant mein mithya tatwon nirupan (S).
Meerut, 1972.

1597. Acharya, V.K. Seshadri
The philosophy of visistadvaita in relation to other system of philosophy.
Annamalai, 1967.

1598. Adinarayana, P.
Mukti in visistadvaita Vedant: A critical study.
Venkateswara, 1990.

1599. Agrawal, Brahma swaroop
Sankara and spinoza: A comparative study.
Agra, 1960.

1600. Agrawal, Madan Mohan
The Vedant kustibha prabha of Kesavakas miri Bhatta: A critical study (D. Litt.).
AMU, 1990.

1601. Alston, A.J.
Early post Sankara Advaita.
BHU, 1969.

1602. Ananadan, K.
A critical study of Vedant Rasayanam.
Venkateswara, 1988.

1603. Anontharangachar, N. Srinivasa
The philosophy of sadhana in visistadvaita with

particular reference to Sri Vedant Desika.
Mysore, 1963.

1604. Antarkar, W.R.
Sankara, vijagas: A comparative and critical study.
Poona, 1960.

1605. Awadhesh Prasad
God in Advaita Vedant and stiva siddhanta.
Patna, 1973.

1606. Awasthi, Jaya Rani
Sankaras Vedant mein adhyasvada ka sameekshatmak adhyayan (H).
BHU, 1983.

1607. Awasthi, Vineeta
Bharatiya astik darshan sampradaya mein dvaita vichardhara (H).
Saugar, 1988.

1608. Baldha, C.V.
Contribution of Vidyananya Swami in Advaita Vedant (S).
Saurashtra, 1990.

1609. Bandhyopadhyay, Abha
Jiwanmukti in Advaita Vedant (S).
Burdwan, 1982.

1610. Banerjee, Arati
Advaita Vedant pramanya vichara (S).
Jadavpur, 1982.

1611. Banerjee, Mitra
Advaita Vedanta vyakarane mayostulanatmak adhyayanam.
BHU, 1994.

1612. Bharadwaj, Krishna Dutt
The bhakti school of Sri Ramanuja.
Delhi, 1952.

1613. Bhaskar, Anuradha
Advaita Vedant evam Kashmir shaiv darshan mein sadhana ka sameekshatmak adhyayan Geeta Bhasya ke sandarbh mein (H).
BHU, 1986.

1614. Bhaskara, Satya Narayana
The doctrine of being and knowledge in Advaita Vedant.
Andhra, 1989.

1615. Bhatnagar, Vijay
Vedant sampradayon mein naitik karam sampratyay vishleshan (H).
Durgawati, 1986.

1616. Bhattacharya, Adityanath
Sangata Sankaradvaita veda sameeksha (S).
Burdwan, 1983.

1617. Bhattacharya, Amar Prasad
Sri Nimbark O Dailidvaits darshan.
Calcutta, 1965.

1618. Bhattacharya, Asutosh
Studies in post Sankara dialetic.
Calcutta, 1933.

1619. Bhattacharya, Deba Prasad
The world in relation to final emancipation form the stand point of Advaite Vedanta.
Calcutta, 1962.

1620. Bhattacharya, Hari Prasad
Status of world in Advaita Vedant.
Calcutta, 1969.

1621. Bhattacharya, Jharana
A comparative study of Sankara and Ramjanuja Vedant.
Calcutta, 1962.

1622. Bhattacharya, Karana
Nagarjuna and Sankara: A critical and comparative study.
Calcutta, 1969.

1623. Bhattacharya, Namigopal
The vadantic idealism of Dr. S. Radhakrishnan.
Andhra, 1981.

1624. Bhattacharya, R. Prasad
Monistic philosophy in Mandana Mishras Brahmasiddhi.
Calcutta, 1969.

1625. Bhattacharya, S. Charan
The concept of Adhyasa in Advaita Vedant.
Jadavpur, 1966.

1626. Bhit, Shanti Sad Shivraj
The concept of mokshya or liberation Indian in philosophy with special reference to Advaita Vedanta of Sankara.
Nagpur, 1978.

1627. Bist, Champa
Brahma sutra Sankara Bhasya evam uskee pramukh tikaon mein Vedanta mato ka khindan: Ek adhyayan (H).
Kumaun, 1988.

1628. Bites, Theodore George
The philosophy of Advaita as expounded in the svaragya siddhi of Ganga dharendra Seraswati.
Madras, 1977.

1629. Brahmchri, Dayanand
Vedant dershon ka vibhinna prasthanon mein moksha vichar (H).
BHU, 1986.

1630. Chakraberti, Abhijit
Acharya Nimbhorka metabata Samikshanam (S).
Jadavpur, 1976.

1631. Chakkaborti, Braj Bihari
Vivaranopaniya sakarer dristite panchapadika vavarana or adhyasabhasqer avasykate (B).
Calcutta, 1966.

1632. Chakroborti, Himansu
Amalananda Swamis: A link between Bhamati and Vivarna School.
Jadavpur, 1909.

1633. Chakraborti, Nirad Baron
Studies in the fundamentals of Advaita.
Calcutta, 1958.

1634. Chanchal
Nrismhasnama kriti Vedanta tattva viveka: Ek adhyayan (H), (S).
BHU, 1984.

1635. Chandrakar, Prithvi V.
Ramanuja ke prapatti siddhant ka anusheelan (H).
Ravishankar, 1985.

1636. Chavi, T.B. Narain
Study of tatvamklekalaya.
Osmania, 1986.

1637. Chaturvedi, Girdharilal
The concept of self luminisity of knowledge in advait Vedant (S).
Lucknow, 1971.

1638. Chaturvedi, Krishnakant
Dvaita Vedant tatwa samiksha (H).
Jabalpur, 1966.

1639. Chaturvedi, Shambhudayal
Sankaracharya ke prokeeran granthon ka alochnatmak adhyayan (S).
Jabalpur, 1978.

1640. Chattopadhyay, Iti
Vaisnavati interpratetion of Vedant.
Calcutta, 1977.

1641. Chaube, Madhu
Madhyamik bodh an Advaita Vedant darshan mein nakaratmak padhyati (H).
BHU, 1990.

1642. Chaudhuri, Sumita
A study of Sankaracharyas, Vivekanand meni (S).
Jadavpur, 1987.

1643. Chauhan, Tejbir Singh
A critical study of Sant Sahitya with special reference to the commentaries of Sankara and Nilkanth.
AMU, 1984.

1644. Chetia, Bipin Chand
Advaitavad in Sankaradeva.
Gauhati, 1972.

1645. Das, Ganesh Prasad
Vedanta paribhasa: A work in analytical philosophy by Dharmorajadhavarinda.
Utkal, 1983.

1646. Dutta, Churameni
A comparative and critical study of Bhasyas on the Gita by Sankara and Ramanuja.
BHU, 1970.

1647. Datta, Dhirendra Mohan
The six ways of knowing: A critical and comparative study of the six promanes of Advaita Vedanta.
Calcutta, 1930.

1648. Datta, Tapash Sankar
A study of the philosophy of Vivekanand with special reference to Advaita Vedanta and great universal heart of Buddha.
Gauhati, 1970.

1649. Dev, Jyotsana
Philosophy of Nimbarka.
Allahabad, 1965.

1650. Didmahobham, S.
Parasara Bhattas contribution to vishisteadvaita (S).
Madras, 1986.

1651. Despande, Usha Manohar
Sri Apruvapdeche Vadic dharma va Sanskrit vishayon tatva gyan va tya che sameekshan (M).
Nagpur, 1983.

1652. De, Vries, Jahan Frederik
Advait new platonism: A critical study in comparative philosophy.
Madras, 1958.

1653. Dhruv, Balkrishna Mohanlal
An introduction to the suddhadvaita school of philosophy of Shri Vallabha Charya.
Bombay, 1954.

1654. Dubey, Kaushal Prasad
Vedant mein mahavakyarth: Both evam moksha.
Durgawati, 1991.

1655. Dubey, Rajendra Prasad
Vachaspati Mishrasy Brahmavidya visayak dharmyoh paryalochanam (D. Litt).
Ranchi, 1977.

1656. Dudhatoy, Nam Dev
Shankaracharya Madhavacharya tatha Dayanand ka

tulanatmak parisheelan.
Gurukul, 1987.

1657. Dwivedi, Kamala
A critical study of Dr. V. R. Nagars tantraloka (S).
Udaipur, 1976.

1658. Dwivedi, Sudhakar
Advaita Vedanta darshan mein avidya ka swaroop: Ek vivechnatmak adhyayan (H).
Awadh, 1992.

1659. Gandhi, Ramanlal Hiralal
Sri Gokulnathji's contribution to Suddha Advaita Vedant.
Baroda, 1964.

1660. Ganeshan, T.
Neo Vedantic approach to the philosophy of Advaita Vedant with special reference to Swami Vivekanand (S).
Madras, 1990.

1661. Garg, Karuna
Pratham siddhi ka alochnatmak adhyayan (H), (S).
1977.

1662. Gauri, Ved Prakash
Exitentialism and Indian thought with special reference to the concept of being in Gabriel Marcel and Vedant.
Delhi, 1979.

1663. Goswami, Krishna
Vedantic darsansya unibandhauerupanam (S).
Calicut, 1979.

1664. Goswami, Mahaprabhu Lal
Vivaranka samikshatmak evam Bhamati ke sath tulanatmak adhyayan (H).
Bihar, 1968.

1665. Goswami, Narayan Chandra
Visista advaita Vedant yathur chakhyati swarapam (S).
Calcutta, 1977.

1666. Goswami, Sita Nath
The concept of reality in Vedant: A study of self consciousness and falsity.
Calcutta, 1956.

1667. Goven, Rasika
The absolution of Sankaracharya as compared with Maulana Rumis school of Thought.
BHU, 1958.

1668. Grimes, John
Advaita Vedant and the problem of religious language.
Madras, 1980.

1669. Grant, S.
The concept of relation in Sankaracharya.
Bombay, 1973.

1670. Gujarati, Ashok Kumar
Sudhadvait sampradaya evam Swaminarayan sampradaya ke siddhanton ka tulanatmak evam sameekshatmak adhyayan (H).
Rohilkhand, 1986.

1671. Gupta, Chandra Prakash
A study of the atma tatva viveka of Udayencharya (S).
Delhi, 1986.

1672. Gupta, Kiran Kumar
Visista dvait aur uska Hindi ke bhakti kavya per prabhav (H) (D. Litt.).
Agra, 1960.

1673. Gupta, Sanjukta
Philosophy of Madhusudan Saraswati.
Vishwa Bharati, 1959.

1674. Gupta, Savita
Shankar Vedant mein sakshi kee avadharana (H).
Durgawati, 1995.

1675. Gupta, Sudha
Acharya Basubandhya krit Vidyapit patrata siddhi evam Acharya Shri Shankar krit saririk bhasya ke adhar per vigyanvad tatha Advaita ka tulanatmak adhyayan (H), (S).
Kanpur, 1985.

1676. Gupta, Yogyesh
A critical study of padmapads panchapadika.
AMU, 1980.

1677. Gurudutta
Vedant kee bhakti parampara mein Madhusudan Saraswati ka yogdan (H).
Durgawati, 1995.

1678. Haldar, Sahadev
Sadanandev Vedantsar sameeksha (S).
Ravindra Bharati, 1982.

1679. Handa, Vijay
A study of pre-Sankara Advaita Vedant.
Delhi, 1974.

1680. Harini, H.R.
The fundamental and distinguishing concept of visistadvaita.
Mysore, 1975.

1681. Hatwal, Ram Prasad
Adhya in Sankara Vedant.
Agra, 1965.

1682. Hiremath, Gurusiddhya Deo
Shiva shakti: Comparative study of Advaita and shakla tantra.
BHU, 1972.

1683. Hiremath, Mahant Swamy
The concept of ultimate reality and moksha in veerasaivism and Advaita Vedant: A comparative study.
BHU, 1977.

1684. Inamdar, V.B.
Critical study of Dvaita Vedant as expounded by Shri Jaya Tirth.
Poona, 1962.

1685. Indu Kumari
Vallabh Vedanta ke tattva mimansa ka sameekshatmak adhyayan (H).
BHU, 1987.

1686. Ittuthuran, E.
A philosophy of Advaita with special reference is Anandabadha.
Madras, 1960.

1687. Iyer, Padma K.
Sureshacharya krit Naishanarm Siddhinu vivechanatmak adhyayan (S).
Gujarat, 1988.

1688. Jagateswari, D.
Advaita Vedant of kaivalya navaneetam.
Madras, 1982.

1689. Jain, Sudha
A study of Naiskarmya siddhi of Sureswaracharya (S).
Delhi, 1979.

1690. Jata Shankar
A study of Vedant philosophy in the light of socialist ideals.
Allahabad, 1990.

1691. Jaya Shamusham, N.
Sri Aurobindo and the latest Vedant.
Annamalai, 1979.

1692. Jha, Laxmeshwar,
Vedant siddhant muklavali: Ek adhyayana (S).
Delhi, 1985.

1693. Jha, Shishir Kumari
Pratyabhijandarsan: Ek adhyayan (H).
Bihar, 1968.

1694. Jhingran, Saral
A critical reconstruction of the advaita metaphysics with special reference to the problems of action.
Rajasthan, 1972.

1695. Joseph, Satyanand
Nimbark and his philosophy (S).
Poona, 1985.

1696. Joshi, V. Bhal Chandra Shastri
Vidyaranayas contribution to Advaita (S).
Karnataka, 1987.

1697. Kailash Narayan
A critical study of the Madhava criticism against the Sankara School of Vedant.
Allahabad, 1959.

1698. Kakkar, Sadhana
Study of Iswara in Sankara Vedant (S).
Punjab, 1983.

1699. Kamal, R.
Philosophy of Advaita as expounded by Niscaldas with special reference to his vritti Prabhakar.
Madras, 1981.

1700. Kamjit
Maharishi Dayanand ke Ved bhasya ke paripekshya mein Indra Deva ka adhyayan (H).
Gurukul, 1987.

1701. Kansal, Sadhana
Vigyan Bhikshu ke Vedant siddhanton ka sameekshatmak adhyayan (H), (S).
Banasthali, 1989.

1702. Karmakar, Basudev
Advaita mata sristi tatwa (S).
Jadavpur, 1983.

1703. Karunakaran, B.
Shankaracharya and Narayana Guru: A comparative study of their philosophies (S).
Kerala, 1986.

1704. Karunakaran, R.
The concept of satya in Advaita Vedanta (S).
Kerala, 1977.

1705. Khanna, Ranjana
Advaita Vedant tatha Ajurved ke naitik evam dharmik vicharon ka tulanatmak adhyayan (H).
BHU, 1989.

1706. Killedev, S.S.
A critical translation and study of satagloki ascribed to Sankaracharya with special reference to Anandgiris tika (S).
Poona , 1988.

1707. Kizhavana, P.M.J.
The speaking subject: A preamble to Vedant.
IIT, Bombay, 1991.

1708. Krishnamurty, B.N.
History of Vaidik literature and the philosophy of Madhav as expounded by Jayatirth.
Madras, 1948.

1709. Krishnamurti, B.N.
Some issue of Sankara Vedant.
Karnataka, 1983.

1710. Krishnamoorthy, S.
Self in Advaita Visista Advaita and dwaita: A comparative study.
Madras, 1979.

1711. Krishnan, M.A.V.
The Jijna sadhikarna of the Sribhasya: A study (S).
Madras, 1988.

1712. Kuepfark, Paul Lauis
The Advaiti Vedant: A conception of self-lumunosity.
BHU, 1977.

1713. Kuiti, S. Kumar
Swami Vivekanand Advaita Vedanter adhunik prabakta (S).
Jadavpur, 1987.

1714. Kulkarni
The concept of Viveka in pre-Sankara Vedant in in Sanskrit literature.
Poona, 1965.

1715. Kulshrestha, Saroj
The concept of salvation in Vedant.
AMU, 1984.

1716. Kushavi, Nilima
Theory of Drasti Sristi in Advaita Vedant.
Burdwan, 1979.

1717. Laddha, Varanasi
A critical study of Vedant siddhant.
Muklavali.

1718. Lalitha Kumari
The concept of Karma in Advaita Vedanta Madras.
Madras, 1971.

1719. Lalithambal K.S.
Rupavatara: A critical study (S).
Kerala, 1990.

1720. Mahadevan, T.M.P.
The philosophy of Advaita with special reference to its exposition by Bharata tirtha vidyajanya.
Madras, 1936.

1721. Mahalakshmi, Sitamaha
The philosophy of Advaita with special reference to the siddhana sara sangraha of Appayā Dikshit.
Madras, 1975.

1722. Maheswari, Uma
Sankar Advaita Vedant of Madhu Sudan Saraswati: A reappraisal.
Bombay, 1992.

1723. Mahnot, Indra
Vaishnav Vedant mein mokshya ka swaroop (H), (S).
Jodhpur, 1980.

1724. Maitra, Madhu Sudan
Ethical realism of the recent past: A critical survey from Advaita point of view.
NBU, 1990.

1725. Mallica, G.M.
Philosophy of Advaita as expounded in Srimad Bhagwat.
Madras, 1980.

1726. Mantri, Anand Mayi
Advaita Ratnarkasana.
BHU, 1976.

1727. Marathe, Moreshwar Prabhakar
A critical examination of the philosophy of the Sankaracharya with special reference to the Bruhma Sutra Bhasya.
Poona, 1973.

1728. Marfatia, Mridula Indravadan
The contribution of Vallabhacharya to the Vedant

thought and the problems it involves.
Bombay, 1962.

1729. Marj, K.J.
The rise and development of visistaadvaita and Saiva siddhant in Chola Empire.
Madras, 1986.

1730. Meera Devi
Updeshastri ka vishesh sandarbh mein Shankaracharya ke advaitavad ka alochnatmak adhyayan (H), (S).
Rohilkhand, 1983.

1731. Minuvani
A study of ultimate in Shankar Vedant.
Punjab, 1992.

1732. Mishra, Abha
Nagarjuna ke Madhyamik karika evam Shanker ke Saririk bhasya ka tulanatmak adhyayan ke adhar per Shoonyavad tatha Advaitvad: Ek sameeksha.
Kanpur, 1987.

1733. Mishra, Adya Prasad
The development and place of Bhakti in Sankara Vedant.
Allahabad, 1950.

1734. Mishra, Arjun
Vyakaran darshan mein Advaita vimarsh (H).
Saugar, 1981.

1735. Mishra, Gajendra Narain
Sankars doctrine of Maya and Aurobindos repeatition of it: A critical study.
Agra, 1972.

1736. Mishra, Nirmal Sunder
Is varapratyabhijnavimagini Jhanedhikara: A study (S).
Kurukshetra, 1989.

1737. Mishra, Ram Gulam
Comparative study of the principles propounded by Kamlakar Bhatt and Bhaskaracharya (S).
Darbhanga, 1971.

1738. Mishra, Ram Sajeewan
Visistadvaita darshan mein tulanatmak mukti vimarsh (S).
Awadhesh Pratap, 1982.

1739. Mishra, Satya Deo
A critical and comparative study of the different sub-schools of Abhasaveda in Sankaradvaitism.
Gorakhpur, 1965.

1740. Mishra, Savitri
Criticism of Buddhist school in Advaita Vedant literature from earliest times to the 12th century AD.
Lucknow, 1960.

1741. Mishra, Umarani
Som kaleen Bharatiya darshan mein Vedant ka nav nirman (H).
Vikram, 1974.

1742. Mudgal, S.G.
Impact of Buddhism and sankhya on Sankaras thought.
Poona, 1969.

1743. Mukherjee, Mira
Advaita Vedantamak upasana tattva (S).
Jadavpur, 1985.

1744. Muralidhar
Sankar Digvijay: Ek sameekshatmak adhyayan (H), (S).
BHU, 1987.

1745. Murthy, C.H. Srinivas
The concept of visesa in Dvaita Vedant (S).
Karnataka, 1984.

1746. Murthy, Sabchidanand
Reason and revelation in Advaita Vedant.
Andhra, 1950.

1747. Nachane, Sulochana Anant
Survey of post Sankara Advaita Vedant.
Poona, 1953.

1748. Nag, Anita
Influence of Vedant on vaishavism.
Calcutta, 1988.

1749. Nair, K. Maheswaran
Advaitasiddhi: A study (S).
Kerala, 1989.

1750. Nambudaripad, P.M.B.
The philosophy of Advaita as expounded by Swami Vivekanand.
Madras, 1970.

1751. Nanda, Jayasri
Advaita Vedant Smritiprasthanasya sameekshatmak adhyayan.
Jagannath, 1993.

1752. Nandi, Manoranjan
Philosophy of shribalvada Vidyabhusan: Vaishanava Vedant school of thought,
Bombay, 1950.

1753. Nandkishore
Criteriology in Sankara.
Allahabad, 1942.

1754. Narasimha Chari, Mudambai
Contribution of Sri Yamunacharya to visistaavaita.
Madras, 1967.

1755. Naulekha, Ram Sarup Singh
Sankars Brahmavada.
Agra, 1956.

1756. Neme, Pushpakanti
Achintyabhedabhed mein Bhakti ka swaroop (H), (S).
Rani Durgawati, 1983.

1757. Nigam, Madhur
Vivekanand ka Navya Vedant siddhant evam vyavahar.
Burktullah, 1988.

1758. Norton, James H.K.
Reason and visistadvaita: A study of Nyayakulisa by Atreya Ramanuja.
Madras, 1960.

1759. Pandey, Abhinuklanath
Vedant mein mahavakhyanta vichar: Ek sameekshatmak adhyayan (H).
BHU, 1992.

1760. Pandey, Dina Nath
Sankhya ka dwaitabad: Ek sameekshatmak adhyayan (H).
BHU, 1983.

1761. Pandey, Ghanasyam
Sankhya evam Vedant darshan ka tulanatmak adhyayan (H).
BHU, 1991.

1762. Pandey, Haribansh
Bhakti sahitya Sriramanand male bhakti swarupam.
Sampurnanand, 1976.

1763. Pandey, Indu Bhushan
The ethico religious philosophy of Sri Ramanujacharya.
BHU, 1972.

1764. Pandey, Muralidhar
Srimanchchhon karachayarat purvan Advaitavad (D. Litt.).
Sampurnanand, 1989.

1765. Pandey, Ram Pratap
Sankar Vedanta mein adhyas ka alochnatmak adhyayan (H), (S).
Awadh, 1987.

1766. Pandey, Shailendra Bhushan
Advait Vedant aur Shaiva siddhant mein mokshya kee avadharana (H).
BHU, 1993.

1767. Pandey, Sailendra Nath
The new Vedantic movement in contemporary. Indian Philosophy.
Gorakhpur, 1965.

1768. Pandey, Tarapada
Pre-Nrisimhasrama Advaita teaches (S).
Jadavpur, 1976.

1769. Pandey, Uma
A critical and comparative study of the contribution of Post Sankara Advait. (D. Litt.).
Saugar, 1985.

1770. Pandey, Vijay Prakash
Sankaracharya aur Kant ke darshan mein vichar evam satke sambandh: Ek tulanatmak adhyayan (H).
Gorakhpur, 1996.

1771. Panikar, Sisupal
Vedant kalpatathika: A study.
Kerala, 1993.

1772. Panigrahi, Nirmal Kumar
Advaita Vedanta pratikarmavyavastha (D. Litt.).
Calcutta, 1980.

1773. Pannuswamy, Dharmwathy
Advaita approach to aesthetics.
Madras, 1975.

1774. Pathak, Keshav Prasad
Advaita Vedant mein srishtra prakria ka alochnatmak adhyayan (H), (S).
BHU, 1976.

1775. Pathak, Muralidhar
Vishisthadvaita Siddhant mein jeev aur Iswar ka sambad (H), (S).
BHU, 1966.

1776. Pant, Manyubala
Vishuddhadvaita tatha Kashmir Shaive darshan ka tulanatmak adhyayan (S).
H.P., 1981.

1777. Parashar, Shashi Prabha
Shastriya granthon ka Acharya Vishweshwar krit vyakhoan ka adhyayan (H), (S).
Agra, 1983.

1778. Phillip, Ponvelil John
A study of the Biblical doctrine of salvation and the concept of mukti in Advaita Vedant according to Sankara.
Poona, 1977.

1779. Prasanna Kumari, B.
Vedant philosophy and religion of Swami Vivekanand.
Kerala, 1991.

1780. Prasunaribha, G. Gnana
The vision of Brahman of Advaita Vedant.
Osmania, 1992.

1781. Radha Krishanan, B.
Critique of difference in the philosophy of Advaita Vedant.
Madras, 1986.

1782. Rafia Sultana
Sufism and Advaita Vedanta: A comparative study.
Madras, 1979.

1783. Raghawan, V.K.S.N.
History of visistadvaita literature (S).
Madras, 1977.

1784. Raheja, Sudesh Kumari
Contribution of Buideva Vidya Bhushan to vaishnava philosophy.
Bombay, 1970.

1785. Rajgopal, K.C. Aravinda
The nature of function and types of devotion in visistadvaita.
Venkateswara, 1970.

1786. Rajpal
Nimbark bhasya ka sameekshatmak adhyayan (S).
Kurukshetra, 1981.

1787. Ramakrishanan, S.O.
The advaitik absolutism with special reference to Sankara.
Delhi, 1964.

1788. Ramamurthy, A.
Brahmanabhava in Sankaras, philosophy: A study.
Andhra, 1968.

1789. Ramamurthy, Panyam
Spinozism and Vedanta.
Bombay, 1990.

1790. Rameshchayya, V.
The ethical philosophy of Advaita Vedant.
Madras, 1974.

1791. Ram Prasad
Ramanuja and Hezal: A critical and comparative study.
Ranchi, 1975.

1792. Rangachar, M.E.
The philosophy of visitadvaita as expounded by Vedant desika in nyaya siddhanjana.
Bombay, 1977.

1793. Ranagswami, Sudakshina
The influence of the bancarotra samhita on the visistavaita darshana.
Bombay, 1983.

1794. Rao, B. Kamaleshwar
Advaita Vedant mein vyakti ka swaroop evam sthan (H).
Jabalpur, 1980.

1795. Ravathy, S.
Three little known advaitinas (S).
Madras, 1987.

1796. Ray, Namendra Narayan
Early Vedantic thought from the upanishads to the Brahmasutra.
Gauhati, 1988.

1797. Ruddy, Guillalmus
Comparative poetics as a purely formal science with special application to Advaita Vedant and the phenomenology of Husserl.
Madras, 1979.

1798. Saha, Sukharanjan
The Theory of illusion as in Advaita Vedant.
Calcutta, 1970.

1799. Sahasrabudhe, Madukar T.
Survey of the pre-Sankara Advaita Vedant.
Poona, 1954.

1800. Saini, Sudesh
Concept of reality in Advaita Vedant (S).
Punjab, 1983.

1801. Sarkar, Mahendra Nath
The system of Vedantic thought and culture.
Calcutta, 1920.

1802. Sarma, G. Akhubhatlu
Contribution of Dharma Rajedhvarindra to Advaita Vedant (S).
Andhra, 1982.

1803. Sarma, V. Anjeheya
Chit sukhas contribution to Advaita.
Venkateswara, 1967.

1804. Saraswati, Swami Gurupadnand
Vaidik darshana swatmeswarup vimarshah (S).
BHU, 1983.

1805. Saraswati, Swami Parmanand
Comparative study of Vedant and Kashmir Shaiva philosophy (S).
Kashmir, 1987.

1806. Sarvadanand Paramhans
Sri Sankara siddhant Shri Vallabh Brahm sutrarth siddhantoga samiksha (H).
Sampurnanand, 1965.

1807. Satish Chander
Vigyanvad aur Advaitavad kee dristi se gaurpadkari ka alochanatmak vishleshan (S).
Punjab, 1990.

1808. Seema
Shankar Vedant mein anandvad ke swaroop.
Punjab, 1992.

1809. Sekhawat, Mahendrapal
Vedant and the modern religious reformers.
Vikram, 1969.

1810. Sangupta, Bratindra Kumar
A critique on the vivarana school studies in some fundamental advaitist theories.
Calcutta, 1956.

1811. Sen, Vasana
Badarayan sutrar prayojaniyate (B).
Calcutta, 1956.

1812. Shah, Natwarlal Jethalal
Suddhaadvaita interpretation of Bhagawat Gita.
Baroda, 1964.

1813. Shakuntala
The study of the Pancedesi (S).
Delhi, 1979.

1814. Shanbhag, Dayanand Narsingh
Some problems in Dvaita philosophy surveyed in their dialectical setting.
Bombay, 1962.

1815. Sharma, Arun Kumar
Vedant Deepika: Sameekshatmak adhyayan (H).
BHU, 1989.

1816. Sharma, Awadh Narain
Dashnantra paribrekshya shudhadvait Vedant sameeksha (S).
Darbhanga, 1984.

1817. Sharma, C.D.
Dialectic in Vedant and Buddhism.
Allahabad, 1947.

1818. Sharma, Inderpal
Literary and philosophical study of stotras composed by Shankaracharya (S).
Punjab, 1990.

1819. Sharma, Indra Deo
Nirukta dvaita sameeksha (H).
BHU, 1986.

1820. Sharma, Keshav Deo
Achinty Bhedabhad evam vaishnava darshan (H).
Agra, 1964.

1821. Sharma, Manjula
Vedant parampara mein saririk anubhashy ka Brahma tatwa parak tulanatmak adhyayan (H).
Kanpur, 1978.

1822. Sharma, Raghunath Ramanlal
The system of Shudhadvaita Vedant.
Baroda, 1969.

1823. Sharma, Ram Murti
Shankaracharya ke mayabad ka alochnatmak adhyayan (H).
Agra, 1961.

1824. Sharma, Ram Murti
Advaita Vedant: A critical and comparative study of its history and its tanets (D. Litt.).
Agra, 1967.

1825. Sharma, Ramesh Chander
Shankrapurvavarti Advaita (S).
Delhi, 1984.

1826. Sharma, Rasmi
A study of ultimate principle in sanyavada and Avaita Vedant.
Delhi, 1990.

1827. Sharma, Sangamlal
Ram Charita Manas aur Vedant darshan (H).
Awadhesh Pratap, 1977.

1828. Sharma, Savita
A study of mahabhyadipika (S).
Delhi, 1986.

1829. Sharma, Shashi Bala
Dharma Rajodhvarindra ka Vedant pramana mimansa mein yogdan (H), (S).
Delhi, 1958.

1830. Sharma, Srinivas
A critical and comparative reevaluation of ethics of new-vedant.
Agra, 1973.

1831. Sharma, Suresh Prasad
Madhya Vedantvad ka tulanatmak aur sameekshatmak adhyayan : Shri Aurobindo, Sri Ramkrishna Paramhans tatha Swami Vivekanand ke darshanon ke vishesh sandarbh mein (H).
Bihar, 1983.

1832. Sharma, Urmila
The concept of Urititi in Advaita Vedant.
BHU, 1969.

1833. Shastri. C. Markandeya
Sureswaras contribution to Advaita.
Karnataka, 1969.

1834. Sheshagiri, V.N. Rao
A critical study of Vachaspati Mishras distinctive contribution to Advaita.
Mysore, 1981.

1835. Shobhana, S.
Advaita of Sri Shankara with special reference to Mandukya Karika.
Kerala, 1992.

1836. Shukla, Karunesh
Comparative study in Sankara and Nagarjuna.
Gorakhpur, 1962.

1837. Shukla, Krishnakant
A comparative study of non-dualism of Sankara and Abhina Gupta.
Lucknow, 1968.

1838. Shukla, Prem Shankar Girija Shankar
The contribution of Sri Sankaracharya to the Vedant Philosophy.
Gujarat, 1967

1839. Shukla, Raj Sekhar
Comparative study of phenomenology and Vedant of Sankara.
Allahabad, 1990.

1840. Shukla, Ram Raj
Influence of Buddhism on Sankara Vedant.
Agra, 1969.

1841. Siddappradhya, G.T.
Sakti visistadvaita Vedant.
Mysore, 1966.

1842. Singh, Brajendra
An estimate of Madhu Sudan Saraswatis vindication of Advaita metaphysics.
Allahabad, 1966.

1843. Singh, Dinanath
Visistadvaita dwara Advaita tatwa mimansa ka khandan: Vedant deshik ke vishesh sandarbh mein (H).
BHU, 1989.

1844. Singh, Dinesh
Shankar Vedant aur Kashmir Shaiv darshan mein param tatwa ka tulanatmak adhyayan (H).
BHU, 1988.

1845. Singh, Gurumukh
A study of Advaita in yoga vasistha (S).
Punjab, 1996.

1846. Singh, Neelam
Vallabhacharya, criticism of Shankaracharya and Ramanujacharya.
Sukhadia, 1984.

1847. Singh, Prabhunath
Vaishnava Vedant mein param tatva va Iswar (H).
BHU, 1987.

1848. Singh, Ram Krishan
Nyaya Vedant ke samaj darshan ka sameekshatmak adhyayan (H).
Rohilkhand, 1985.

1849. Singh, Shashi Devi
Chaitanya vaividhya kee samasya. Shankar Vedant ke sandarbh mein (H).
BHU, 1987.

1850. Sinha, Sukesh
Vivekanand ke Advaitavedant mein yoga ka sthan aur mahatwa: Ek alochnatmak adhyayan (H).
Indore, 1977.

1851. Soni, Shatrapa
Sidhantlesa sara sangraha: A study (S).
Delhi, 1977.

1852. Srinivasan, K.
The critical edition and study of Vedant ratna kosa of Mrisimba Sarma (S).
Madras, 1990.

1853. Srivastava, Ayodhya Prasad
Sri Ramanand Sampradaya visista dwaitaveda ke paripekshya mein Swami Bhagwada Charya ji kee

kavya kritiyon ka adhyayan (H), (S).
Kanpur, 1985.

1854. Srivastava, Kaumudi
Advaita Vedant parampava mein jeev kee sandharana ka sameekshatmak adhyayan (H), (S).
Allahabad, 1990.

1855. Srivastava, Kusum
Shankaracharya ke prakaran Granthon ka sameekshatmak adhyayan (H), (S).
Gorakhpur, 1985.

1856. Srivastava, Lalit Kishore Lal
The concept of Jeewan mukti in Advaite Vedant with special reference to the work of vidyaranya muni.
BHU, 1975

1857. Srivastava, Shail Kumari
A critical study of Bhaskara and his place in Vedant.
Allahabad, 1969.

1858. Srivastava, S.N.L.
Sankara and Bradley: A comparative and critical study (D. Litt.).
Allahabad, 1965.

1859. Suman Lata
Visistadvaita kee aachar mimansa (S).
Meerut, 1963.

1860. Sumedha
Maharishi Dayanand ke ved Bhashya ka paripekshya mein agnidevata ka adhyayan (H).
Gurukula, 1988.

1861. Sundavam, P.K.
Advaita expistemology.
Madras, 1960.

1862. Sushila, Kamalesh
A study of Shakti Bhasya on Brahm Sutras : A critical and comparative evaluation mainly in the light of Sankaras Advaita Vedant.
Agra, 1964.

1863. Syam Sunder Das
Ramanandacharya satdiya granth samiksha.
Sampurnanand, 1979.

1864. Thatte, Anuradha Arun
A critical study of the concept of god in the Vedant system (S).
Patna, 1977.

1865. Tiwari, Indira
Vadic vangamay mein manas tatwa (H).
Saugar, 1980.

1866. Tiwari, Munni
Vedant tattvaḷok: Ek sameekshatmak adhyayan (H).
BHU, 1986.

1867. Tiwari, R.N.
The ethics of Sankaracharya.
Allahabad, 1947.

1868. Tiwari, Ram Pratap
Sankar Vedanta mein adhyas ke alochnatmak adhyayan (H), (S).
Awadh, 1983.

1869. Tripathi, Devendra Kumar
Conception of revelation institution and reason in the Vedant of Sankara.
BHU, 1983.

1870. Tripathi, Syama
Sri Chaitanya Mahaprabhu evam unke pramukh

shishyon kee vaishnav Vedant ko den (H), (S).
Kanpur, 1985.

1871. Tripathi, Yogendra Jagnnath
Kevaladvaita in Gujarati poetry.
Baroda, 1993.

1872. Trivedi, Madan Mohan
An Advaita appraisal of the philosophy of F.H. Bradley.
Gorakhpur, 1983.

1873. Trivedi, Prabhakar
The notion of absolute in Sankara and some neo Hegẽliars (D. Litt.).
BHU, 1949.

1874. Upadhyay, Beermani Prasad
Some aspects of Advaita philosophy as expounded by Sureswar (D. Litt.).
BHU, 1947.

1875. Varshney, Poonam
The concepts of Adhyasain Advaita philosophy (S).
AMU, 1983.

1876. Vasan, Ramanan, J.R.S.
The Advaita mata: A study (S).
Madras, 1988.

1877. Uasantha Kumar
Advaita in contemporary Indian thought.
Madras, 1974.

1878. Vataya, Hemraj Sharma
Doctrine difference in post Sankara Advaita with special reference to siddhantalesha sangrah.
Punjab, 1966.

1879. Veezhinathon, Narayan Swami
Samksepasariraka: A work on Advaita Vedant by Servajnatham.
Poona, 1963.

1880. Verma, K.S.
The philosophy of Sri Vallabhacharya.
Agra, 1949.

1881. Verma, Neelam
Shankaracharya ke mayabad ke paripekshya mein Shri Aurobindo ka mayabad (H).
BHU, 1986.

1882. Victor, P. George
Social philosophy of Vedant.
Andhra, 1986.

1883. Vinaya Kumar, V.A.
Structure of Advaita: A attempted reconstruction.
IIT, Kanpur, 1988.

1884. Vyas, Ram Narayan
The Bhagawat Bhakti cult and the three Advaitacharyas: Sankara Ramanuja and Vallabha (D. Litt.).
Agra, 1969.

1885. Wanchoo, Vinita
An appraisal of Vedant in the light of modern Indian thought.
Allahabad, 1971.

1886. Warrior, A.G. Krishna
The concept of mukti in Advaita Vedant.
Madras, 1951.

1887. Yadav, Bhabhuti Singh
Appearance in Nagarjuna and Sankara.
BHU, 1970.

7

WESTERN PHILOSOPHY

1888. Amin, Sonal K.
Studies in the philosophy of Karl Jespars.
Jabalpur, 1973.

1889. Amruthamme, Dodla
Philosophy of Bertrand Russell. A study with special reference to religion and society.
Andhra, 1989.

1890. Annie, K.A.
Asceticism and mysticism. A search through the doctrine of St. John of the cross.
Kerala, 1983.

1891. Awasthi, Jamuna Prasad
The instrumental philosophy of John Dewey. A critical study.
Agra, 1968.

1892. Bagga, Urmila
Social philosophy of Bertrand Russell.
Allahabad, 1963.

1893. Benerjee, Kalpana
Some aspect of the philosophy of Charles Peirce.
Vishwa Bharati, 1977.

1894. Banerjee, Sadashib
Absolute as an unconditioned principle with special reference to British idealism.
Allahabad, 1954.

1895. Bandgopadhyay, Krishna
Essence and aesthetics in the philosophy of George Santeyana.
Calcutta, 1983.

1896. Baral, Raj Kishore
Critical studies in the philosophy of Descartes.
Poona, 1984.

1897. Basuroy, Mukti
The concept of the men in the philosophy of Jean Paul Sartre.
Jabalpur, 1976.

1898. Bahera, Satrughna
Wittganstein kripke and rule following a critical examination of rule secpticism.
Hyderabad, 1993.

1899. Bhandari, Dhanpal Raj
The social philosophy of Plato in the Republic.
Jodhpur, 1974.

1900. Bharadwaj, Shanti
G.E. Moore's common sense philosophy.
Delhi, 1975.

1901. Bhattacharya, Ratnavali
Kants critique of taste with special reference to the concept of disinterestedness and its bearing on recent Indian thought.
1994.

1902. Bhattacharya, Susmita
A critical evaluation of non-naturalism of G.E. More.
Patna, 1977.

1903. Bhalka, S.E.
The concept of will and obligation in the philosophical thought of Jean Jacques Rousseau.
Poona, 1978.

1904. Bodale, Malti Manjaram
Bheraliya samajawar Buudh dharmachha.
Prabhav (M), 1992.

1905. Bosak, Jyotish Chand
A critical study of Russels socio-political philosophy and its contemporary relevance.
AMU, 1996.

1906. Celeamma, Vishwanadhapalli
Peace humanistic elements in scholigue philosophy with reference to the writing of 1st Augustine. St Aquines etc.
Andhra, 1995.

1907. Chakraborti, Tapan Kumar
Humes theory of casuality.
Calcutta, 1977.

1908. Chakraborti, Tapan Kanti
John Dewey: His naturalism and its relevance to the problems of philosophy.
Calcutta, 1993.

1909. Chattarjee Ira
Aesthetic trends in modern weste n philosophy.
BHU, 1970.

1910. Chatterjee, Rita
Science, technology and man in the philosophy of John Dewey.
Osmania, 1989.

1911. Chattopadhyay, Pritibhusan
The philosophy of Jogiah Royee's: A critical exposition.
Calcutta, 1984.

1912. Cletus, Chakwu Nwawkike
Jespers analysis of human action responsibility and Goa.
Punjab, 1993.

1913. Dakshene, J.P.
Philosophy Josiah.
Rajasthan, 1968.

1914. Das, Parthsarathi
A study of Collingueds philosophy.
Ravindra Bharati, 1986.

1915. Das, Sinanshu Bhushan
Studies in Royees philosophy.
Calcutta, 1960.

1916. Datta, Kritidipa
Some problems in Russels early philosophy.
Burdwan, 1995.

1917. Datta, Nira
Freud and Adler on man and society.
Calcutta, 1975.

1918. Deb, Ratna
Henri Beagson ka darshanik adhyayan (H).
Jabalpur, 1978.

1919. Dwivedi, Deokinandan
Wittgenstein and his infulence on contemporary English philosophy.
Allahabad, 1969.

1920. Gabriel, Teresa
Plotinus in the light of vedant and Indian mysticism.
Rajasthan, 1962.

1921. Ganapathi, T.N.
Bertrand Russells philosophy of sense data.
Nagpur, 1972.

1922. Gandhi, Ramchandra
Apprehension in reality. A study in the philosophy of Alfred North white head.
Delhi, 1967.

1923. George, Vensus A.
From being in the world to being toward being. Mertin Heidagiers philosophy of the authentic human person.
Madras, 1995.

1924. Ghosh, Sisir Kumar
Aldous Huxley: A cynical Salvationist.
Calcutta, 1950.

1925. Goindi, Suchet
The revolution of aesthetics and ethics in Greak-thought with special reference to the views of plato.
Allahabad, 1962.

1926. Gopalkrishnaiah, Vellanki
Philosophy of Jose ortega Gasset.
Andhra, 1979.

1927. Grey, Ernest Siman
20th century philosophies of religion in English and America.
Lucknow, 1960.

1928. Gupta, B.P.
The self in Spinoza and Ibuul Arabi.
Allahabad, 1954.

1929. Haider, Hiralal
Hegelianism and human personality.
Calcutta, 1910.

1930. Hola, Sabitarani
A critical study of the concept of philosophy with special reference to L. Wittagesteins G. Ryle and J.L. Astin.
Kurukshetra, 1993.

1931. Indira Prasad
Common sensism in philosophy of Peiree.
Patna, 1973.

1932. Jagannathan, A.
A critical study of hermenauties as a philosophical method.
Osmania, 1995.

1933. Kapoor, Usha Rani
Wittgensteins theory of meaning.
Allahabad, 1977.

1934. Kashyap, Subhash Chandra
Political and social philosophy of Neitzzoche.
Allahabad, 1966.

1935. Kelkev, M.P.
A critical examination of spinozas concept of substance attributes and modes.
Poona, 1979.

1936. Koshy, Abhey
De construction of theory in Nietsche philosophy.
JNU, 1995.

1937. Kuttanickal, Joseph
Status of women in catholic Christianity. A religious philosophical study since veticon counal II.
Andhra, 1994.

1938. Madhuri Devi
Philosophy of sense date in contemporary western philosophy with special reference to Moore, Russell and Price.
Patna, 1978.

1939. Maitra, Keya
Reference and internal realism. An enquiry into Hillary Patnams philosophy of language.
Hyderabad, 1995.

1940. Mallick, Mohini
Russells theory of sense data.
Lucknow, 1959.

1941 Mary, Joseph
A study of F.H. Bradleys philosophy.
Madras, 1971.

1942. Mehta, Jarvalal
The philosophy of Martin Heidegger.
BHU, 1964.

1943. Mirza, Nasim Jahir
The empirical tradition in 20th century British philosophy with special reference to Bertrand Russell and A.J. Ayer.
Lucknow, 1963.

1944. Mishra, Lallanji
Language and fact in the philosophy of L. Wittgentein
Magadh, 1984.

1945. Mitra, Esha
The concept of object in contemporary Western philosophy.
Vishwa Bharati, 1992.

1946. Mukherjee, Nilratna
R.G. Collingwood: A analytical study.
Jadavpur, 1983.

1947. Mukherjee, Sheryar Kevas
F.H. Bradleys approach to life.
Bombay, 1965.

1948. Murty, T. Narsimha
Philosophies of Moore, Russell and Wittgenstein.
Andhra, 1975.

1949. Nag, Bhitta Ranjan
The impact of Christianity on the life of Mizos. A study

of their social philosophy.
Gauhati, 1975.

1950. Nag, Gargi
Theories of psiphenomena: A critical study.
Burdwan, 1993.

1951. Naidu, N. Venketrao
A critical and comparative study of A.S. Edingtons philosophy of science.
BHU, 1972.

1952. Namboodary, C.P.M.
Moral value and their gradation a study in Nicolai Harmans.
BHU, 1977.

1953. Pandey, Sachidanand
The Indian temper in plotonic thought.
Delhi, 1988.

1954. Pathak, Diwakar
A comparative study of the philosophy of David Hume and A.J. Ayer (D. Litt.).
Ranchi, 1975.

1955. Patil, D.L.
Philosophy of G.E. Moore.
Mysore, 1974.

1956. Paul, Kadavil
The orthodox Syrian Church. Its religion and philosophy.
Kerala, 1959.

1957. Pradhan, Ramesh Chandra
Language and experience: An interpretation of the later philosophy of Wittgentein.
BHU, 1977.

1958. Premchand, B.
Karl Poppers theory of falsification. An appraisal.
Madras, 1993.

1959. Raghubansi, Mala
Proper names and descriptions with special reference to Russell and Strawson.
BHU, 1993.

1960. Rai, Asheem Kumar
A critical study of partner concept of wing.
Kashi, 1993.

1961. Rai, Motibir
Kants philosophy of mathematics.
Calcutta, 1977.

1962. Rajgopal, Ladapuram Varadochar
The philosophy of A.N. White head : The concept of reality and organism.
Mysore, 1960.

1963. Rajinder Kaur
The concept of experience in John Dewey.
Punjab, 1976.

1964. Ramanujam, A. Appan
A study of the development of the philosophy of Henri Bergson.
Annamalai, 1949.

1965. Rao A. Pampapathy
Problem of meaning with special reference to Wittgentein.
Saugar, 1961.

1966. Ray, Dilip Kumar
The philosophy of George satayana.
Calcutta, 1971.

1967. Ray, Ritendra Kumar
Hume and Hussert: A critical comparative study.
Calcutta, 1993.

1968. Roy Chaudhuri, Udayashankar
The nature and function of imagination Hume nad Kant.
MBU, 1996.

1969. Roy, Shambhunath
Concept of religion in contemporary western philosophy.
Ranchi, 1976.

1970. Roy, Sunil
The human subject. A study in Kants philosophy.
Burdwan, 1997.

1971. Sabastin, K.
The nature of the philosophical problems in Gabriel Moral.
Karnataka, 1978.

1972. Sandha, Gurcharan Singh
A critique of social philosophy of Bertrand Russell.
Panjabi, 1976.

1973. Sanjeev, M.P.
The question of state and Marxist response. A philosophical analysis in the light of the late 20th century.
Kottayam, 1996.

1974. Santosh Kumar
The revival of scepticism in contemporary British philosophy.
Allahabad, 1950.

1975. Sarin, Madhu
Hegel and Marx: A reinterpretation.
Delhi, 1991.

1976. Saxena, Rakesh
A comparative study of ontology and epistemology of Spinoza and of Marx Engels.
JNU, 1993.

1977. Saxena, Supriya
Bharatiya evam pashchatya anishwarvadi darshnikon ka samalochnatmak adhyayan (H).
Jiwaji, 1988.

1978. Sharma, Ramesh Chandra
The main issues of process philosophy.
Rajasthan, 1968.

1979. Shastri, Prithiviraj
The dialectics of negation in Sartre.
Poona, 1983.

1980. Shukla, Sanjay Kumar
Kants copernican revolution and its epistemic implication.
BHU, 1993.

1981. Singh, Harinarayan
The concept of being in existentalism with special reference to Martin Heideggar.
Osmania, 1977.

1982. Singh, Raghvendra Pratap
A critical examination of Immanuel Kants philosophy.
JNU, 1985.

1983. Singh, Vidya Sagar
Chauvaka aur Hume: Ek tulnatmak darshanik adhyayan (H).
Bihar, 1983.

1984. Sinha, Gayatri
Studies in the philosophy of Jo Saiah Royce.
Jabalpur, 1977.

1985. Shina, Susil
Problems related with the synthetic apiori in Kants criticism.
NBU, 1995.

1986. Srikala Devi, S.
Concept of men in the works of Dostoyavsky.
Calicut, 1993.

1987. Srivastava, Ramesh Chandra
The concept of single one in the philosophy of Martin Buber.
Gorakhpur, 1992.

1988. Srivastava, Surendranath
Plastic eros and psychoanalysis.
Allahabad, 1957.

1989. Sugna, Kumari S.C.
Albert Schwertzers philosophy of civilisation. A study.
Andhra, 1981.

1990. Sundarajan, R.
Studies in the later philosophy of Wittgenstein.
Madras, 1966.

1991. Tennyson, Samraj
Central theme in Sartre: A conceptual analysis.
Poona, 1984.

1992. Thekkar, Chadraman
Amriki darshan mein Nebastubad ka aprikshan (H).
Magadh, 1968.

1993. Thiruvengadathen, Viraraghava
Henri Bergson and Karl Juisper: A comparative study.
Bombay, 1970.

1994. Tripathi, Ramakant
Spinoza, in light of Advailism (D. Litt.).
BHU, 1949.

1995. Tripathi, Ramesh Kumar
G.E. Moores defence of common sense. A critical study.
Kashi, 1979.

1996. Trivedi, Madan Mohan
An advaitic appraisal of the philosophy of F.M. Bradley.
Gorakhpur, 1983.

1997. Venketkrishan, B.
The conception of salvation in the philosophy of Schopenhuner.
Osmania, 1956.

1998. Verma, J.G.
Empirical legacy of contemporary British thought.
Allahabad, 1948.

1999. Verma, Kamleshwar Prasad
The concept of reality in the philosophy of F.H. Bradley.
Bihar, 1977.

2000. Vijaylakshmi B.V.
Poppers critique of historicism: A mark on analysis.
Osmania, 1995.

2001. Vyas, Koshavlal, B.
The absolation in modern Western philosophy.
Gujarat, 1954.

2002. Wahagham, Satyavama Devi
J.L. Austin and ordinary language.
BHU, 1977.

2003. Yadav, Manmohan Singh
R.M. Hare ke adhiniti shastriya vicharon ka adhyayan.
Jodhpur, 1986.

2004. Yogesh Chander
Anevaluation of the analytical approach to ethical language with special reference to C.L. Stevenson and R.M. Hare.
Kurukshetra, 1989.

2005. Zaccheas, Dorothy
Faith and reason in Paul Tillich.
Osmania, 1987.

2006. Zulshi, Urmila
Critical study of the philosophy of James Ward.
Allahabad, 1971.

8

COMPARATIVE PHILOSOPHY

2007. Agera, Cassian Rok
Faith, prayer and grace: A comparative study in Ramanuja and Kierkegaard.
Delhi, 1977.

2008. Alrega, Harnam Singh
Manav niyati aur swatantra sankhya: Baudh aur Advait darshan ke vishesh sandarbh mein (H).
Ravishankar, 1995

2009. Bagchi, Reeta
The concept of self and liberation in Hinduism and Christianity.
BHU, 1979.

2010. Bharucha, F.P.
Einsteins theory of relativity and Buddhist conception of Karana.
Bombay, 1978.

2011. Chaurasia, H.L.
A comparative study of the philosophy of Josiah Royee and Radhakrishnan.
Jabalpur, 1978.

2012. Dutt, Tripti Rattan
Sankara and Plato.
Bihar, 1978.

2013. Dubey, Umesh Chand
Sri Aurobindo aur Bradley ke darshan mein param satt ka swaroop (H).
BHU, 1977.

2014. Khan, Gulam Moh. Yahiya
The concept of transendence in British and Indian philosophy with special reference to Bradley and ke Bhattacharya.
Gorakhpur, 1976.

2015. Padmawathi, G.
The concept of social futurism in Alvin Toffler and Sri Aurobindo.
Osmania, 1995.

2016. Samtani, L.T.
Problem of one and many in Indian and western ultraphysics: A critical and comparative study.
Gujarat, 1979.

2017. Savitri Devi
A critical study of the concept of creativity in philosophy with special reference to Bergson Whitehead and Sri Aurobindo.
Kurukshetra, 1977.

2018. Sema, V.C. Kanite
Western humanism and Advait Vedant: A study of spiritual revolution with special reference to Teilhardde Chardin.
Madras, 1980.

2019. Singh, Ram Dutt
Jain aur Baudh dharmon kee nirmandhara ka tulanatmak adhyayan (H).
Magadh, 1980.

2020. Sinha, Priti
Conception in ultimate reality, man and salvation in

Sankara, Sri Aurobindo and Paul Tillich.
BHU, 1977.

2021. Speneer, Anand
The concept of world in Christianity and Sikhism.
Panjabi, 1980.

2022. Varadan, Geetha
Truth and freedom: A study of philosophies of Martin Heideggar and Sankara.
Madras, 1987.

2023. Vempony, Ishanand
The doctrine of Avatar in Bhagavat Gita and the incornotion in the new testament.
Gujarat, 1979.

2024. Verma, Anil Kumar
Vaidik evam Baudh dharma kee manyatayen. Ek adhyayan (H).
Bihar, 1995.

2025. Vijay Kant
The concept of the absolute in the philosophy of Sri Aurobindo and Hegal.
BHU, 1977.

2026. Yaruingam, A.S.
Hinduism and Christianity in Manipur: A comparative study of Vaishnavism and Baptist sect.
JNU, 1996.

9

ETHICS

2027. Agrawal, Niti
A phenomenological study of moral decredation in contemporary India.
Gorakhpur, 1978.

2028. Alfred, Marney Paul Mary
Basic concept of ethics in the darshana.
Madras, 1978.

2029. Anantharamu
A critical study of moral philosophy of the early Dharmasu.
Mysore, 1980.

2030. Ansari, Mohd. Abdul Haq
Ethical philosophy of Miskawach: An exposition and critical examination.
AMU, 1961.

2031. Antarkar, Shivaram Sadashiv
Metaphysical ethics.
Bombay, 1968.

2032. Ashok Kumar
Ethics of John Dewey in the context of social change in U.S. in 20th century.
BHU, 1983.

2033. Balkrishanan, S.
Some contemporary assessment of Kants. Critique of pure reason.
Madras.

2034. Bandiste, D.D.
A study of ethics of Bartrand Russell.
Saugar, 1974.

2035. Bharadwaj, Vijay Kumar
Naturalistic ethical theory. A critical study in the light of G.E. Moores criticism and certain recent development in ethical theory.
IIT, Kanpur, 1969.

2036. Bharucha, L.A.
A study of the concept of peace.
Bombay, 1991.

2037. Bhatia, Mangat Ram
Neeti Parayen pustak malon ka mulyankan. Manava mulya kee dristi se, (H).
Panjabi, 1985.

2038. Bhattacharya, Rajlakshmi Devi
Some implications of the concept of personality.
Poona, 1972.

2039. Chandel, Bhuwan
Marxian ethics: An analysis of its nature and character.
Punjab, 1970.

2040. Chaturvedi, Abha
A study of nature of moral judgements.
Lucknow, 1973.

2041. Chaudhuri, Chandra
A study of the problem of adjustment in adolesednce.
Calcutta, 1972.

2042. Chaurasia, Maheswar Prasad
A critical study of the metaethics of C.L. Stevension.
Bihar, 1985.

2043. Das, Bishwambhar
The nature and input of Gandhis moral philosophy.
Agra, 1980.

2044. Dave, Shivlal
Moral thought and practice in contemporary India.
Udaipur, 1975.

2045. Deepak Kumar
Gandhi darshan evam Jain darshan ke naitik vicharon ka tulnatmak adhyayan, (H).
BHV, 1989.

2046. Devraj, Pamela
The moral nature of man relating to love and compassion and his liberation according to St. Paul, Shankara and Ramanuja.
Madras, 1993.

2047. Ghosh, Nripendra Bhushan
The moral philosophy of the Mahabharata.
Rohilkhand, 1985.

2048. Ghosh, Radha
The nature of ethical statement with special reference to A.J. Ayer and R.M. Hare.
Kanpur, 1975.

2049. Gnanapragasan, M.
Professional ethics: Its nature and justification.
ITI, Bombay, 1990.

2050. Gopinath Sudha
Analytic philosophy with special reference to moral philosophy.
Banglore, 1990.

2051. Guha, Samarendu
Some semantic studies of ethical sentences.
Calcutta, 1996.

2052. Gupta, Nandita
Geeta, Kant aur Vivekanand ke niti darshan mein gyan aur karma ka samanwaya, (H).
Ravishankar, 1984.

2053. Jafri, Tanveer Fatma
Seikh Sadika naitik darshan: Ek vivechnatmak anusheelan, (H).
BHU, 1989.

2054. Jain, Phool Chand
Malachar ka samikshatmak adhyayan, (H).
BHU, 1977.

2055. Jain, Pushpa
A Charanga sutra ka neeti shastriya adhyayan, (H).
Awadhesh, 1985.

2056. Jagatpal
The nature of moral principles.
IIT, Kanpur, 1980.

2057. Jatadharpal
The philosophy of Gandhi.
Calcutta, 1984.

2058. Jalihal, G.A.
The ethical contribution of the late Prof. M. Hiriyanna of Mysore.
Mysore, 1975.

2059. Jha, Ramakant
Sortsanhate ka alochnatmak adhyayan, (H).
Kashi (S), 1982.

2060. Jha, Shivendra
Guru Shukrayo rudayostedi vichar viva hopanayanadi

Sankharet praba bhavashch.
Darbhanga, 1985.

2061. Joshi, Arvind Sadashiv
Bharataleel naitik va adhyatmik shikshan avashyakata and disha (M).
Nagpur, 1975.

2062. Kanwar, Deepak Prakash
Sri Aurobindo ke naitik siddhanta kee sameeksha.
Ranchi, 1990.

2063. Kapoor, Veena
Nature of moral reasoning.
Delhi, 1980.

2064. Kaushik, Krishna Sharma
Sanskrit mein auchitya kee saidhyantik evam proyogik paksha, (H).
Panjabi (S), 1985.

2065. Khambate, Zarindira
Dimensions of G.E. Moores ethical theory. A critical study.
Devi Ahilya, 1990.

2066. Khanna, Neelam
A critical and comparative study of Marxian Gandhian social and moral philosophy.
Saugar, 1986.

2067. Khanna, Renu
A critical analysis of Hobbs' moral philosophy.
IIT, Kanpur, 1981.

2068. Khosla, Kamal Kanta
Ethical foundation of social and political philosophy of Z.S. Mill.
Punjab, 1979.

2069. Kotzamanis, Linda
A philosophical interpretation of the nature and socio-ethical implication of psychriatic ideology.
Venkateswara, 1991.

2070. Lyndom, Samuel R.
The nature of values in the new testament.
NEHU, 1992.

2071. Lyngdoh, Marnina
The concept of virtue in the khashi world view
NEHU, 1992.

2072. Mahajan, Joginder Kaur, J.S.
The dichotomy of 'IS' and ought.
Nagpur, 1975.

2073. Malhotra, Veena
Ethics of C.L. Stevenson and R.N. Hare. A critical and comparative study.
Panjab, 1975.

2074. Mandal, S.
Health policy ethics and human values.
NBU, 1991.

2075. Mishra, B.P.
Elements of ethics in the Mahabharata.
Patna, 1969.

2076. Mishra, Hirdaya Narayan
Comparative ethical study of T.H. Green and Bhagawat Gita.
Agra, 1962.

2077. Mishra, Ram Shankar
Moral reasoning: A critical study with special reference to C.L. Stevenson, S.E. Toulimin, R.M. Hare, and K. Baier,
IIT, Kanpur.

2078. Mohd. Abdul Hamid
A study of Moores ethics.
Panjab, 1982.

2079. Muley, Dattatray Govind
The stevensionian tradition in ethics.
Nagpur, 1976.

2080. Muthukamaraswamy, R.
Thiruvallurar, vagutha pudunarioru oppeettairu (T).
Madurai, 1991.

2081. Naganathan, Ghanakumran
Maya fact of fiction.
Durgawati, 1987.

2082. Natarajan, Kanchana C.V.
The Vidhi Viveka of Mandan Mishra. A study in the analysis of language of moral injuction.
Delhi, 1990.

2083. Nesy, D.
Existentiality trends in Hiezshe.
Kerala, 1980.

2084. Pachi, Deepa
An analytical approach to the ethical philosophy of the Bhagwat Gita.
Utkal, 1991.

2085. Pandey, Kanchan
Concept of moral standard in Indian Materialism.
Gorakhpur, 1978.

2086. Pillai, J.K.
Thomes Danial: The relation between religion and morality with special reference to A.G. Hogg and Rein hold Naibahr.
Madras, 1984.

2087. Pinsaong, Phramaha Kitti
A critical study of Therauvada Buddhist ethics.
BHU, 1977.

2088. Pradhan, Sushama
A critical and comparative study of the elements of ethical idealism in Geeta Devatma and Swami Shivanora and its relevance in the present age.
Bihar, 1990.

2089. Prasanna Kumari, U.P.
The concept of freedom in Marxian ethics.
Calcutta, 1996.

2090. Radha, S.
Gandhian ethics: A critical study.
Calicut, 1984.

2091. Rai, Balasunder
Contribution of Mahatma Gandhi, to the contemporary ethical philosophy.
Punjabi, 1984.

2092. Rai, Pratap Singh
Buddhism with ethics of self perception.
MBU, 1993.

2093. Ramkrishayya, D.
An experimental study of the errors in reasoning.
Andhra, 1940.

2094. Ray, Shrimati
Ethical implications of the Maya Hermonuties in recent Indian thought.
MBU, 1993.

2095. Roy, Shambhu Nath
The concept of good in contemporary ethical thought.
Allahabad, 1962.

2096. Saxana, Chitra
Adhunik Bharatiya chintakon ka nitishetra mein

sameekshatmak adhyayan, (H).
Rohilkhand, 1987.

2097. A phenomenological enquiry into the upanishadic concept of self realisation.
IIT, Kanpur, 1986.

2098. Sharma, Meenakshi N.
A comparative study of the influence of moral values on parent child relationship in the age group of 9-16 in Northern Indians and in state of California.
Durgawati, 1987.

2099. Singh, Kamini
Dharam Sutron aur dharma shastron ka neeti shastra, (H).
Bhagalpur, 1984.

2100. Singh, Meera
Thervad aur sarvastivad sampradaya mein vinay: Ek tulnatmak adhyayan, (H).
BHU, 1987.

2101. Singh, Param Hans
Institutionalism in recent ethical thought.
BHU, 1973.

2102. Singh, Pushpa
Mahabharat ke naitik mulyon ka sameekshatmak adhyayan, (H).
Durgawati, 1989.

2103. Singh, Rama
The origin and evolution of Indian ethics.
Bihar, 1972.

2104. Singh, Ravindra Nath
Vidur ka aachar darshan: Udyog parva ke paripekshya mein, (H).
BHU, 1992.

2105. Singh, Satrughan
Nature and function of reason and intiution.
Magadh, 1981.

2106. Singh, Syam Nandan
An analysis of the concept of morality in contemporary society.
Bihar, 1990.

2107. Sinha, Himmat Singh
A comparative study of the philosophy co-ethical doctrine of communism and Ashaktiyoga.
Meerut, 1974.

2108. Sinha, Hrishikesa Prasad
The nature and basis of ethical judgement.
Bihar, 1970.

2109. Sinha, Indradeo Narayan
A critical study of Humes ethical thought and its impact on analytical ethics.
Bihar, 1978.

2110. Sinha, Lakshmi
Humanistic trends in contemporary Indian ethics with special reference to Radhakrishanan and M.N. Roy.
Bihar, 1974.

2111. Sinha, Rameshwar Prasad
A study in the ethics of mimansa.
Bihar, 1990.

2112. Sinha, Vimalendu Narayan
The nature of moral valuation. A study in contemporary ethics with special reference to G.E. Moore, John Dewey and C.L. Stevenson.
IIT, Kanpur, 1969.

2113. Srivastav, Anand
An appraisal of Bradlay criticism of Kantian and

Hedonistic ethics.
Allahabad, 1982.

2114. Srivastava, Prakash, K.
The existentialist ethics with particular reference to Jean Paul Sartre.
Rajasthan, 1972.

2115. Srivastava, Renu
Astitvavadi neeti sastron ke prakash mein Kant ke neeti shastra, ka mulyankan, (H).
Gorakhpur, 1992.

2116. Suther, Rohtas Kumar
A critical study of the socio-ethical values in Ramcharit Manas.
Kurukshetra, 1992.

2117. Tahtinan, Unto
Non-violence as an ethical principle.
BHU, 1958.

2118. Talghatti, Shankar Ram Chandra
The concept of moral obligation.
Patna, 1969.

2119. Tandon, Nirmala
Recent Indian ethical thought.
BHU, 1965.

2120. Tiwari, B.G.
Some tendencies in modern ethical thought of India, (D. Litt.).
Agra, 1953.

2121. Unterman, Alan
Morality and religion: A investigation of the nature of morality thought study of the relationship between morality and religion in the Judaco Christian and Indian tradition.
Delhi, 1970.

2122. Vaidya, Nirmala
A study of relationship between the development of moral concept in children and the moral values of parents.
Rani Durgawati, 1983.

2123. Vanlalnghak
Value and interest. An alternative to fact value distinction R.B. Perrys ethical theory.
IIT, Kanpur, 1988.

2124. Vaz, Joans Clement
Eastern spirituality and christian ethics.
Bombay, 1977.

2125. Verma, Ved Prakash
Subjectivism and emotionism in contemporary ethics. A critical study.
Delhi, 1968.

2126. Yadav, Jagat Narayan
Problem of moral crisis in modern Indian society.
Magadh, 1982.

2127. Yadav, Sarvajit Singh
Prescriptivism as an ethical theory. A study in the philosophy of R.M. Hare.
BHU, 1990.

2128. Yadav, Usha
Gita ka karmayoga aur Kant ke naitik vichar, (H).
BHU, 1992.

10

LOGIC

2129. Acharya, Satish Chandra
Mediaeval school of Indian Logic.
Calcutta, 1108.

2130. Agarwal, Padma
A psychological approach to symbolism.
BHU, 1950.

2131. Bagahi, Sitanshu Sekhar
A study of tarka reasoning. Its nature and role in Indian logic (D. Litt.).
Calcutta, 1949.

2132. Bandyopadyay, Mamta
Dummelt on fregers sense and reference.
Calcutta, 1996.

2133. Basu, Dalip Kumar
Some problems conceiving the nature of logic.
Calcutta, 1973.

2134. Basu, Khana
A study of poppers logic of knowledge.
Vishwa Bharati, 1983.

2135. Basuri, Benuker
A comparative study of the classical and modern treatment of disjunction.
Vishwa Bharati, 1977.

2136. Bhadka, Madhu Sudan Vasudev
A critical reconstruction of the epistemological basis of logic.
Poona, 1973.

2137. Bhattacharya, Birendra Kumar
An enquiry into the foundation of logic (D. Litt.).
Calcutta, 1949.

2138. Chandra Sekhar, Reena
Dignaga's contribution of Indian logic and epistemology.
Bombay, 1989.

2138a. Chattopadhyay, Supria
Proposition and fact.
Calcutta, 1992.

2139. Dalai, Balkishore
The relation of inference in Indian logic.
Poona (S), 1987.

2140. Dalai, B.K.
The relation of inference in Indian logic.
Poona, 1987.

2141. Das, Prabhati
Hypothesis and evidence.
Vishwa Bharati, 1983.

2142. Dixit, Krishna Kumar
Indian logic. Its problems as treated by its schools.
Bihar, 1964.

2143. Dixit, Suresh Pratap Singh
Madhyamik darshan mein tarka ka sthan.
BHU, 1987.

2144. Duperkayastha, Govind Chandra
Reason intution and reality.
1994.

2145. Ghosh, Kanaidas
Some proposed application of devaint logic. A philosophical enquiry.
Jadavpur, 1988.

2146. Gohale, P.P.
An investigation in fallacies discussed in Indian logic special reference to Ancient nyaya and Buddhism.
Poona, 1980.

2147. Goswami, Arati
The apriori in recent philosophy.
Calcutta, 1966.

2148. Goswami, Chinjoy
Logical structure of casual statements with special reference to G.H. Von Wright.
BHU, 1979.

2149. Guha, Dinesh Chandra
Some basic theories and techniques of Navya Nyaya system in logic. (D. Litt.)
Calcutta, 1963.

2150. Jain, Asha
A comparative study of Jain logic and modern money value and logic.
Allahabad, 1979.

2151. Jha, Kishore Nath
The problem of theism in Indian logic and special reference to the work of Jnanesrimitra.
Bihar, 1967

2152. Ketkar, B.Y.
Problems of relations in Indian logic with special reference to nyaya logic.
Poona, 1980.

2153. Khan, Ramdas
Critiques of pure reason.
Calcutta, 1914.

2154. Kothari, Jagdish Prasad.
Akghar sama mnaya ka shastriya adhyayan, (H).
Rohilkhand (S), 1986.

2155. Kothia, Darbarilal Jain
Treatment of inference in Jain logic: A historical and critical study.
BHU, 1968.

2156. Mangal, Shanti Ram
Aristrolle's theory of induction: A critical study.
Ravindra Bharati, 1984.

2157. Mishra, Ramesh Dutt
The theory of propositions in modern logic.
Lucknow, 1907.

2158. Mishra, Revati Raman
They theory of logical construction in contemporary British philosophy.

2159. Mukesh, Ragini
The problem of justification in induction.
MBU, 1992.

2160. Mukherjee, Jatil Kumar
Illusion and its correction. A comparative and critical study of Indian theories.

2161. Mukhopadhyay, Ranjan
The justification of deduction.
Jadavpur, 1988.

2162. Nippani, Gururaj K.
Vadirajas yuktimallika. A critical study.
Karnataka (S), 1987.

2163. Pal, Ramchand
Studies into the fundamentals of induction.
Calcutta, 1953.

2164. Pandey, Sri Ram
Advaita Vedant Gur Madhyamik darshan mein Tark ka sthan, (H).
BHU, 1977.

2165. Pandit, Mrityunjaya
Some philosophical problems in logic and mathematics.
NBU, 1993.

2166. Patel, J.A.
A study of the effect of religion understanding in moral reasoning.
Gujarat, 1990.

2167. Pradeep Kumar
The native of arguments in western logic.
Panjabi, 1996.

2168. Rajbanshi, Bibha
Ksana bhangasiddhi of Ratna kirti: A study.
Kurukshetra.

2169. Rao, Kumari Rama
A critical evaluation of Bertrand Russells conception of mathematical logic.
Meerut, 1977.

2170. Sakata, Harish Chandra
Logic of imparatives and its significance in to mural reasoning.
Rajasthan, 1983.

2171. Samanti, Bimalendu
The concept of meaning verifications and necessity as in theme and logical positivism.
Burdhwan, 1987.

2172. Sengupta, Pradeep Kumar
Some aspects of logic and methodology.
Calcutta, 1961.

2173. Shaidu, Sullan Ali
Naturalistic fallacy: Its impact and relevance in ethics.
Delhi, 1969.

2174. Sharma, Neelam Kumar
Mokshakar Gupta kee tark bhasha mein praman sameeksha, (H).
BHU, 1989.

2175. Sharma, Bankelal
Inference (Anamena) in Indian philosophy.
Punjab, 1968.

2176. Sharma, Brajnarayan
Inference in Hindu philosophy,
Vikram, 1968.

2177. Sharma, Girish
A critical study of Kants philosophy of logic.
Gauhati, 1969.

2178. Shrimathi E.
Justification of indication: A study.
Madras, 1989.

2179. Siddheswara Prasad
The problem of indication in Indian logic with special reference to nyaya vaisasika system.
Venkateswara, 1983.

2180. Singh, Badri Prasad
A critical study of the logical doctrine in the nyaya manjari of Jayant Bhatt.
BHU, 1966.

2181. Singh, Ram Lal
The nature and status of reason in kants and Sankara.
Allahabad, 1966.

2182. Singh, Prithpal
The logic of ethical arguments.
Panjabi, 1996.

2183. Sinha, Ramesh Chandra
Conception of reason and intution in the 20th century Indian thought with special reference to Sri Aurobindo, ke Bhattacharya and Radha Krishanan.
BHU, 1969.

2184. Veezhinathan N.
The tarks Sangraha Dipika Prakasika with the commentary Balapriya Part-I with commentary prasajana Part-II.
Madras (S), 1985.

2185. Verma, Rooprakha
The problem of synthetic apriori proposition.
Lucknow, 1968.

11

LINGUISTIC PHILOSOPHY

2186. Ahmad Neeser, T.K.
A philosophical enquiry into the foundation of meening and Grammar.
IIT, Kanpur, 1985.

2187. Aminul Haque
Some linguistic problems about private experiences.
Burdwan, 1976.

2188. Chakraborti, Jhuma
Problem of syntax and sementies with special reference to Chomsky.
Jadavpur, 1993.

2189. Kantamani, A.
On linguistic competence: A study of the development of N. Chomsky 5 principles of competence.
Madras, 1976.

2190. Kiyoshima, Hideke
Indian philosophy of language with reference to Vakyapadiya.
Delhi, 1985.

2191. Lungalang G. Zoquizo
Language and action.
NEHU, 1989.

2192. Mitra, Keya
Reference and internal realism. An enquiry into Hilavy patnams philosophy of language.
Gujarat, 1995.

2193. Mishra, Arun
Synonymy.
Delhi, 1987.

2194. Moudgal, Asha
Some main problems of Withgensteins later philosophy.
Hyderabad, 1989.

2195. Mukhopadhyay, Arundhati
On linguistic competence: A critical analysis of Chomsky.
Jadavpur, 1987.

2196. Pandey, Harprasad
Wittgensteins philosophy of Grammar: A reconstruction.
Hyderabad, 1993.

2197. Panja, Girija Shankar
Theory of translation.
Vishwa Bharati, 1990.

2198. Primala, C.P.
The problem of induction.
Mysore, 1991.

2199. Prabhakaran, V.
The concept of evidence with special reference to the doctrine of language in Edmund Husserls phenomenology.
Calcutta, 1995.

2200. Prakashvir
Meaning in ordinary language philosophy. A critical study of the Wittgensteinian and Post Wittgensteinian

conception.
Kurukshetra, 1990.

2201. Raman, L.
Language rules and grammar in the later philosophy of Wittgenstein.
IIT, Bombay, 1985.

2202. Roy, Manju
Similarity and language.
NBU, 1984.

2203. Sharma, Rajendra Prasad
Shabda shastriya vigyanam praman hankarika.
Rajasthan, 1989.

2204. Tripathi, Laxman Kumar
Language subjectivity and inter subjectivity in Edmund Husseri. A critical study.
Poona, 1993.

12

RELIGIOUS PHILOSOPHY

2205. Adhani, Theophil
Journey to the Centre: Religious symbolism and its manifestation in secred structures.
Bombay, 1992.

2206. Agrawal, Sandhya
Ishwar evam uske astitva kee dharana ka alochnatmak adhyayan (H).
Bihar, 1987.

2207. Anusuya Devi, A.R.
Tradition and modernity in contemporary religio-philosophic movement.
Venkateswara, 1988.

2208. Arora, Kamals
A philosophical study of Sri Sattya Sai Baba in the context of contemporary religious philosophical milliece.
Delhi, 1989.

2209. Arora, Veena
The concept of Awtar with special reference to Shri Aurobindo.

2210. Arya, Devkanya
A critical study of Sat Sandarbha with special reference

to Srikrishna and Bhakti sandarbha.
Delhi, 1965.

2211. Babra, Daya Kaur
Dharma ke darshanik adharon ka samalochanatmak adhyayan (H).
Reni Durgawati.

2212. Bajpai, Suman
Radhaswami mat ek darshanik adhyayan (H).
Vikram, 1990.

2213. Bandyopedhyay, Krishna
Some modern criticisms of the idea of God.
Calcutta, 1972.

2214. Bandyopodhyay, Ranjeet Kumar
Vedanter alok Srimad Bhagwat (S).
Burdwan, 1979.

2215. Banerjee, Aruna
Parsi dharma tatha somestic dharma mein moksha kee dharana (H).
BHU, 1973.

2216. Basavaraju, T.B.
Shri Radhakrishanans contribution to world religions.
Mysore, 1990.

2217. Basu, Manju
Importance of religion in the perfection of modern philosophy.
Ravindra Bharati, 1986.

2218. Bhagat, Jagdish Kumar
Swami Vivekanand: Dr. Bhagwan Das and S. Radhakrishanan universal religion: A critical and comparative study.
Bhagalpur, 1984.

2219. Bhagat, Vimala Sain
The concept of prayers in modern Indian religious thought.
Delhi, 1981.

2220. Bhandari, Prem Dayal
Possibility and process of human freedom in the Bhagwat Gita.
Agra, 1979.

2221. Bharadwaj, Savita
Adhunik yug mein dharma shastron kee prasangikta (H).
BHU, 1990.

2222. Bharati, Manju
Bhakti ka artha evam uski awadharanayon ka vikas (H), (S).
Gorakhpur, 1986.

2223. Bhattacharya, Amarnath
Foundation of theism: An Indian approach (S).
Burdwan, 1983.

2224. Bhattacharya, Chandan
Some aspects of phenomenology of religion.
Ravindra Bharati, 1992.

2225. Biswas, Dulal Chandra
Srisri Chaitanya Charitamrita Iswartattws.
Ravindra Bharati, 1986.

2226. Bangala, S.R.
White Heads, concept of God.
Bombay, 1984.

2227. Bora, Purna Chandra
The philosophical outlook and religion of Sri Sankardeva.
Dibrugarh, 1984.

2228. Cardoze, J.C.
Religious dynamism: Its degeneration and revitalisation.
Bombay, 1977.

2229. Chakravarthi, Ramanuja C.N.
Nine fold relationship between the human and devine according to Sri Pillai Lokacharya and Madam H.P. Blaratsky.
Madras, 1993.

2230. Chakraborti, Sudhindra Chandra
A critical exposition of the philosophical foundations of Bengal vaishnavism (D. Litt.).
Calcutta, 1964.

2231. Chandra Mohan
A critical and comparative study of Buddhism. Hinduism and Christianity.
Rohilkhand, 1985.

2232. Chandra Prabha
Philosophical implications of Krishna legend.
Meerut, 1988.

2233. Chandratra, P.D.
The methodology of major Bhasyas on the Brahmasatra.
Gujarat, 1957.

2234. Chatterji, Chhanda
The philosophy of gaudiga vashnavism.
Delhi, 1984.

2235. Chatterjee, Mitra
The concept of destiny of the individuals in the Bhagwat Gita as interpretted by Sri Aurobindo.
Ravindra Bharati, 1979.

2236. Chaudhuri, Piyash Kanti
An enquiry into the nature validity and value of

religious experience.
Nagpur, 1975.

2237. Chaudhuri, Raghav Prasad
Panchratnagam Nadiya samhita: Ek vivechnatmak adhyayan (H).
Bihar, 1978.

2238. Chirappanath, A.K.
Karma and original sin with reference to the problem of evil.
Karnataka, 1980.

2239. Conio, Caterino
The Mondkye karika in relation to Buddhism and Vedant.
BHU, 1969.

2240. Cooper, Rustam Jahangir
God in human experiences.
Bombay, 1946.

2241. Crtiz, Javier Ugaz
A hermaneuties of symbolic special" terms akasa vyoman kha, sunya and their relation to the centre Heart. Hrgdeya in the shavism of Kashmir.
BHU, 1989.

2242. Dadheech, Jyotsna
Kabir ke darshanik chintan ka shodh parak adhyayan (U).
Jodhpur, 1990.

2243. Dasgupta, Dipika
An examination of some approaches to the concept of God.
Vishwa Bharati, 1967.

2244. Dasgupta, D. Shuabhra
Critical study of Vivekanand towards religion.
Bihar, 1973.

2245. Dass, Madhu
The concept of sin and faith in world religion and their corelation.
Bombay, 1978.

2246. Datta, Jay Kumar
A critical survey of the contribution of William James to different problems of philosophy of religion.
Calcutta, 1985.

2247. Datta, Prajaranjan
Rajadharma in ancient India.
Jadavpur, 1967.

2248. Dattaray, Sunil Kumar
The Bhakti school of Indian philosophy.
Calcutta, 1968.

2249. Dave, K.S.
The social philosophy of Bhagawat Gita.
Saurashtra, 1986.

2250. Devnath, Pabitra Kumar
Religion and religious establishment of Kamate. Kochking dam.
NBU, 1995.

2251. Deleury, G.A.
Cult of Vinoba
Poona, 1952.

2252. Desai, Subhash Kesavrao
The relevance of modern scientific conclusions to religion.
Shivaji, 1991.

2253. Despande, Vishnu Wama
The impact of ancient Indian thought on Christianity.
Bombay, 1989.

2254. Dhulia, Yohan
God man relationship in vaishnavism and Christianity with special reference is Ramanuja and S.P. Paul.
Devi Ahidlya, 1996.

2255. Dwivedi, Dinesh Kumar
Hindi sahitya mein Gautam Buddh aur unke chintan kee abhivyakha (H).
Bundelkhand, 1992.

2256. Dwivedi, Vishwambhar Nath
Gita kee vivid vyakhyaon kee aitihasic evam tulnatmak sameeksha: Sankar Ramanuj, Tilak, Gandhi, Vinoba evam Radhakrishnan ka vicharon ke vishesh adhyayan (H), (S).
Kanpur, 1986.

2257. Emmanuel, Damera
An resurrection: A critical appraisal of John Hicks position on resurrection and life hereafter.
Hyderabad, 1991.

2258. Gabriala, Gastaldello
Bhakti movement: Its aesthetic philosophical, ethical perspective.
BHU, 1986.

2259. Gabrial, M.
Subjectivity and religious thruth in the philosophy of Soren Kierkegaurd.
Madras, 1997.

2260. Gangadhar, Dangar Alia
Dharma aur samajik jeevan. Sarvapally Radhakrishnan aur Rein hold Hiebuhr ka tulanatmak adhyayan (H).
BHU, 1973.

2261. Ganguli, Alpana
God and the absolute with special reference to Sri

Aurobindos philosophy.
Vishwa Bharati, 1985.

2262. Garg Manorama
Hindu aur Isai, acharshastra ka tulanatmak adhyayan. Manusmriti, Bhagwat Gita aur New Testament ke vishesh sandarbh mein (H).
BHU, 1970.

2263. Ghosh, Eva
Conceptoin of God in contemporary modern thought: A critical Study.
Ranchi, 1967.

2264. Ghosh, Nripendra Bhushan
The moral philosophy of the Mahabharat: A critical study.
Gurukula, 1978.

2265. Ghosh, Piyush Kanti
A study of the Bouls their philosophy and religious practices.
Ravindra Bharati, 1992.

2266. Giandemenica, Tamiozza
Prayer in Islam and christianity: A comparative study.
BHU, 1989.

2267. Goel, Divya Abha
Samkaleen Bharatiya darshan mein dharma kee avadharana (H).
Indore, 1981.

2268. Gole, Leela Dattatraya
God as the supreme value. Analysis and interpretation of the idea of the God from the stand piont of value.
Poona, 1959.

2269. Gopal Krishnan, T.
A study into the secular values of Ramayan and their

relevance to the modern society.
Banglore, 1990.

2270. Govind Rajalu, D.
Thava thiru pamban Shrimad Kamara Gurudesa Adhigolarin thathuva kolgai (T).
Madras, 1993.

2271. Grou, Claude
The religious background of philosophy in modern Maharashtra: A study of the influence of Hinduism. Charistianity and Islam on the evaluation of philosophical ideas in Maharashtra between 1818 to 1920.
Poona, 1974.

2272. Guha, Debashis
God in relation to the external world and the energy concept.
Jadavpur, 1988.

2273. Gupta, Ramesh Chandra
Tirthankar Buddh aur Awatar kee avadharna: Ek tulnatmak adhyayan.
BHU, 1986.

2274. Hiremath, Neelkantha Sharma
A critical and comparative study of the tattva Pradeepika of Sri Chitsukhacharya.
BHU, 1969.

2275. Hiremath, Nuranda Swami
Veershaiv aur Kashmir Shaiva darshan mein maukshya ka swaroop: Ek sameekshatmak adhyayan (H).
BHU, 1990.

2276. Harikesh
A critical study of the psycho analytic approach to religion.
Karukshetra, 1990.

2277. Hunibou, Newmai
The concept of God and Godly men in liangmai Naga tradition.
NEHU, 1993.

2278. Igneshius, I Maria
Historising as a method for a new philosophical understanding of the problem of religious language.
Poona, 1980.

2279. Indira, K.
comparative study of the religious philosophies of Tagore and Radhakrishnan.
Calicut, 1991.

2280. Indubala
Kierkegaurdis analysis of religious experience.
Punjab, 1973.

2281. Indumati, B.
The study of Sri Aurobindos interpretation of Isha and the Keha upanished from the stand point of Sankara.
Madras, 1978.

2282. Isac A.I.
The doctrine of Grace in Vaishavism and Christianity.
BHU, 1989.

2283. Jacob, Gaddam
Religious experience: A critical study with reference to Sadhu Sunder Singh.
Andhra, 1990.

2284. Jain, Deepak Lata
Concept of soul Karma Moksha in sudhadvaita and Jainism: A comparative study.
Sukhadia, 1986.

2285. Jain, R.C.
Jain darshan ke nishchay aur vyaharon ka

sameekshatmak analysis (H), (S).
Bhopal, 1980.

2286. Jain, Shiv Kumar Muni
The doctrine of liberation in Indian religions with special reference to Jainism.
Punjab, 1978.

2287. Jaiswal, Sushila
Pramukh upanishadon aur Shrimad Bhagwat Gita mein Bhakti tatwa (H).
BHU, 1979.

2288. Jalihal, M.R.
Whitehead and veerashainism with special reference to some Vachanakarsas.
Karnataka, 1992.

2289. James, L.E.
The concept of guilt in christianity and Hinduism with special reference to Paul Tillich and Mahatma Gandhi.
Jabalpur, 1973.

2290. Jha, Sangeeta
Dharma aur darshan kee khetra mein Acharya Hari Bhadra ka yogdan (H).
BHU, 1991.

2291. Jha, Upendra Narayan
The way out of crisis: Theology in the light of aesthitic Jainism and Buddhism and Advaita Vedanta.
Magadha, 1972.

2292. Jose, Elemenpassery
The philosophy of religion in Karl Marx: An exposition and critique.
Poona, 1980.

2293. Joshi, Anju
The role of religious belief in North Eastern India.
NEHU, 1983.

2294. Joshi, Laduram
Idea of God.
Rajasthan, 1955.

2295. Joshi, Neela J.
Dhavadavas philosophy of religion with special reference to mysticism and humanism.
Gujarat, 1985.

2296. Kampchen, Martin
The concept of the holy in world religions: The concept of holiness in Hinduism and Christianity as exemplified by the lives of Ramakrishna and Fransis of Assise.
Vishwa Bharati, 1987.

2297. Karkar, D.B.
Bharatiya Iswar darshan.
Gujarat, 1991.

2298. Kasai, Minoru
A comparative study of Hinduism, Buddhism and Christianity in the light of the Bhagawat Gita the Bodhicaryara Tara and Gospel according to John.
BHU, 1965.

2299. Katagihallimath. M.K.
Veeraghavism and imagination of Aurobindo.
Karnataka, 1992.

2300. Kayarohanam, P.C.
The concept of God as realised by the Siddhas.
Madras, 1986.

2301. Kerkotta, Paulas
Theism in the philosophy of Gandhi and Christianity.
Ranchi, 1974.

2302. Khan, Abdul Ahmed
Muslim economic thought during second and third century of Hijjal.
AMU, 1978.

2303. Khastigir, Amitabha
Theism: A critical survey.
Ravindra Bharati, 1972.

2304. Koottiyanial, Annamma
Sprituality of selfless action for meaning ful file today: An exploration into the ideal of Bhagawat Gita and St. Francis of Assisi.
Madras, 1993.

2305. Krishna Chander
Rajdharma: A critical study.
Punjab (Police), 1980.

2306. Kukrati, Vishnu Datt
Nagpanth: Garhwal ke paripekshya mein (H).
Garhwal, 1985.

2307. Kumkum Kumari
A study of religio-social philosophy of some contemporary Indian thinkers with special reference to Vivekanand and Gandhi.
Patna, 1981.

2308. Kundu, Azit Kumar
Self and reality in saivism.
Burdwan, 1993.

2309. Leitanthen, Diven Singh
A philosophical study of the worship of Umanglai forest in Manipur.
Gauhati, 1992.

2310. Mahadevappa. N.G.
The viva saiva concept of sakti.
Mysore, 1978.

2311. Mahanta, Bina
The concept of heaven and hell.
NEHU, 1983.

2312. Mehta, H. Pherozshah
Iranian idea of impurity. Being an analysis of a phase of Zorbastian religion contended as a source book of psychology and sociology of religion.
Bombay, 1944.

2313. Manikkam, Thomas M.
A comparative study of the social and moral idea of Dharamshastras and old testament with special reference to Manusmriti and Panta toush.
BHU, 1974.

2314. Minoo, Jai, Murzban
The concept of Fetishism in Marx: An analysis of some recent interpratation.
Punjab, 1993.

2315. Mishra, Alka Sundari
Devantedhu Ishwar tatwon samalochnatmakam adhyayanam (S).
Jagannath, 1991.

2316. Mishra, Mahesh
A study of the Kanada Rahasya of Shankar Mishra.
Lucknow, 1960.

2317. Mishra, Prem Niwas
Swami Dayanand tatha Swami Shivanand ke dharma darshan ka tulnatmak evam sameekshatmak adhyayan (H).
Bihar, 1190.

2318. Mishra, Rakesh Dutt
Bharatiya darshan mein Bhakti kee avadharana (H).
BHU, 1992.

2319. Mishra, Saroj Kumar
Aghor mat : Siddhant, sadhana aur sampradaya (D. Litt.), (H).
Ravishankar, 1991.

2320. Mishra, Satyendra Nath
Bharatiya bhabaney dharma-o-Ishovar.
Ravindra Bharati, 1990.

2321. Mishra, Surendra Kumar
Bharatiya Sanstri tan Daivisakti Vimersh.
Jagannath, 1986.

2322. Mishra, Sriniwas
Bharat mein dharma aur Rajneeti Secularism. Dharma nirpekshyata ke vishesh sandarbh mein (H).
BHU, 1994.

2323. Mitoma, Ryojan
Saddharmapundarika sara: A textual and philosophical study.
Delhi, 1985.

2324. Mohammad Hayat
The religious thought of Syed Ali Hamedance.
AMU, 1986.

2325. Mohammad Miraj
Sufimat ka darshanik vivechan.
Kashi, 1993.

2326. Mohammad Noor Nabi
Development of Muslim religious thought in India from 1200 A.D. to 1450 A.D.
AMU, 1954.

2327. Mohanlal
Absolution in the East and West.
Rajasthan, 1953.

2328. Mahonty, Malaya Kumar
A critical study of some important views about religion with special reference to Marx, Freud and Willian James.
Kurukshetra, 1989.

2329. Mukherjee, Anandmay
Brahma Dharma-o-sree Ramkrishna (D. Litt).
Ravindra Bharati, 1986.

2330. Mukherjee, Sadhana
The absolute and God in Bradley and Sankara.
BHU, 1971.

2331. Mukhopadhyay, Pooran Chandra
Impact of upanishads on the ninteenth century Western thought.
Calcutta, 1981.

2332. Mundle, Swati
Sri Aurobinda ka dharma darshan.
Vikram, 1981.

2333. Muthuraman, M.
The idea of soul and the place of grace of God in philosophy of Saiva siddhanta.
Madras, 1966.

2334. Navathe, Kalinde Vasudeo
A study of the philosophical thinking Mohanubhava cult about the concept of God and the life of the Lord Krishna dipicted in the literature.
Shivaji, 1992.

2335. Neelam Kumari
Mahabharat mein dharma kee avadharana (H).
BHU, 1994.

2336. Padmavathi, Kilambi
A phenomenological examination into the essential of major religions of India: A search for integration of consciousness of India.
Osmania, 1995.

2337. Padmavathi, N.G.
The concept of death and immortality in Katha and

Isha Upanishads.
Osmania, 1978.

2338. Pahari, Lakshmi Kanta
Bhakti tatwa sameeksha (H).
BHU, 1990.

2339. Pal, Bimal Chandra
Socio-religions thought of Radhakrishnan.
BHU, 1991.

2340. Pal, Subodh Kumar
Atheism in Indian thought.
Vishwa Bharati, 1988.

2341. Pandey, Durgadutt
Dharma visayak arvacheen ak shepon kee sameeksha (H).
Awadh, 1988.

2342. Pandey, Madan
Gita ke alok mein manas ka darshanik evam sanskritik vivechan (H).
Ranchi, 1980.

2343. Pandey, Parmanand
Bharatiya darshan mein Iswar kee avadharana (H).
BHU, 1994.

2344. Pandey, Rameshraya
Jain evam Baudh darshan mein upasana ke swaroop ka alochnatmak adhyayan (H).
Gorakhpur, 1991.

2345. Pandey, Uma
Conception and nature of Bhakti in vashanav darshan.
Saugar, 1970.

2346. Pandit, Sukhi Chand
Gandhi's concept of God.
Bhagalpur, 1985.

2347. Paramjit Kaur
Prachya dharma darshano ka naitik evam alochanatmak adhyayan (H).
Rohilkhand, 1986.

2348. Paranjape, Kalpana Manohar
Beganning of philosophic religious and scientific thoughts in the history of mankind nd the Indian contribution to it.
Poona, 1981.

2349. Parikh, M.P.
Bhagawat Gita teachings and modern man: Application in psychotherapy.
Bombay, 1992.

2350. Parekh, Pushpa
The religion and philosophy of Sh. Chaitanya and his school: A comparative and critical study.
Ravindra Bharati, 1987.

2351. Patyaiying, Paitoon
Modern Hindu approach to comparative study of religion. Radhakrishnan.
Vishwa Bharati. 1989.

2352. Pathak, Ajay Kumar
Sadhana Paddhati ka tatwa vimershiya adhar: Ek sameekshatmak adhyayan (H).
Kashi, 1993.

2353. Pathak, Ramesh Kumar
Ramcharit Manas mein gyan karma evam Bhakti ka swaroop (H).
Burktulla, 1989.

2354. Pathi, Narayan Chandra
Doctrine of karma.
Utkal, 1988.

2355. Pathrose, C.D.
The concept of samanyasa in Indian religio-philosophical traditions.
BHU, 1992.

2356. Pillai, P. Arulswamy
Some problems in inter religious dialogue.
Karnataka, 1982.

2357. Plat, J.C.
Philosophy of devotion: A comparative study of bhakti and prapathi.
BHU, 1956.

2358. Pooranandam, Vemuri
The personal and impersonal native of God head.
BHU, 1969.

2359. Premlata Devi
Religious philosophy of the Boros of the Brahmaputra valley.
Gauhati, 1993.

2360. Rai, Girija Shankar
Validity of religious experience.
BHU, 1962.

2361. Rai, Suresh Vrat
Recent developments in Indian philosophy of religion with special reference to the work of Dayanand, Ramtirtha, Maharishi Raman, Ranade and Krishna Murthi.
Allahabad, 1964.

2362. Rajagopalan, Vasudha
The Shri Vaishnava understanding of Bhakti and prapatti.
Bombay, 1978.

2363. Raju, G.R. Venkatapati
Contemporary Indian religious thought: A study with reference to the philosophies of Ravindra Nath Tagore, Mahatma Gandhi. Sri Aurobindo and Radhakrishnan.
Andhra, 1989.

2364. Ramakant Kumar
Sceptical approaches to religion.
Patna, 1971.

2365. Rao, P.N.
A comparative study of the religious philosophy of Alfred North Whitehead and the Advaita Vedanta of Sankara (D. Litt.).
BHU, 1995.

2366. Rathore, Rekha
Ishwar ke astitva hetu prastut paramparagat pramanon ka nyayadershan ke sandarbh mein tulnatmak adhyayan (H).
BHU, 1986.

2367. Raut, Rameshraya
Sant Kabir ka darshan: Ek adhyayan (H).
Bihar, 1990.

2368. Razia Khatoon
Problem of evil in Christian and Muslim philosophy with special reference to St. Augustine. St. Thamsa quines and Imam A.L. Ghazati.
AMU, 1976.

2369. Roberts, H.R.
A study of the Wittgensteian philosophy of religion.
Madras, 1978.

2370. Sadanand
Method of God realisation in Indian religions with special reference to theistic religious system of India.
BHU, 1970.

2371. Safia Bano
Maulana Azads reconstruction of religious thought in Islam.
Osmania, 1977.

2372. Sahay, Keshavanand
Some contributions to the religious synthesis: A comprehensive and critical study of the theology. Din Iilahi Lala Bhagwan Das, R.N. Pagare and Radhakrishanan.
Bihar, 1971.

2373. Sahay, Radhika Raman
A critical study of the religious philosophy of William James.
Patna, 1973.

2374. Sahu, Gangadhar
God in Indian philosophy: A conceptual analysis.
Sambalpur, 1993.

2375. Sajivan Prasad
Religion and reason.
Patna, 1973.

2376. Samvasivan, S.
The philosophy of Saiva siddhant with special reference to their Vandhigar and Thirakalitrupadiyar.
Madras, 1980.

2377. Santosh Kumari
Philosophical concept of Krishna cult.
Durgawati, 1992.

2378. Sanyal, Batukdas Sadadhar
Religion as the realisation of the subline in theory.
Bombay, 1958.

2379. Saran, Bina
Dharam kee Bhashya mein nihit samasyayen: Ek

sameekshatmak vishleshan (H).
Magadh, 1990.

2380. Saran, Om Prakash
A study of religion and its different expressions with special reference to Brahamanical, Buddhist and Jain religious movement.
Magadh, 1967.

2381. Sarma, Sibbnath
A critical study of religious philosophy of Eudolt Otte.
Gauhati, 1985.

2382.. Sarvate, Shobhana
Maharashtra, santon ka vaishnav darshan ke sandarbh mein darshanik adhyayan (H).
Saugar, 1991.

2383. Sehgal, Saroj Kumari
Philosophical implications of Ram Legend.
Rohilkhand, 1986.

2384. Sen, Sabujkali
Possibility of religious knowledge.
Vishwa Bharati, 1985.

2385. Sengupta, Krishna
A study of Sri Aurobindos and B.G. Tilaks interpretation of the Gita.
NBU, 1990.

2386. Seshasayee, T.
The concept of pravana: Its meaning and significance in Hindu religion.
Madras, 1988.

2387. Shahi, Poonam
A critical study of the mein philosophical concepts of Christian and Hindu religion.
Gorakhpur, 1992.

2388. Shankaran, K.P.
Critique of religion by Marx and Freud: Analysis and evolution.
Madras, 1982.

2389. Sharma, Asha
Religious values and their doctrinal bases with special reference to Hinduism, Buddhism and Christianity.
BHU, 1971.

2390. Sharma, Asha
Shrimad Bhagwat Gita ka Shankar, Ramanuja evam Aurovindo ke Geeta bhasyon ke aloke mein ek sameekshatmak adhyayan (H).
BHU, 1989.

2391. Sharma, Chandrakanta
A study of psycho analytic conception of religion.
Gauhati, 1991.

2392. Sharma, Dev
Ramanuj darshan mein Bhakti ka swaroop (H).
Gurukul, 1978.

2393. Sharma, Dwijendra Prakash
The concept of God in the Bhagwat Gita and neo-vedantic thinkers: A comparative study.
Rohilkhand, 1993.

2394. Sharma, Gyaneshwar
Religious experience according to William John.
Bhagalpur, 1985.

2395. Sharma. J.D.
God in the philosophical systems of the world.
Agra, 1949.

2396. Sharma, Kamaleshwar
The philosophy of Karmayog according to the Bhagwat Gita and Swami Vivekanand: A comparative and critical study.
Bhagalpur, 1978.

2397. Sharma, Prakashwati
Dharmik anubhaon mein satya kee sameeksya (H).
Rajasthan, 1976.

2398. Sharma, Rajendra Prasad
Upanishadik darshanik Satyakam Jabal aur unka darshan (H).
Patna, 1980.

2399. Sharma, Shraddha
Bharatiya darshan mein Bhakti evam upasana ka adhyatmik evam darshanik chintan (H).
Rohilkhand, 1985.

2400. Sharma, Suman
Madhyakaleen Bhakti andolan ka samajik vivechan (H).
BHU, 1972.

2401. Shiv Shankar
The ethico religious philosophy of Bhaskara Bhasya.
BHU, 1970.

2402. Shastri, Chhagan Lal
Acharya Bhikshu aur unka tatwa darshan (H).
Bihar, 1968.

2403. Shivaji, A Barlow
A comparative study of the philosophical and religious principles of christianity and vaishnavism.
Vikram, 1967.

2404. Shukla, Deena Nath
Bhamati mat mein bibhram ka nirupan (H).
Durgawati, 1985.

2405. Shukla, Hiralal
Dendharanga kee sanskritic pristibhumi (H), (D. Litt.).
Ravishankar, 1978.

2406. Shukla, Rajendra
Ramanujacharya ke darshan mein Iswar siddhant (H).
BHU, 1987.

2407. Shukla, Vishwanath.
A comparative study of the Bhakti philosophy of Srimad Bhagwat and Ram Charita Manas.
AMU, 1984.

2408. Singh, Chhaya Rani
Swami Vivekanand ke dharma kee avadharana (H).
BHU, 1994.

2409. Singh, Jai Prakash
Sri Sankaracharya evam Ramanujacharya ke Ishwar sambandhi siddhanton ka vivechan (H).
BHU, 1990.

2410. Singh, Kaushilya
Awatar kee dharana: Ek sameekshatmak adhyayan. Bhagwat Gita, Ram Charit Manas aur Sri Sat Sai Baba ke krition ke vishesh sandarbh mein (H).
Bihar, 1985.

2411. Singh, Meher
Humanist elements in Gita and Gospel: A study in comparative religion.
Durgawati, 1987.

2412. Singh, Phramaha Suthan
The concept of God in western philosophy of religion.
BHU, 1991.

2413. Singh, Pratibha
Baudh dharma darshan ko Acharya Shanti Deo ke dan (H).
Gorakhpur, 1992.

2414. Singh, Poornima
The role of Indian religions in moulding the religious

life of South East Asia.
Magadh, 1985.

2415. Singh, Rajnath
Conception of devotion in vaishnavism at Christianity.
BHU, 1973.

2416. Singh, Ram Suresh
Religious movements in modern India with special reference to Brahma Samaj and Arya Samaj.
Magadh, 1979.

2417. Singh, S.
Katholik Isai mission: Ek adhyayatmik adhyayan (H).
Kashi, 1972.

2418. Singh, Sri prakash
Shrimad Bhagwat Gita evam Charak-Samhita ke darshanik tatwon ka tulnatmak adhyayan (H).
BHU, 1987.

2419. Singh, Samar Bahadur
Samkaleen vishleshnatmak dharma darshan mein Iswar mimansa virodhi pravittiyon ka alochnatmak adhyayan. L. Vitgestine A.J. Ayer and R.M. Hane ke vishesh sandarbh mein (H).
Gorakhpur, 1992.

2420. Singh, Sudarshan
The socio-religious philosophy of Arya Samaj.
Osmania, 1990.

2421. Sing, Vikram
A critical and comparative study of the nature and meaning of theological statement from cognitive and non-cognitive stand point of religious language.
Punjab, 1993.

2422. Sinha, Sushant Kumar
Study of conversion in religion.
Bhagalpur, 1985.

2423. Sinha, Anjani Kumar
Jungs psychology of religion.
Bihar, 1967.

2424. Sinha, Shakuntala
Ethical evolution of Ram Charit Manas.
Vikram, 1966.

2425. Singhal, Jwala Prasad
Changiable and changeable in religion.
Agra, 1947.

2426. Soloman, Esther Abraham
Avidya and the cognate concepts in vadik Buddhist and Jain darshanas.
Bombay, 1954.

2427. Srinirasachar, S.M.
A study of satadasani.
Madras, 1949.

2428. Srivastava, Alpana
Sankhya darshan mein Iswar kee avadharana (H).
Gorakhpur, 1992.

2429. Srivastava, Ranjana
Adhunik yug mein dharma: Sarvapally Radhakrishanan ke vicharon ka sameekshatmak adhyayan (H).
BHU, 1989.

2430. Srivastava, Sudha
Rudolf Ottos analysis of religions consciousness with special reference to Advaita Vedant.
BHU, 1975.

2431. Srivastava, Suresh Chandra
A study of Vijanna Bhikshu and his place in Indian philosophy.
Allahabad, 1965.

2432. Srivastava, Ushakiran
Bharatiya darshan mein dharmik chintan ka swaroop (H).
Ravishankar, 1978.

2433. Sujati, Patu
A study in the tantras philosophy with special reference to the mahanirvana tantra.
BHU, 1968.

2434. Sarun, Tribhuwan Nath
The religious philosophy of Josiah Royee.
Ranchi, 1970.

2435. Takauchi Kaiji
A study of Brahma technology with the special reference to Ram Mohan Roy and Devendra Nath Tagore.
Vishwa Bharati, 1985.

2436. Teyab-El-Edrous, Habeeb
The religious thought of Shah Walcullah.
Osmania, 1973.

2437. Thapliyal, Sakalanand
The puranas and the Greek philosophy: A comparative and critical study.
Agra, 1973.

2438 Theerapantha M. Pramaha
A comparative study of Dhammapad and Tirukkural.
Madras, 1993.

2439. Thomas, M.V.
Study of the role of the Church in Vidarbha.
Nagpur, 1983.

2440. Tikadar, Pavitra Mohan
Mahaprabhu Sri Chaitanya ke bhakti ke bhakti darshan ka samalochnatmak adhyayan (H).
Ravishankar, 1991.

2441. Tiwari, Kedar Nath
An analytical study of religious belief.
Magadh, 1967.

2442. Tripathi, Alok Mani
A study of Pasupat Saiva philosophy and religion on the basis of the Pasupat status and the Gankesika of Bhasarvayna.
Gorakhpur, 1986.

2443. Tripathi, Gyaneshwar
Bhagwat Gita mein loksangrah ka adarsh: Ek mulyankan (H).
Gorakhpur, 1990.

2444. Urankar, Ramchandra Vishnu
The Gita philosophy: An ontological perspectives.
Bombay, 1990.

2445. Vanhlauva, C.
Religious belief and custom amongs the Mizos before advent of Christianity.
Gauhati, 1981.

2446. Varghese, Joseph Manimala
Inter subjectivity: A study of the philosophies of Jean Paul Sartre and Gabrial Marcel with special reference to the concept of Sangha in Buddhism.
Madras, 1988.

2447. Varickyil, Robert
The relevance of Max Webers theory of religion to the economic development in India.
Bombay, 1975.

2448. Varshanay, K.M. Girijesh
Ardhanari Swaraim Sanskrit literature (S).
AMU, 1980.

2449. Vasmatkar, Kusum Chimanrao
Tagore aur Shri darshan mein Ishwar kee dharana (H).
BHU, 1986.

2450. Verma, Balbir Singh
Comparative study of the concept of perfection in the teaching of Kant and Gita.
Punjab, 1962.

2451. Verma, Krishna Kumar
The concept of God in contemporary Indian philosophy.
Bihar, 1964.

2452. Verma, Meena
Parmarth sar ka ek alochanatmak adhyayan.
BHU, 1987.

2453. Verma, Sashi Bhushan
A study of some correlates of religiously.
Bihar, 1974.

2454. Verma, Shiv Kumar
Swami Vivekanand evam Mahatma Gandhi ke dharmik vicharon ka tulnatmak adhyayan (H).
Awadhesh Pratap, 1987.

2455. Verma, Sunita
Bharatiya vaishnav Shiv Sampradayashyatma tatwa sameekshanam (S).
Meerut, 1989.

2456. Vilasini, C.P.
Dr. S. Radhakrishnan approach to religion: A critical relation.
Calicut, 1985.

2457. Vyas, S. Rao
Doctrine of reincornation in Hinduism and Christianity.
Uduaipur, 1980.

2458. Vyas, Girija
A comparative study of ethical teaching in the Gita and the Bible.

2459. Vyas, Nalin Kumar J. Lal
The problem of evil: A study in comparative religion.
Baroda, 1979.

2460. Waray, Ganesh Shridhar Shastriya
The philosophy of Vija ne Bhikshu.
BHU, 1963.

2461. Wilson, James Gilbert
The grounds of religious belief in Indian philosophy.
BHU, 1968.

2462. Yadav, Arun Kumar
Mahatma Gandhi kee dristi mein Hindu dharma: Ek sameekshatmak adhyayan (H).
BHU, 1986.

2463. Yadav, Parasuram
Vishudhi marga ka sameekshatmak adhyayan (H).
Gorakhpur, 1992.

2464. Yadav, Umesh
Yurush Mantram mein adoyatma bhavna: Ek alochnatmak anusheelan (H).
Punjab, 1992.

2465. Yajjanik, Jayendra Kr. Anandji
Swaminarayan sect: A comprehensive study.
Baroda, 1967.

2466. Yashray
Sri Chakradhar Swami ka dharma darshan (H).
Meerut, 1983.

HINDU PHILOSOPHY

2467. Agrawal, Krishna Mohan
Shrimad Bhagwat ka kavya shastriya perisheelan (H).
Magadh, 1968.

2468. Aiyer, Indira S.
Durga as Mahisasur mardini.
Bombay, 1991.

2469. Aiyer, T.K.K.
Asvins in the Vedas.
Dibrugarh, 1970.

2470. Arumugapevamal, A.
Worship of village deities and festivals in Agarteeswaran Panchayat Union.
Madurai, 1996.

2471. Asha Kumari
Hinduism and Buddhism: A relative study on the basis of the literature of Thailand.
Magadh, 1990.

2472. Bala Subramanyam, R.
The Taittiriyopanishad — Bhasya vartika of sureswara (D. Litt).
Madras, 1975.

2473. Bamore, Punita
Shaiv dharma aur nritya parampara (H).
Burktulla, 1993.

2474. Bangert, Fekhard
A critical study of the vimalakivtinidesa sutra.
Panjabi, 1974.

2475. Baruah, Archana
The religious form of life in Assam with special reference to the Vaishnavism of Shankaradeva.
NEHU, 1991.

2476. Baruah, Bharati
A study of the socio-religious ceremony of upanayana in the sutras and the Dharma sastras.
Gauhati, 1976.

2477. Basu, Anil Chandra
Concept of Bhakti in Goudiya Vaishnavism: A comparative and critical study.
Calcutta, 1965.

2478. Basu, Sakti Prasad
The concept of Brahma: Its origin and development (S).
Calcutta, 1984.

2479. Beidler, William
The concept of self in the Upanishads and the Bhagawat Gita.
Osmania, 1958.

2480. Betai, Ramesh. S.
A reconstruction of the original interpretation of the Manusmriti.
Gujarat, 1956.

2481. Bhaskaran, G.
Evaluation of the proofs for the existence of God with special reference to Saiva siddhant.
Madras, 1983.

2482. Bhattacharya, Debabrat
Europiya-o-Bharatiya da kinitantras (B).
Ravindra Bharati, 1990.

2483. Bhattacharya, Narendra Nath
Indian mother Goddess.
Calcutta, 1965.

2484. Bhukhanwala, Anjani Arun Kumar
Aspect of dance of the tenth skanda of the Bhagawat Puran: A study in Ancient Indian culture.
Bombay, 1988.

2485. Bimal Kumar
Recent trends in Hinduism with special reference to Arya Samaj.
Bihar, 1982.

2486. Biswas, Mohan Kali
Gauriya Baishnav darshan abakshyer karan sangathanik durbalate.
Calcutta, 1993.

2487. Borah, Meera
Later history of Vaishnavism faith and movement in Assam.
Gauhati, 1989.

2488. Brahmachari, Shivanand
Veer shaive dharma darshan mein veer Bhadra Shaiv Charya ji ka yogdan (H).
BHU, 1994.

2489. Chakraborti, Atreya
Studies in the evolution of the concept of female deities (S).
Jadavpur, 1987.

2490. Chakraborthi, Bharat Chandra
A study of the Brata with special reference to the worship of Durga from the standpoint of Sharma Sastras (S).
Calcutta, 1983.

2491. Chander Narayan Prasad
Shrimad Bhagawat Gita audharmpad ke naitik evam samajik siddhanton ka tulanatmak adhyayan (H).
Rajasthan, 1984.

2492. Chatterjee, Harambha Nath
A critical and comparative study of the forms of marriage in ancient India.
Calcutta, 1958.

2493. Chatterjee, Krishan Nath
The evolution of Hindu marriage.
Calcutta, 1965.

2494. Chattopadhyay, Ashok
Maithilas martah Shri Dutto padhayastasya sam pradipasheha (D. Litt.).
Sampurnanand, 1969.

2495. Chaturvedi, Kusum
Shrimad Bhagwat Gita ke Shachiknihitarth (Edu.).
Agra, 1982.

2496. Chaudhury, Birendra Kumar
Spiritual religion of the Bhagwat Gita and its meaning for the modern world.
Ranchi, 1979.

2497. Chaudhary, Shyam Nandan
Mahabharat shanti parva mein rajniti (H).
Bihar, 1972.

2498. Chinnappa, Gawda K.
Bhootaradhana : Ondu adhyayan.
Mangalore (K), 1988.

2499. Chinnappa, K.
Worship of small deities at thioumangatam taluk.
Madurai, 1984.

2500. Chinnaswami, P.
Philosophy of Vamana.
Madras, 1973.

2501. Dabral, Santi Kumar
Uttarakhand mein shakti mat ka vikas evam Hindu ko ushka yogdan (H).
Garhwal, 1985.

2502. Das, Ram Mohan
The position of women in Manu and his seven

commentations.
Bihar, 1961.

2503. Das, Sevarani
Mahima Dharma: Its doctrine and development.
Utkal, 1992.

2504. Das, Sudhir Ranjan
Folk religion of Bengal: A study of the Kumari Uratas.
Calcutta, 1956.

2505. Datta, Ashim Kumar
Jagannath and the ancillary images at Puri. Are they Savara Gods adopted into Hinduism.
Calcutta, 1980.

2506. Datta, Nilima
Influence of Sri Sri Syam Nanda of middle Bengali vaishnav religion and literature.
Calcutta, 1984.

2507. Devasenapathi, V.A.
Saiva sidhanta as expounded in the Sivagnana. Siddhiyur and its six commentaries.
Madras, 1949.

2508. Dhar, Lalita
Prominent saiva shrines of Jammu: A study in philosophical and religious perspectives.
Jammu, 1990.

2509. Dhongade, Lata
Economics of pilgrimage: A case study of Deval Gaopur.
Gulbarga, 1992.

2510. Dubey, Brij Kishori
Hindu Dharma me yoga ka sthan (H).
Agra, 1970.

2511. Dwivedi, Vijay Shankar
Kashmir Shaiv darshan aur Sankhya darshan main

shristi ka swaroop (H).
BHU, 1980.

2512. Ganapathiraman, S.
Tirunatveli pakthiyil siru theiva vazhipadu (T).
Madurai, 1983.

2513. Gangai, P.
Periapuranathil mupporal nilai (T).
Bharathidasan, 1990.

2514. Gangopadhyay, Alok
Tantricism. Its fundamental concept and practical aspects (S).
Ravindra Bharati, 1989.

2515. Gangopadhyay, Jayadev
Study of Dharma shastra in Mathili.
Calcutta, 1960.

2516. Garg, Ravindra Kumar
The upanishadic teaching of devotion, dedication and service and its bearing on the present day world.
Meerut, 1971.

2517. Ghosh, Atreyi
The concept of reality in Gaudiya vaishnavism.
Calcutta, 1970.

2518. Giri, Raghunath
The philosophy of Puranas with special reference to the Siva Parana.
BHU, 1960.

2519. Goyal, Jai Bhagwan
Guru Pratap Suraj ke kavya prakash ka adhyayan vishestah Chhanda alankar kee dristi se (H).
Punjab, 1964.

2520. Gopalan, S.
Hindu social philosophy: An inter presentation.
Madras, 1965.

2521. Gosavi, R.R.
Samarth sampradayik virachit prachine Marathi Samarth Chaitra: Ek abhyas (M).
Poona, 1985.

2522. Goswami, Bhagwan Chandra
Shri Sankaradeva and neo-vashnavism in India.
Agra, 1970.

2523. Goswami, Harishikesh
Evolution of Godiya vaishnavism on the vaishnava philosophy of the Chaitanya school.
Calcutta, 1950.

2524. Goswami, Krishna Gopal
Studies in the law of inter caste marriage in ancient India.
Calcutta, 1969.

2525. Gupta, Mahesh Prasad
The Arya Samaj movement and its impact on education in Western U.P.
Meerut, 1981.

2526. Gupta, Neelam
Kashmir Shaiva darshan mein Samanoga ka sthan.
Jammu, 1990.

2527. Gupta, Prasant
Shakti shrine of Jammu region: A study in religious perspectives.
Jammu, 1989.

2528. Handiya, Laxmi
Ram Charit Manas mein darshan ke tatwa (H).
Indore, 1974.

2529. Haripriya, Rangarajan
Historical and cultural study of the spread of vashnavism in Gujarat up to 16th century A.D. with

special reference to I conic vishna and his incornation.
Gujarat, 1987.

2530. Harishankar Prasad
Shaiva darshan: Ek sameekshatmak adhyayan.
Bihar, 1990.

2531. Hingorani, Gopi
Bhagwat Gita Avesta tatha John kee Gospel mein Ishwar ka swaroop (H).
BHU, 1970.

2532. Hunashal, S.M.
Virasaiva philosophy.
Lucknow, 1955.

2533. Iyer, B.P. Subhaiah
The conception of nish kama karma in the Bhagwat Gita.
Bombay, 1984.

2534. Jacab, Planthodathil S.
Christian influence in modern Indian thought with special reference to the Brahma Samaj.
Poona, 1973.

2535. Janson, Roos
The Hindu concept of Sin: A comparative study.
Delhi, 1965.

2536. Jesudass, D.I.
Studies in the religious experience of the Saiva Samyacharyas.
Annamalai, 1967.

2537. Jeyapandian, C.
Working of little duties in Madurai city.
Madurai, 1987.

2538. Jha, Awadh Bihar
Parasarasmriti: A study.
Bihar, 1967.

2539. Jha, Badri Prasad Vireet
Bharatiya Arya dharma mein danadharma kee mahima (H).
Bihar, 1973.

2540. Jha, Praboth Chandra
The vadic religion in the Brahmanas: A study.
Bihar, 1983.

2541. Jha, Raghubansh
Brhedaranyaka upanishad: Ek sameekshatmak adhyayan (H).
Bihar, 1972.

2542. Jha, Umesh
A critical study of chandyoga upanishad with special reference to its philosophical significance.
Bihar, 1973.

2543. Joshi, Labha Shankar Mohanlal
Lalita Saharsanama stotra: A study in the light of the commentary of Bhashavaya Makhindra (S).
Baroda, 1984.

2544. Jothmani, R.
Bathirakalivalipada.
Madurai, 1990.

2545. Kabadgi, Manikamma Subanna
A socio-cultural study of Ratnakar.
Karnataka, 1996.

2546. Kadirvel, C.
Salem mavatta Chiva Deivangat (T).
Annamalai, 1982.

2547. Kalia, Ashok Kumar
Laxmi tantra: Ek darshanik adhyayan (H).
Lucknow, 1968.

2548. Kaniya Parambi, James
Biblica upanishadic philosophy of life for the modern men.
Poona, 1974.

2549. Kapoor, Satish Kumar
Swami Vivekanand: A study of his sojourns and impact on the west 1893-96.
Punjab, 1981.

2550. Kappuswamy, C.
Sankara and Aurovindo on the Gita: A critical examination.
Madras, 1981.

2551. Katre, Shripad Nilkanth
Sri Gyan devancha santmanatal vangamaya ani samaj yan che anubandh: Ek abhyas (M).
Shivaji, 1991.

2552. Kesavraj, V.
A study of south India hero stones.
Kerala, 1986.

2553. Khan, Benjamin
The concept of dharma in Valmiki Ramayan.
Agra, 1962.

2554. Khandave, Subhash Gulabrao
Awdhut sampradaya ka tyanche vangmay (M).
Amrawati, 1987.

2555. Khandekar, Arundati C.
Hindu dharma, Hindu Sanskriti: Ek samalochna.
Bombay, 1993.

2556. Khandelwal, Ramesh Nath
Philosophy of shabda Brahman and its application in life.
Agra, 1972.

2557. Kothari, Puranima
Prasamarati aur umashagati (H).
Rajasthan, 1980.

2558. Krukkal, K. Kailasanatha
Study of saivism of epic and Puranic period together with its ancillary cult with special reference to saiva religious practices prevalent in South India and cylon.
Poona, 1968.

2559. Kulkarni, Prabhakar Vishvanath
Vishnu sastri Chiplannkar: A study (M).
Karnataka, 1980.

2560. Kundu, Mamta
A critical study of universal religion of Ramkrishna Paramhansa.
NBU, 1985.

2561. Kundu, Nandlal
Nondualism in Saiva and Sakla philosophy.
Calcutta, 1963.

2562. Lal, Syam Kishore
Female devinities in Hindu mythology and ritual.
Poona, 1977.

2563. Lala, Chaganlal
A reflective study of the philosophy of bhakti in its developing stages with special reference to Sri Vrahad Bhagawati smitom of Shri Sanatan Goswami.
Agra, 1972.

2564. Limaye, Sridhar, Krishnerao
Influence of mimansa rules of interpretations on principal commentators of Dharma sastras viswa rupa madhatithe, Vijnaneswara, Aporar ka and Kulluka.
Nagpur, 1970.

2565. Maithani, Vachaspati
Garhwal mein pramukh devatoyon kee samajik va sanskritik adhyatmik pristibhoomi (H), (S).
Garhwal, 1986.

2566. Maitra, Susil Kumar
The ethics of the Hindus.
Calcutta, 1928.

2567. Malarvizha, C.T.
Religion and tradition of worship in Pallavi Period.
Bharatihar, 1990.

2568. Malladevaru H.P.
Saiva grames and upanishads.
Karnataka, 1970.

2569. Menonmana. M.
Saivism in Kanganndi: An enquiry.
Bharatihar, 1990.

2570. Mathur, Rita
Revelation and reason in Paul Tillich and Advaita vedanta.
BHU, 1976.

2571. Manickvelu, M.A.
Thamizh naatill netarasarvazhippada (T).
Madras, 1992.

2572. Midori, Meri
A critical study of some modern interpretion of the Bhagwat Gita.
BHU, 1988.

2573. Mishra, Anand Nath
Shrimad Bhagawat Gita mein sankalpa swatantraya aur niyativad (H).
Rohilkhand, 1992.

2574. Mishra, Ballabh Saran
Vaishnav Stutiyon kee sameeksha (H).
Gorakhpur, 1983.

2575. Mishra, Bibhuti Bhusan
Religious movement in Orrisa in ninteenth century.
Sambhalpur, 1991.

2576. Mishra, Kamalkar
Philosophy of Abhinava Gupta with special reference to tantralok.
BHU, 1989.

2577. Mishra, Kanhu Charan
The cult of Jagannath.
Calcutta, 1965.

2578. Mishra, Rama
Vadic kaladarabhya vaivahiki shastriya vyavastha (S).
Sampurnanand, 1968.

2579. Mishra, Ram Preeti
Bhagawat Gita mein sthit pragya ka swaroop evam uskee samsamayik prasangikata (H).
Gorakhpur, 1983.

2580. Mishra, Ram Shankar
Rudrayamall uttar tautra ka parisheelan (H), (S).
Awadh, 1982.

2581. Mishra, Udaikant
A critical study of the tantra sastra with special reference to netyasodasika Navya tantra.
Bihar, 1968.

2582. More, Sadanand Shridhar
The Gita: A theory of human action.
Poona, 1982.

2583. Mukherjee, Anil Kumar
The philosophy of Abhinav Gupta: A comparative and

critical study of Kashmir Saivism.
Calcutta, 1963.

2584. Mukherjee, Govind Gopal
The absolute and its realisation according to the upanishad.
Calcutta, 1958.

2585. Mukherji, Lily
Role of Govind Temple of Vrindaban in the context of religious based social life in the Northern India 1590-1970.
Vishwa Bharati, 1991.

2586. Mukherjee, Ranjit Kumar
Mediaval vaishnava religion and literature the ado dhara sect and critical study of Jayanandas Chaitanya Mangala.
Jadavpur, 1980.

2587. Mukhopadhyay, Manisha
Indra worship in ancient India.
Calcutta, 1990.

2588. Mukhopadhyay, Somnath
Goddess Chandi and folk daity of Bengal.
Calcutta, 1990.

2589. Murthy, H.V.S.
Vaishnavism of Sankaradeva and Ramanuja: A comparative study.
Gauhati, 1961.

2590. Muthu Lakshmi, A.
A study of village daily worship in and around patini.
Madurai, 1987.

2591. Narayan, V.
Upanidathangalin the live sivag nona bothan (T).
Madras, 1989.

2592. Nalinibai, M.V.
Narayaniya: A critical study (S).
Madras, 1978.

2593. Narharrao, Deo Ashok
Sanskritik sahilyavat vyat Jhalele Dharmshastriya vichar (M).
Marathwada, 1993.

2594. Neeha,
Grhastha Ratnakara of Candeswara: A study (S).
Delhi, 1979.

2595. Narkan, Pushpa
Dharmashastra dwara istriyon ke liye vihit achar ka alochnatmak adhyayan (H).
Agra, 1967.

2596. Negi, Surendra Singh
A critical study of philosophical trends in Mahabharata.
Saugar, 1973.

2597. Nirankari, Ramdas
Systematic study of the Pre-Bauddhistic upanishads.
Delhi, 1972.

2598. Niyogi, Nilkamal
Growth and development of Lakshmi worship in ancient India.
Calcutta, 1996.

2599. Ojha, Rama Devi
Kalarnavatantra ka parisheelan.
Awadh, 1987.

2600. Pakhamode, Guruprasad Govindrao.
Shri Eknath Maharajancharya abhangga the cha vivechanatmak abhyas (M).
Nagpur, 1987.

2601. Pandey, Deokishan
Shritontrasya sameekshatmak menusheelanam (S).
Sampurnanand, 1990.

2602. Pandey, Govind
Bhakti rasarnava sameeksha.
BHU, 1977.

2603. Pandey, Hira Ballabh
Milya shodh shikainava tantra kee tikaon ke tulanatmak adhyayan (H), (S).
Awadh, 1983.

2604. Pandey, Lakshman Kumar
Saivism in Orissa,
Utkal, 1981.

2605. Pandey, Mohini
Upanishadon mein mana evam pran ka swaroop tatha sambandh (H).
1983.

2606. Pandey, R.B.
The origin, history and significance of the Hindu Sanskaras (D. Litt).
BHU, 1937.

2607. Pandey, Surendra
Kashmir shaivagam tatwa vivechan (S).
Sampurnanand, 1968.

2608. Pandey, Uma
Concept of ultimate: A reality as value in principal upanishads.
Saugar, 1977.

2609. Pandey, Uma
Saiva darshan peethika per Kanth Haritam ka alochanatmak adhyayan (S).
Kanpur, 1982.

2610. Pandit, Baljit Nath
A comparative study of Kashmir Saivism.
Punjab, 1967.

2611. Paramasivam, T.
Alogakoil temple (T).
Madurai, 1981.

2612. Parameswaran, E.G.
Psychological symbolism in some Hindu Sankaras secramental rites.
Madras, 1961.

2613. Param Jyoti, Eliza V.
Saiva Siddhanta.
Madras, 1935.

2614. Parkha, A.M.
A critical edition of Bhargava Canedipika (S).
Poona, 1977.

2615. Parmanand
Reguveda adi Bhasha bhoomika of Swami Dayanand Saraswati translated into English from original Sanskrit with critical introduction and notes.
Panjab, 1987.

2616. Parthsarathy. V.
The historical evolution of the rituals connected with the temple festivals in Vishnu temples of southern India.
Bombay, 1983.

2617. Patel, Sushil Kumar
Vishnu worship in Orissa.
Sambhalpur, 1991.

2618. Pathak, Jainendra Kumar
Bharatiya dharma aur sanskriti mein Brahma (H).
Gorakhpur, 1981.

2619. Pathan, Yusuf Khan Mohd. Khan
Maharashtra ke dharma sambradayon ka samikshatmak adhyayan (H).
Ranchi, 1977.

2620. Pati, Kamdev
The shakti cult of Orissa.
Utkal, 1992.

2621. Pillai, Shanmugham
A research in vaishanava temple at Tirupathi Saram in Kanya Kumari district.
Kerala, 1992.

2622. Prajapati, Sheo Prasad
Shaiva Siddhant aur Kashmir Shaiva darshan mein koksha ka swaroop (H).
BHU, 1983.

2623. Pratap, K.
Studies in Saumya moorthis of Siva with special reference to Dakshinamurthi Siva (S).
Venkateswara, 1987.

2624. Promasen, Phramaha Sanworn
The study of the Doctrine of Paieca Samuppada in Athervavada.
BHU, 1973.

2625. Rai, Pushpa
Sanskrit Sahitya mein mahashakti: Ek parisheelan (H).
BHU, 1992.

2626. Rajgopalachari, R.
The contribution of Sri Pillai Lokacharya to Srivaishnavism.
Venkateswara, 1992.

2627. Rao, T. Gopal Krishna
Ramayana as depicted in folk poetry of Telagu and

Kannada.
Mysore, 1982.

2628. Ray, Manmathnath
Position of Shudras in ancient India (D. Litt).
Allahabad, 1937.

2629. Rath, Ghansyam
Odisarevaisnava dharmara nutane abhimukshya, soda sa satebdira adhybhaga (O).
Sambhalpur, 1985.

2630. Rath, Pratiya Manjari
Rudra cult: A study.
Utkal, 1992.

2631. Rath, Ravi Charan
Hindu dharamasya vattatva vimarsha.
Jagannath, 1991.

2632. Rathina Sabapthy, P.
The conception of bhakti in Indian philosophy.
Annamalai, 1991.

2633. Ray, Suprasad
A critical examination of the concept of personal God in Vaishnavism.
Gauhati, 1983.

2634. Roy, Janmajit
The Hindu theory of Awatar and Lord Chaitanya.
Gauhati, 1981.

2635. Roy, Juthika
A critical study of Agni Purana.
BHU, 1968.

2636. Rukmabai, Babasaheb Guru
Madhya yageen Krishna Bhakti sadhana ka samakaleen vivechan (H).
Meerut, 1983.

2637. Subarwal, Kanchan Lata
Concept of Shiva in saivism.
Lucknow, 1952.

2638. Sadashivaiah, H.M.
Comparative study of two veerasaiva manestaries in Mysore state: A study in the sociology of religion.
Mysore, 1960.

2639. Satya Swaroop
The philosophy of the ethical religion of the Vishnu Puran.
Agra, 1965.

2640. Savaliya, R.T.
Gujratha Hindu devetonom pratma vichar.
Gujarat, 1987.

2641. Sehgal, S.R.
Comparative study of the mantras of the Riguvadic Grhya Sutras *i.e.*, Shakhuyana kau shitaka and Asvalayana Gryya Sutras with critical introduction.
Punjab, 1983.

2642. Sheshadri, V.S.
History of vaishnavism from vadic times to the end of the 16th century with special reference to its rise as the Vijay a Nagaraj empire and the role played by the 1st pentiff of Shri Ahobite Mithe.
Madras, 1987.

2643. Shah, Asha
Uttarakhand mein prachalit dharmon ka itihas (H).
Kumoun, 1980.

2644. Shahpurkar, P.G.
The origin and evolution of the cult of Sri Ganesha.
Bombay, 1987.

2645. Shan Mugasundarana, K.
Thiruvarangam Ranganather thirukkoil

thirurizhakkalum pazhekkava hakkangatam (T).
Bharathidasan, 1992.

2646. Sharma, Baldev Raj
The concept of Atma in the principal upanishads.
Delhi, 1967.

2647. Sharma, Dhan Prakash
Vivah swaroop ka varn per prabhav (S).
Durbhanga, 1984.

2648. Sharma, Giriraj Prasad
Shri sampradaya ke stotra sahitya mein panchastva ka sthan (H), (S).
Agra, 1982.

2649. Sharma, Jagdish Kumar
A critical and comparative study of vijnanabhaijava and tantrasara.
Punjab, 1986.

2650. Sharma, Laxmi Nidhi
Aspects of Kashmiri Saivism is related to Advaita Vedants.
BHU, 1960.

2651. Sharma, Nand Kishore
Constructive survey of the philosophy of the Puranas and its relation to some of the contemporary philosophers of India.
Rajasthan, 1966.

2652. Sharma, Neel Kamal
Shakti worship in ancient India up to the end of Gupta age.
Jodhpur, 1982.

2653. Sharma, Rani
Bratas in the Smrities and the Puranas with special reference to upavasas (S).
Delhi, 1978.

2654. Sharma, Santosh
Hindu dharma mein Sarvabhaumik evam vaigyanik tatva (H).
Agra, 1978.

2655. Sarma, Shashi Bala
Tikakar Rajank Ramkanth: Kashmir shaira darshan mein (S).
Jammu, 1987.

2656. Sharma, Suresh Chandra
Pramukh Smritiyon mein rajdharma swaroop (H), (S).
Delhi, 1978.

2657. Sharma, Tulsi Ram
Ethical technical in the sectorian upanishads.
Delhi, 1969.

2658. Sharma, Vijay Kumar
Vaishanavism in Jammu: A study based on the Jammu region (H).
Jammu, 1987.

2659. Shastri, C.L.
Udarrahan of Shakalya Mulla Mallacharya: A critical study and editing the some (S).
Saurashtra, 1978.

2660. Shastri, Motilal Khaddar
Bharatiya parampara mein Shiv ka swaroop (H).
Gorakhpur, 1992.

2661. Sastri, Vishnudutt
Malinivijay Hara Tantra: A source book of Trika Shastra of Kashmir togather with the English translation, critical notes on its philosophy and religious significance.
Punjab, 1957.

2662. Shaivamurthaiah, T.
A critical study of the suta samhita.
BHU, 1977.

2663. Shivaraman, K.
The philosophy of saiva siddhanta.
BHU, 1963.

2664. Shri Ram
Social philosophy in some later smritiyon.
Rajasthan, 1968.

2665. Shukla, Sachchidanand
Pratapudriya: Ek adhyayan (S).
Gorakhpur, 1988.

2666. Shurti, Sheel
Metaphical conception in Riguveda.
Baroda, 1976.

2667. Singh, Ambika Prasad
Prarambhik puranon ka samajik evam arthik adhyayan (H).
Awadh, 1981.

2668. Singh, Harmail
Banisri Guru Ramdas, Srijnatmak darshanik adhyayan (H).
Punjabi, 1976.

2669. Singh, Hridaya Narayan
Major brahminical religious and schools of philosophy in the shantiparva of the Mahabharat.
Gorakhpur, 1981.

2670. Singh, M. Ibotom
Hinduism in modern Indian society.
Manipur, 1991.

2671. Singh, Mrigendra Kumar
Geeta mein yuddh samvadi samaj ka pradipadan (H).
Rohilkhand, 1993.

2672. Singh, Radhika Raman
Hindu dharma mein sristivada: Ek darshanik adhyayan

Veda evam Puran ke sristi vichar ke vishist sandarbh mein.
V.K. Univ., 1997.

2673. Singh, Rajdeo
Sant aur sant mat (H), (D. Litt.).
Punjab, 1972.

2674. Singh, Ramji
The concept of Omniscience in ancient Hindu thought. (D. Litt.).
Ranchi, 1973.

2675. Singh, Ram Naresh
Shivpuran: Ek sankritik adhyayan (H).
Magadh, 1985.

2676. Singh, Ranjit
The Hindu concept of Dharma.
Allahabad, 1966.

2677. Singh, Rudra Narayan
Vajrayan aur Advait Shaiv darshan mein tantra sadhana (H).
BHU, 1987.

2678. Singh, Sankatha Prasad
The revival of upanishadi thought in contemporary Indian philosophy.
Allahabad, 1955.

2679. Singh, Vijay Laxmi
Ram Charit Manas mein samaj darshan (H).
Bihar, 1984.

2680. Srinirupan
Prachin Bharatiya Dharmashastria sahitya mein shudron ke isthiti (H).
Agra, 1967.

2881. Srivastava, Kiran Kumari
Vishnu Puran ka dharma darshan (H).
BHU, 1967.

2682. Srivastava, Renu Kumari
Bharatiya parampara mein Shiva ka swaroop.
Gorakhpur, 1992.

2683. Srivastava, Saral
A critical study of the varnashram system.
BHU, 1963.

2684. Srivastava, Shankar
Hinduism in South East Asia.
Magadh, 1987.

2685. Subhamma, P.C.
A study of Sankaranands Alam puranam.
Madras, 1968.

2686. Subhurathinam, S.
Karuppanasami Vazhipattil Mandira Sadangugal.
Madras, 1993.

2687. Sunita Kumari
Nature and function of Sakti in Kashmir Saiva darshan (S).
Jammu, 1987.

2688. Surinder Pal
Shaiv strotan kee darshanik pristibhoomi ka alochanatmak adhyayan: Prarambh se lekar dharshan shatabdi tak (S).
Punjab, 1986.

2688a. Swami, B. Siddalinga
Maleya Mahadeshwara: A study.
Mysore, 1988.

2689. Thilagavaithe, S.
Thiruthindar puranathil vatipatta muraikal (T).
Bharathidasan, 1990.

2690. Thiyagamani, S.
Harish Chandra puranam and the birth of Jab: A comparative study.
Venkateswara, 1990.

2691. Tiwari, Devendra Nath
Brahadaranyu ko panishad ka ek darshanik adhyayan (H).
BHU, 1979.

2692. Trigunayat, Vishwa Dev
The philosophy of life as depicted in upanishads.
Agra, 1969.

2693. Tripathi, Avinath Nath
Shaiva darshan kee sadhana paddhati.
BHU, 1988.

2694. Tripathi, Krishnamani
Puranetihasayo sankhyayoga darshan vimarsha (S).
Sampurnanand, 1985.

2695. Trivedi, Sudha
Shrimad Bhagwat Gita evam Shrimad Bhagawat mein karma kee avadharana: Ek tulanatmak adhyayan.
Durgawati, 1995.

2696. Uma Devi
The concept of punishment according to the Mahabharat and the Manusmriti.
Patna, 1974.

2697. Umamaheswari, P.B.
Tirunalveli Nellappar Temple.
Madurai, 1982.

2698. Upadhyay, Radhe Syam
Srimad Bhagwat Gita evam adhunik jeevan (H).
BHU, 1983.

2699. Vaidya, Kamal
Ek natha Bhagwat: A critical study (M).
SNDT, 1987.

2700. Velkar, Neela Anjanani Kumar
Upasana in the upanishads.
Bombay, 1969.

2701. Verma, Krishna
Recent interpratation of the Bhagwat Gita.
Delhi, 1974.

2702. Verma, Om Prakash
Chhattisgarh mein ṣaharikaran va oudyogikaran ke dharmik abhivrittiyon per prabhav: Raipur va Bhalia kshetra kee gaveshana per adharit (H).
Ravishankar, 1993.

2703. Vidyalankar, Sumetha
A critical study of the Shanti Parva in Mahabharat with a view to find out similarities and difference between Buddhism and Mahabharat.
Delhi, 1973.

2704. Vijayal, A.
A study of Kanya Kumari Amman Temple.
Madras, 1990.

2705. Vyas, Hansa
Prachine Malva mein Shiv Dharma (H).
Vikram, 1986.

2706. Vyas, Ram Narayan
Concept of Ishwara Prakriti and Jeeva in the Bhagwat Puran.
Agra, 1963.

2707. Vijaylakshmi. P.
Akam conventoris in Alwar Hymns (T).
Madurai, 1985.

2708. Yadav, Ram Nath
Tantra sar: Ek sameekshatmak adhyayan (H).
BHU, 1992.

2709. Yamunadari Brahmachyarini
Bhagwat Gita theiatic or absolute.
Bombay, 1983.

2710. Zachariah, Aleyamma
Social action in the Gita according to Sri Aurobindo: An analysis of the interpretationship of social responsibility and mtaphysics.
Mysore, 1983.

BAUDH PHILOSOPHY

2711. Abe, Join
A study on the first and second chapter of the Visuddhimarga and its commentaries (S).
Poona, 1979.

2712. Abha Rani
Abhindh math sangrahon ka shastriya anusheelan (S).
Magadh, 1987.

2713. Acharya, Chitra
Buddhism Outside India. Mainly Buddhist literature in Central Asia, China and Japan.
Calcutta, 1989.

2714. Agrawal, Alka
An analytical study of Majahima Nikaya.
Delhi, 1983.

2715. Akhileshwar Kumar
Sthiti Pragya aur bodhistava ke adarsh ka tulanatmak adhyayan: Gita aur Vimal krit ke vishesh Sambandh mein (H).
BHU, 1994.

2716. Anita Rani
Deegha Nikaya ka samajik evam sanskritik anusheelan (H).
Magadh, 1989.

2717. Apte, Keshav Vaman
Criticism of Buddhism and Jainism in Brahma Sutras.
Bombay, 1964.

2718. Arya, Namita
Baudh dharma ke siddhant: Ek neeti samhita (H).
Bhopal, 1985.

2719. Badlamani, Venkata
Satya saibaba: Faith and devotion in Buddhism.
Andhra, 1985.

2720. Barua, Amal Kanti
Mind and mental factor in early Buddhist psychology.
Calcutta, 1983.

2721. Barua, Hemnendu Bikas
Buddhism and Buddhist of West Bengal.
Calcutta, 1983

2722. Barua, Pran Ranjan
Buddhism in Nepal.
Calcutta, 1983.

2723. Barua, Pranab Kumar
Buddhist culture, in Bangladesh in the post Pale period.
Calcutta, 1985.

2724. Barua, Ranjit Kumar
King Pasenada and his reign.
Delhi, 1987.

2725. Barua, Sukomal
Psychological attitude: A study of mind in early Buddhist text.
BHU, 1986.

2726. B.C. Sam
The impact of Buddhism in Cambodian social life.
Poona, 1978.

2727. Bhanot, Neeraj
Pale abhilakhon mein pratipadita Buddha Dharma tatha darshan (H).
Delhi, 1988.

2728. Bhatnagar, Raka
Swatantrayottar Hindi katha sahitya mein Baudh dharma ke tatwa. (H).
Delhi, 1995.

.2729. Bhikchhu, P.T.R.
Buddhism and social progress in the control of modern Thailand.
BHU, 1987.

2730. Bhikcchu, Ratrupal
The concept of God in Pali tripitakes.
Magadh, 1970.

2731. Bhutia, T. Dorjey
The contribution of Padma sambhava to Tibetan. Buddhism.
Delhi, 1989.

2732. Bijolwan, Chakradhar
A critical and comparative study of Jayantas theory of knowledge.
Delhi, 1972.

2733. Bimalendu Kumar
An analytical study of the pattbana pakarna with special reference to philosophy of religion.
Delhi, 1990.

2734. Bindal, Meera,
Prachin yug ke jan jeevan mein para Baudh ka prabhav (H).
Agra, 1989.

2735. Biswas, Kalpana
A critical study of the Dasabhumikesutra.
Delhi, 1979.

2736. Cheechean, P. Sanggom
An analytical study of the Kenkhavi Tarni.
Delhi, 1991.

2737. Chakravarthi, Jhavna
Japan mein Baudh sampradayon ke darshanik siddhant tatha pratimanon tatha Bharat aur Kuchhunga Baudh darshan se unki tulana (H).
Garhwal, 1992.

2738. Chakraborti, Uma
Social dimensions of early Budha.
Delhi, 1987.

2739. Chandrkaew, P.C.
The concept of nirvana in early Buddhism.
Madras, 1977.

2740. Chaubey, Shiv Kumar
Dakshin Poorva Asiai deshon ke samajik jeevan per Baudha dharma aur darshan ka prabhav (H). 1992.

2741. Chaudhury, Sudesh
The doctrine of Bodhisattva in the Saddharma Pundarkaka Sutra.
Delhi, 1989.

2742. Chou, Hsiang Kuang
An outline of the history of Buddhism in China.
Delhi, 1955.

2743. Chunekar, Mridula
A critical study of the concept of anatta and samghata with special reference to Buddhism.
Poona, 1977.

2744. Chuntharin, P.C.
Buddhappa vattivinicahaya (S).
BHU, 1987.

2745. Dobnale, Jagannath Ram Chandra
Dr. B.R. Ambedkars interpretation of Baudha doctrine Dharma.
Kolhapur, 1997.

2746. Das, Sidhartha
Studies in Tabatan Buddhism.
Calcutta, 1982.

2747. Dass, Pradeep Kumar
Laddakh sthit Gonpanam Shravakyandrishtya Mahayan drishtya cha tulanatmak sanskritakam cha nusheelanam.
Sampurnanand, 1993.

2748. Davidson, Jermy HCS
An Shyhgau the man and translation.
Delhi, 1982.

2749. Deodikar, Sanjay, G.
Some points of contact between early Buddhism and upanishads.
Poona, 1980.

2750. Dhar, Sachitanand.
A survey of the avadana literature with special reference to sumaga dhera dena from Indian and Tebatan sources.
Calcutta, 1956.

2751. Dharam, Rashmi
Theravad Baucha vangamaya mein vimukti ka upaya: Ek adhyayan (H).
BHU, 1992.

2752. Dhammaratan, Uruwala
Nairatmiya doctrine in early theravada in the light of sunyavada.
Calcutta, 1959.

2753. Dubey, Akhileshwar Prasad
Baudh rajneeti darshan ka sameekshatmak adhyayan (H).
Saugar, 1985.

2754. Dubey, Preeti Kumar
A critical edition and evolution of the Cakkevala Dipani.
Delhi, 1992.

2755. Dubey, S.H.
Doctrine controversies in early Buddhism with special reference tọ Kathyvastu.
Rajasthan, 1968.

2756. Dwivedi, Rajendra Narayan
A critical and cultural study of the Amarkosa and Trikardasesa, two major works of Buddhist taxicographies.
Delhi, 1975.

2757. Eksanbang, P.V.
Analytical study of Karma and Heaven in Buddhism.
BHU, 1994.

2758. Framha Surachitsang Sukal
Thervad Mahayannikikayeshu panchhat thaha nirupanam.
Sampurnanand, 1978.

2759. Gangopadhyay, Purbi
Buddhist econography: A comparative study in India and outside India.
Calcutta, 1989.

2760. Gian Chand
A study of the dravya sangraha in relation to early Buddhist philosophical texts.
Delhi, 1993.

2761. Gond, Dashrath
Pali Jatak sahitya ke adhar per Budha dharm ka ek adhyayan (H).
BHU, 1989.

2762. Gupta, Indu
A comparative study of Buddhism and Vedant. Based on a comparison between Malamadhyamak Karika of Nagarjuna and Mandukya Karika of Goudopada.
Delhi, 1981.

2763. Gupta, Meenakshi
Concept of suffering in the early Buddhist tradition.
Delhi, 1991.

2764. Gupta, Neena
Contribution of the Laity in the development of early Buddhism form 6th century B.C. to 1st Century B.C.
Delhi, 1982.

2765. Gupta, Ramdas Prasad
A critical study of humanism in Indian philosophy with special reference to Buddhism.
Bihar, 1979.

2766. Gyi, Khin Maung
An examination of the concept of asankhatadhatu in the Dharma samgani.
Delhi, 1987.

2767. Haldar, Aruna
Some psychological aspect of early Buddhism as based on Abhidharm kosa.
Calcutta, 1960.

2768. Hardikar, Vasundhara
Baudh vaicharik parampara mein nirman (H).
Saugar, 1986.

2769. Harihar Prasad
Magadh mein Baudh dharma ka prarambhic itihas. Tritiya shatabdi isvipura tak (H).
Magadh, 1984.

2770. Hikosaka, Shu
Budhism from Tamil sources with special reference to Manimakalai and Chitapathikaran.
Madras, 1984.

2771. Hisamtsu, Ric
A critical study of the Paramaitha Vinichaja.
Delhi, 1983.

2772. Indasara, Ittademaliya
A study of the ethical development of the personality in early Buddhism.
Delhi, 1988.

2773. Jaideo
Prak Baudh-Jain vihar ke dharmik chintan dharanayon aur uska chintak (H).
Bihar, 1967.

2774. Jain Dharma Chand
Baudh praman ved ka Jain drishti se parikshan (H), (S).
Rajasthan, 1989.

2775. Jain, Ramesh Chandra
Baudha darshan kee shastriya sameeksha: Sanskrit Granthon ke adhar per (D. Litt.), (H).
Rohilkhand, 1981.

2776. Jain, Vijay Kumar
Samyutta nekaya: Ek adhyayan.
BHU, 1983.

2777. Jamuna Prasad
A study of the economic condition as depicted in the Mohayana Sutras.
Delhi, 1993.

2778. Janyun Hua
The vicissitudes of Buddhism in China.
Vishwa Bharati, 1964.

2779. Jha, Rajendra,
Adhunik Bharatiya samajik sanskritic vichardhara per Baudha prabhav (H).
Jabalpur, 1969.

2780. Kacheruji, Shashrao
Buddhist Maharashtra: A cultural study.
Marathwada, 1986.

2781. Kamdeo, Duen
The ethical philosophy of Buddhism.
Magadh, 1982.

2782. Kamzao, N.P.S.
The concept of Samadhi in early Buddhism.
Vishwa Bharati, 1970.

2783. Kantecara, B.P.K.
Buddhist philosophy in its social and educational relevance in modern Thailand.
BHU, 1987.

2784. Kaushik, Jabir Singh
A socio cultural study of the inscription of sravasamodhanam.
BHU, 1987.

2785. Kher, C.V.
Buddhism as presented by Brahmanical systems.
Poona, 1970.

2786. Khormomklang, P.J.
Budhasasana deva samodhanam (S).
BHU, 1980.

2787. Kim, H.O.U.
Fundamental philosophy of Nagarjuna's madhyamika and early madhyamika in China.
Delhi, 1975.

2788. Kim, Soonkaum
The concept of causality in Buddhism specially in the field of Indian Buddhism and won Buddhism of Korea.
Delhi, 1985.

2789. Kiran Kumar
A critical study of the Yandhada in Buddhism.
Jammu, 1996.

2790. Konditya, Bhikshu
Influence of Buddhism and Pali on taikhamiti and their literature.
Delhi, 1977.

2791. Kotsuka, P.
Bharatiya Darshan samatasya atmatattvasya prarambhic Baudh dharma dristitaya. Plato dekarta kant kadi pashchatya darshnik drashtya tulanatmak sameekshatmakam cha vashulanam (S).
Sampurnanand, 1990.

2792. Koves, Morgit
Comparative study of suvarana prabhasa in Turkish and Tibetan versions.
Delhi, 1980.

2793. Krishnaiha, M.V.
Early Buddham and Jean Paul Sartre: A study in comparative philosophy.
Andhra, 1985.

2794. Kusum Kumar
Prarambhic Baudh darshan mein nirman evam nirvantmak tantra: Ek adhunik adhyayan (H).
Magadh, 1985.

2795. Labh, Vaidnath
Panna: A philosophical analysis with special reference to Visuddhimarga.
Delhi, 1987.

2796. Laxmi Kumar
Pali Tipitaka mein parilaxit loka jeevan: Ek vivechanatmak sameeksha (H).
Delhi, 1992.

2797. Macharaon, Bhikkha P.
Some aspects of democratic elements of the early Buddhist institutions.
BHU, 1977.

2798. Madhusudan V.
Buddhism in Andhra Pradesh.
Vikram, 1986.

2799. Mahapatra, Bimal Chandra
Buddhism and socio-economic conditions of Bengal and Orissa from 8th to 12th century A.D.
Delhi, 1992.

2800. Mahinda, Kollupitiya
Origin and development of the practices of Dhutan gas with special reference to Theravada Buddhism.
Delhi, 1988.

2801. Maiti, Syam Sunder
Plarya dristite Buddha O Buddha dharma.
Calcutta, 1993.

2802. Mandal, Syambabu Prasad
Buddha darshan dharma Chakra pravartan Sutra.
BHU, 1994.

2803. Manju Rani
The doctrine of pratitya samutpada in Buddhist schools.
Magadh, 1986.

2804. Mansure, P.M.
Neelakesiyill samaya kot pattugal.
Bharathidasan, 1992.

2805. Maunglang, Naglot
A study of Buddhism among the national minorities of Yuhan (China).
Delhi, 1985.

2806. Maung, Maung Myint
Abhidhammika interpratation of man in Buddhism.
BHU, 1977.

2807. Meghram, L.G.
Baudh dharma ke vikas mein Ambedkar ka yogdan (H).
Nagpur, 1986.

2808. Mishra, Deepali
Baudh darshan mein parivartan kee samasya (H).
Rajasthan, 1985.

2809. Mishra, Harshnath
A critical study of Chandra Vyakaran vritti on the basis of new manuscripts.
Delhi, 1972.

2810. Mishra, Manu
Baudh darshan mein Pragya (H).
BHU, 1987.

2811. Mishra, Neelam
Baudh Nyaya (H).
BHU, 1994.

2812. Mishra, Poonam
Baudh darshan mein pratyaksha kee avadharana (H).
BHU, 1994.

2813. Mishra, Prabhakar
The concept of Tathagat in Buddhism.
Magadh, 1983.

2814. Mishra, Vijay Shankar
Mahayan Baudh darshan mein chetna ka swaroop (H).
BHU, 1985.

2814a. Mithileshwar, Prasad
Kama and rebirth in the context of Theravada Buddhism.
Magadh, 1982.

2815. Mohd. Abdul Mazid
The concept of man Buddhism in the Vedant: A critical study.
Gauhati, 1994.

2817. Manoharana, Surendra Kumar
Development of Tantrik Buddhism in Orissa.
Utkal, 1987.

2818. Mukhopadhyay, Satkari
The Buddhist philosophy of universal flux.
Calcutta, 1932.

2819. Nag, Deepa
A philosophical study of Buddhist Art symbols India 2nd century B.C. to 7th century A.D.
Delhi, 1969.

2820. Naik, Chandrasekhar, Dejibaji
Inequality of religions and need of conversion with special reference to Buddhism and Dr. Ambedkar.
Nagpur, 1995.

2821. Naik, Sushila Tulshiram
Bharatiya Baudha shakshanik sanstha, tulanatmak adhyayan (H).
Nagpur, 1993.

2822. Nanda, S. Sasna
History of Buddhism in Assam.
Magadh, 1982.

2823. Nand Kishore Prasad
A comparative study of Buddhist Vinay and Jaina acora.
Bihar, 1965.

2824. Nandlal
Abhidhamma: Baudha darshan mein Manodaihik chikitsa (H).
BHU, 1983.

2825. Nanesuwan, Pramana T.
A comparative study of Dhammapada and Tirukkural.
Madras, 1993.

2826. Negi, Vengchhungdorji
Vajrayansadhana prokarannom sameekshatmak adhyayan (S).
Sampurnanand, 1990.

2827. Ngugen, Thi Hon Bhikhuni
Buddhism in South East Asia.
Magadh, 1989.

2828. Okkantha, Ashimsiri
History of Buddhism in Arakan.
Calcutta, 1992.

2829. Palram, Phramahba Bue
The Buddhism and its effect on social welfare.
Magadh, 1984.

2830. Pandey, Kamaleshwar
Lalita vistara ke Sahityik evam bhasagat dristi se sameekshatmak adhyayan (H).
Magadh, 1989.

2831. Pandey, Satyendra Kumar
A critical and analytical study of the Dharmas as dȩpicted in the Abhidammatt hasangaho.
Delhi, 1989.

2832. Pandey, Sharmistha
Studies in the Avadana literature with special reference to the Devyaradana.
Delhi, 1971.

2833. Pandey, Vishwanath
Nature of consciousness in early Buddhism.
Bombay, 1976.

2834. Panth, Ravindra
A critical edition of the Mohaviechedani abhidha mmamalika tthavannana with exahaustive introduction and explanatory notes.
Delhi, 1987.

2835. Pathak, Om Prakash
Prayogika manovigyana: Piggala Pannatti paripekshya mein (H). Delhi, 1987.

2836. Pezzali, Analia
The optical discipline of Buddhism.
BHU, 1958.

2837. Pharmaha, Phidhure V.
Buddhism in Thailand: Its impact on the life.
Marathawada, 1993.

2838. Phesode, P. Chalta
Buddhism in south East Asia.
Magadh, 1984.

2839. Phrngsai, Upashika Arree
A critical on analytical study of the therigathe and its atthakatha with special reference to their historical aspect.
Magadh, 1983.

2840. Pin-Askorn Phramaha Tuen
Buddhist concept of Karuna and world peace.
BHU, 1989.

2841. Poonam Rani
Hindu Baudh and Jain dharmon ke sandarbh mein manushyon ke swaroop aur uski karam niyati: Ek tulanatmak adhyayan (H).
Bhagalpur, 1988.

2842. Pratap Chandra
The concept of self in early Buddhism.
Saugar, 1970.

2843. Purohit, Anupam Gopal
Buddhism during the Kushan period with special reference to arts and architecture.
Delhi, 1995.

2844. Rada, Ivekovic
The problem of soul in Pali Buddhism (Supported by evidence from the Satta-Patika and the Milindapanho): A critical and Comparative Study.
Delhi, 1973.

2845. Raghavendrachari, S.V.
A comparative study of the Chinese and Tibetan versions of Patitavistara with an introduction to Lalita vistara as a Mahayana text.
Delhi, 1968.

2846. Rai, Jiwan
Prachina Afganistan mein Buddhisattva: Ek vishleshan (H).
BHU, 1990.

2847. Raja Ganeshan, D.
Buddha myth and complex: The problem of world alienation in the human life cycle.
Madras, 1987.

2848. Rajiv, Ram Subhag Singh
Attitude towards meal eating Buddhism from the beginning to the end of the 8th century A.D.
Delhi, 1987.

2849. Rakkhita, B.S.
A critical study of house holders discipline in Thervada Buddhism.
Poona, 1968.

2850. Ramteka, Deodas Liluji
A study of revival of Buddhism in the 20th century India.
Delhi, 1983.

2851. Rana, Ram Kumar
A study of Buddhist Laity in Chinees society from 4th to 8th century A.D.
Delhi, 1989.

2852. Ravindra Kumar
A study of the Dohakasa.
Delhi, 1991.

2853. Rastogi, Reena
Bharat mein Baudh sanskriti ka uday aur vikas: Ek adhyayan (H).
Lucknow, 1990.

2854. Rawal, Bimala
Dhammapade ka sanskritik adhyayan (H).
Delhi, 1986.

2855. Rewatha, Dadangoda
Buddha Dharma mein yog sadhana (H).
BHU, 1990.

2856. Racha, Sosaria Santana
Towards the Abhidhamma theory of interpretation: A critical analysis of the Attasalini.
Delhi, 1993.

2857. Sadhukhan, Sanjit Kumar
Uddyotakaras repulation of the Buddhista (S).
Calcutta, 1991.

2858. Sahay, Vinod Kishore
The concept of jeewan mukli according to the Gita and the Dhammapada.
Bihar, 1975.

2859. Saini, Sunita
Social and political history of the sixteen Mahajinapadas.
Delhi, 1991.

2860. Sakyabhinand, P.W.
Buddhism and Marxist ideology.
BHU, 1988.

2861. Samanatissa, V. Modagoda
A study of social and moral norms as depicted in the Vinay Patrika.
Delhi, 1986.

2862. Samerchit, P.S.
Buddha sasana kammavadessa avadharana.
BHU, 1987.

2863. Sanjiah, P.
The development of Buddhist study in Thailand and India.
Magadh, 1985.

2864. Santina, Krishna Datta
A few Tibatian Buddhist deities.
Delhi, 1981.

2865. Santina, Pater Della
Madhyamika schools in India.
Delhi, 1979.

2866. Sappadantree, Chavalit
History of Buddhism in Thailand.
Vishwa Bharati, 1994.

2867. Saroa, K.T.S.
Origin of Buddhism.
Delhi, 1996.

2868. Sarma, Rakeshranjan
The studies in the philosophy of Buddhist vijnanavada.
Calcutta, 1935.

2869. Sekido Nario
The study of the Mahayana Buddhism with special reference to the Saddharma Sutra and the Mahabharata Bhism Puran and Shantiparva.
Delhi, 1992.

2870. Seneviratna, S.D. Suresh
Social base of early Buddhism in South East India and Sri Lanka 3rd century. B.C. to 3rd century A.D.
JNU, 1987.

2871. Seth, Ved
Study of biographies of the Buddha Based on Pali and Sanskrit sources.
Delhi, 1988.

2872. Sharma, Ambika Dutt
Baudh darshan mein swalakahana kee avadharana.
BHU, 1988.

2873. Sharma, Bhagat Ram
The influence of Buddhism in the life of the people of Japan.
Delhi, 1992.

2874. Sharma, Mathura Lal
The origin and development of magic and magical beliefs and superstitions in Buddhism (D. Litt.).
BHU, 1931.

2875. Sharma, Meera
Sarnath ke vishesh sandarbh mein Porvi Uttar Pradesh evam Bihar mein Baudh pratimanon ka vikas (H).
BHU, 1989.

2876. Sharmopadhyay, Phupdev
Acharya Nagarjuna krit vi grah vyavastniya granthasya samikshatmak adhyayanam (S).
Sampurnanand, 1993.

2877. Shamsi, B. Begam
Theory of creation in Tripatakas:
AMU, 1984.

2878. Sharma, Shiva Kumar
A comparative and critical study of the ethics of Buddhism, Jainism and Bhagwat Gita.
Bihar, 1967.

2879. Shashi, Bala
Japani Baudh kala mein dwadash Hindu dev pauranik vaidik tatha Baudh sanskriti sahitya ke alok mein (H), (S).
HP, 1982.

2880. Shastri, Nikhilesh
A critical study of the Gridha vyahasutra with its Chines and Tibetan versions: Aselected study.
Delhi, 1989.

2881. Shastri, Srinivas
Vachaspati Mishra dwara Boudh darshanik sampradayon ka nirupan (H).
Agra, 1962.

2882. Shastry, Y.S.
Mahayanasutralenkar of Asanga: A study in vijananavada Buddhism
Bombay, 1988.

2883. Shadhka, Om Prakash
Buddha Dharma ka Nath Sampraya per prabhav (H).
Delhi, 1993.

2884. Shendga, Malati Janardan
A study the system of vajrayana literature with special reference to Havajratantra.
Delhi, 1967.

2885. Shiraishi, Ryokai
Ascerticism early Bdddhism and dharmasutras: A comparative study.
Delhi, 1995.

2886. Shukla, Aswani Kumar
Therwad ko Buddhi ghosh kee den (H), (S).
Gorakhpur, 1982.

2887. Shukla, Kamalesh
Baudh tantrik darshan ka sameekshatmak adhyayan: Sadhna sahitya ke vishesh sandarbh mein (H).
Gorakhpur, 1992.

2888. Shukla, Kunj Biharilal
A comparative study of Abhidhammatha Sangrah and Abhibharama Kosa.
Delhi, 1996.

2889. Shukla, Rama
Abhidhammapit kee Chittavimansa (H).
BHU, 1994.

2890. Singh, Arun Kumar
Origin and development of Buddhist images up to the Gupta period.
Delhi, 1990.

2891. Singh, Arun Kumar
Baudh manav evam atimanava: Ek anusheelan (H).
BHU, 1986.

2892. Singh, Balram
Baudh dharma darshan mein pratitya samulpadvad (H).
BHU, 1981.

2893. Singh, Birendra Kumar
The Buddhist theory of perception.
Bihar, 1972.

2894. Singh, Brahma
Live and contribution of Anagarika Dharmapal towards the revival of Buddhism in India.
Delhi, 1990.

2895. Singh, Chandra Sekhar
Bhikshu, Sangh ka swaroop tatha Bharcharys (H).
Gorakhpur, 1987.

2896. Singh, Durg Vijay
Baudh Siddhant: Nyaya bindu ke sandarbh mein (H).
BHU, 1992.

2897. Singh, Gopal Saran
Baudh sadhna: Udhav vikas aur swaroop.
Pali Tripatik se lakar Baudh Dhosh kal tak (H), (S).
Magadh, 1982.

2898. Singh, Jai Prasad
Meditation: A way to enlightment.
Delhi, 1987.

2899. Singh, Jitendra Pratap
Mahayan Baudh darshan mein Nirvan kee sameeksha (H).
BHU, 1992.

2900. Singh, Kaushal Kumar
Baudh praman pariksha Vachaspati Mishra ke alok mein (H).
BHU, 1994.

2901. Singh, Madhuri
Baudh tantra ke adhyatamik gaveshana (H).
Gorakhpur, 1989.

2902. Singh, Mrityunjay
Mahayan Baudha darshan mein parmita: Ek sameekshatmak adhyayan (H).
BHU, 1984.

2903. Singh, Priya Sen
A historical study of the ethics of vinaya with particular reference to the Vinay Sutra.
Delhi, 1988.

2904. Singh, Ram Chandra Prasad
Element of pragmatism in Buddhistic philosophy.
Bihar, 1969.

2905. Singh, Ram Nandan
From Hinayana to Mahayan: A study in the historical development.
Jammu, 1991.

2906. Singh, Ran Vijay
Baudh gyansiddhanta: Tarka shastra ke alok mein (H).
BHU, 1994.

2907. Singh, Shashi
Mahayana Baudh dharma, darshan mein trikayavad (H).
BHU, 1988.

2908. Singh, Sheela
Dakshin Poorvi Asia kee sanskriti mein Boddhi briksha.
BHU, 1986.

2909. Singh, Sheo Shankar
Vinaya Patrika mein pratibmbit Samaj (H).
Magadh, 1986.

2910. Singh, Shiv Kumar
Origin, growth expansion and decline of Buddhism in India and abroad (D. Litt.).
Bihar, 1973.

2911. Sinha, Jaydhari
Baudhdharma mein tantrik siddhant (H).
Bihar, 1967.

2912. Sobti, Harcharan Singh
The concept of Nbhana in early Buddhism.
Delhi, 1983.

2913. Sohan Lal
Contribution made by India towards the spread of Buddhism in Tibet from B.C. 600 to 1050 A.D.
Punjab, 1990.

2914. Srivastava, D.C.
Dharmakirties theory of inferential knowledge: A study in Nyaya bindu.
IIT, Kanpur, 1991.

2915. Srivastava, Priya
Prachin Baudh granthon mein vernit dhatu evam dhatukarma (H).
BHU, 1992.

2916. Srivastava, Sushil Kumar
Samajik, Dharmik pravittiyon evam Baudh dharma ka udaya (H).
Awadh, 1986.

2917. Sud, Meena
Dakshin Bharat mein Baudh dharma.
Delhi, 1987.

2918. Sukhram Pal
Milina Prashva: Ek sansritic adhyayan (H), (S).
Meerut, 1989.

2919. Suphacharapong, Bhikshu P.D.
The way of mental development in Buddhism: Theory and Practice.
Magadh, 1980.

2920. Surendra Kumar
Baudh sangeetayan ka sameekshatmak adhyayan (H), (S).
Magadh, 1983.

2921. Swaroopanand, Bhikshu
Dhammpad beerkayoh tulanatmak sameekshatmak adhyayanam (S).
Sampurnanand, 1993.

2922. Tafu, Chou
Three Buddhist Hymns restored into Sanskrit from Chinese transliteration of the 10th century A.D.
Bombay, 1944.

2923. Takahashi, Takahide
The role of foreigners in the evolution of Indian Buddhism from 1st to 7th century A.D.

2924. Takasaki, Jikido N.
Study on the Ratnagotravibhaga (Uttarutantra): Being a treatise on the tattagatrbha theory of Mahayana Buddhism.
Poona, 1957.

2925. Telwatte, Rahul
A critical study of the Mahavasta.
Delhi, 1972.

2926. Tanika, Chalam Rani
Deva Dharmachud early Buddhism: A study in comparision.
Bangalore, 1990.

2927. Tenzin, Suman Gyantso
Buddhism in Sikkim: A historical, cultural study of its introduction, growth and development in 17th, 18th and 19th century A.D.
Satya Sai, 1989.

2928. Thero, Ven I.P.
A critical assessment of Sanyata with special reference to Pali text.
Calcutta, 1966.

2929. Thero, Vilegoda Ariyadeva
The theory of social revolution in early Buddhism.
BHU, 1994.

2930. Tiwari, Mahesh
An examination of the concept of personality in Buddhist thought.
Bihar, 1961.

2931. Tiwari, Parashuram
Baudh niti darshan ka sameekshatmak adhyayan (H).
Saugar, 1986.

2932. Tiwari, Rekha
History of social and monestic enactment in Pali vinaya.
Delhi, 1992.

2933. Tripathi, Dinesh Chandra
Acharya varrupa sidhpada ni vattamtri kane, parisheelanam (S).
BHU, 1988.

2934. Tsering, Nawang
The doctrine of the Pramnabhuta Buddha.
Panjabi, 1987.

2935. Tsering, Phuntsok
A study of rise of sects in Buddhism in Tibet. 800 A.D. to 1600 A.D.
Delhi, 1985.

2936. Upadhyay, Muralidhar
Dhammasangani: Ek darshanik anusheelan.
Magadh, 1984.

2937. Uyesugi, Nobauti
A study in the psychology of the Padi abhidhamma, (S).
Poona, 1986.

2938. Veena Kumari
Buddhist doctrine in Sanskrit Mahakavyas till 400 A.D.
Delhi, 1985.

2939. Verma, Pushpa
A historical and cultural history of Saddharmapandarika sutra.
Delhi, 1992.

2940. Vijay Laxmi
A comparative study of Buddha Charita and Raghubansha.
Delhi, 1986.

2941. Vijay Rani
The Buddhist philosophy as propounded in Mimansa sloka varttika.
Kurukshetra, 1978.

2942. Vyanjana
Theravada Buddhist ethics with special reference to visiddhimaya.
BHU, 1990.

2943. Vyas, Chandra Sekhar
Buddhist theory of perception with special of reference to pramanayavarttaka of Dharmakriti.
BHU, 1989.

2944. Yadav, Giridhar
Baudh darshan mein vyapti aur hatwabhas (H).
BHU, 1995.

2945. Yamunelal
Buddhist missionaries and their activities in India and abroad from earliest times to 10th century A.D.
Lucknow, 1989.

2946. Yooyod, Upasika Suman
Conception of Nibbana in Theravada Buddhism.
Vishwa Bharati, 1978.

JAIN PHILOSOPHY

2947. Atre, Shri Ram Vasudeo
Philosophy of Mahabira: A critical study.
Poona, 1963.

2948. Bhargava, Dayanand
Jain ethics.
Delhi, 1968.

2949. Bhattacharya, Manjula
Jain dharma mein Ishwarvad kee samalochana (H).
BHU, 1992.

2950. Bhayani, Harivallabh C.
The Paumchater of Suayambhu deva.
Bombay, 1952.

2951. Bothra, Puspa
The Jain theory of perception.
Calcutta, 1970.

2952. Chandra, K.R.
A critical study of Paum Charia and other related topics.
Bihar, 1963.

2953. Chhabra, Raj Kumar
Jain darshan mein dravya kee avadharana aur karan karya sambandh.
Rajasthan, 1990.

2954. Dalal, M.N.
A critical and comparative study of Jain spiritualism.
Poona, 1985.

2955. Dige, Arhaddas Bandoba
Jain yog ka alochanatmak adhyayan (H).
BHU, 1969.

2956. Divya Prabha
Arhint Tattwa: Ek alochanatmak adhyayan (H).
Vikram, 1969.

2957. Gadsu. P.S. Mashram
Conception of anupraksa in Jainism and Buddhism.
Nagpur, 1984.

2958. Ghosh, Pralay Kanti
Jain concept of omniscience: A critical study.
Vishwa Bharati.

2959. Gundappa Kalshatge Vavanu
Jain psychology. Jain theory of soul: Some problems of Jain psychology.
Karnataka, 1959.

2960. Jain, Ashok Kumar
Theory of anekantvad in Jain philosophy (S).
Garhwal, 1986.

2961. Jain, Bhag Chandra
Studies in Jainism and Buddhism through Sanskrit Sources (D. Litt.).
Nagpur, 1990.

2962. Jain, Charitra Lata
Jain agman mein straman.
Rajasthan, 1993.

2963. Jain, Darshan Prabha
Jain darshan ko Acharya Haribhadra Surika Yogdan (H), (S).
Rajasthan, 1989.

2964. Jain, Harindra Bhushan
Jain Aagumshastra ke anusar manav ka vikas (H).
Saugar, 1957.

2965. Jain, Hemant Kumar
Bhatta Kalankrit-logheey strya: Ek darshanik vivechan (H).
BHU, 1990.

2966. Jain, Jai Kumar
Parsvantha Charita ka samikshatmak adhyayan (H), (S).
BHU, 1977.

2967. Jain, Jitendra Kumar
Philosophical evaluation of Jain literary work of 10th century A.D.
Sukhadia, 1993.

2968. Jain, Komal
Jain agam mein nari (H).
Vikram, 1985.

2969. Jain, Lal Chand
Jain sahitya mein Mahabharat Puran ke vishesh sandarbh mein (H), (S).
Vikram, 1988.

2970. Jain, Lal Chand
Jain darshan mein atam vichar: Alochanatmak evam tulanatmak adhyayan (H).
BHU, 1977.

2971. Jain, Mahipal
Jain karma siddhant ka ek tulanatmak alochanatmak adhyayan (H).
Agra, 1978.

2972. Jain, Narendera Kumar
Jain darshan mein valankya ka swaroop (H).
Rohilkhand, 1987.

2973. Jain, Rajkumar
Jain darshan mein gyan ka swaroop (H).
Rajasthan, 1989.

2974. Jain, Rekha
Jain Shravakochar paranpara mein Acharya Sumantra Bhadra ka yogdan (H), (S).
Kanpur, 1985.

2975. Jain, Sadhvi Dharamshilaji
Sanskrit Granthargat Jain darshan a til navtatve (M).
Poona, 1978.

2976. Jain, Sadhvi Priyadarshana
Jain sadhana paddhati mein dyan yog (H).
Poona, 1988.

2977. Jain, Sagarmal
Buddha evam Gita ke achar darshan ke sandarbh mein Jain achar darshan ka tulanatmak evam samalochanatmak adhyayan (H).
Jiwaji, 1971.

2978. Jain, Sumati Chand
The structure and frontier of the soul in Jainism.
Agra, 1960.

2979. Jan, Shanti
Jaina mysticism.
Udaipur, 1971

2980. Jain, Sudeshan Lal
A philosophical study of the Uttaradyanasutra.
BHU, 1967.

2981. Jain, Sudha
Jain Shravakercharka Adhyayan.
Dharmamrit ke vishesh sandarbh mein.
Saugar, 1989.

2982. Jain, Sukhnandan
Jain darshan mein nyayavad: Ek sanskritic adhyayan (S).
Meerut, 1977.

2983. Jainarya, Susheta Kumari
Jain Diwakar Muni-Shri Chauthamalji Maharaj aur unka Hindi Sahitya (H).
SNDT, 1988.

2983a. Janyanprabha, Jaingadhvi
Jain darshan mein jeevatma.
Poona, 1991.

2984. Jayadarshita, Shriji Sadhvishri
Philosophy of sachana of Jainism.
Bhavanagar, 1989.

2985. Lodha, Kanchan
Jain mat mein Saiyabad ka tarkik adhyayan (H).
Jodhpur, 1979.

2986. Lakhanda, Kulbhushan
Jain strota sahitya ka alochanatmak adhyayan (H).
Vikram, 1986.

2987. Mallick, Jagdish Narayan
Influence of Jainism on Sarvodaya philosophy.
Bihar, 1966.

2988. Manorama
Jain darshan mein karma siddhant ek adhyayan (S).
Dayanand, 1987.

2989. Maghani, Suraj Labh Chand
The special contribution of Jainism to Indian philosophy.
Bombay, 1988.

2990. Mahta, Manjula
Trisastisalakapurush Charita mein varnit Mahabir

Charit ka tulanatmak adhyayan (H).
BHU, 1977.

2991. Mehta, Mukul Raj
Concept of spiritual development and liberation of Jainism.
BHU, 1987.

2991a. Mehta, Sangita
Jain sanskrit sahitya ka alok mein Vardhaman Mahabir: Ek adhyayan (H).
Devi Ahilya, 1991.

2992. Muti Prabha
Jain dharma mein yog: Ek alochanatmak adhyayan (H).
Vikram, 1988.

2993. Pancholi, Badri Narayan Sharma
Shrivigya Bhikshu darshan vimarshakhya (D. Litt.).
Darbhanga, 1986.

2994. Pandey, Brij Kishore
Jain darshan ke sandarbh mein
Acharya Sumant Bhadra ke achar siddhant ka samikshatmak adhyayan (H).
Magadh, 1977.

2995. Pandey, Madan Mohan
Dhammpad ka sahityik evam darshanik parisheelan (H).
Magadh, 1986.

2996. Pandya, H.O.
Jain sammat Gyancharya Vishishtahmaley Giri krut Nanda Tika ne adhare (G).
Gujarat, 1979.

2997. Rajande, B.B
Jain conception of Mokshya.
BHU, 1958.

2998. Rajjan Kumar
Jain dharma mein samadhimaran kee avadharana (H).
BHU, 1989.

2999. Rana, Jagmohinder Singh
The concept of Panch permesthi in Jain philosophy.
BHU, 1992.

3000. Rathanakara, A.B.
Jain dharma in Rahnatans work.
Mysore, 1981.

3001. Sahu, Anand Chand
Jainism in ancient Orissa.
Vishwa Bharati, 1987.

3002. Santappanavur, P.B.
The ethics religious doctrine as discussed in Karakanda Chariu: A study.
Karnataka, 1993.

3003. Sekhar, B.
Dharma in Sramanic traditions with a special reference to Jana tradition.
Madras, 1995.

3004. Shabeen Ahmad
A critical study of the Sravagarammjon (S).
AMU, 1986.

3005. Shah, H.J.
Theism and Jainism.
Gujarat, 1990.

3006. Shah, Jagrati M.
Jain darshan and sankhya yoga bhasyan satadarshan (S).
Gujarat, 1969.

3007. Shah, S.P.
Karma theory in Jainism based on Jain Agames in

philosophy.
Bombay, 1983.

3008. Sharma, Ajit Shah Deo
Agam sahitya mein Jain achar (H).
BHU, 1968.

3009. Sharma, I.C.
Terapanthi sect of Jainism belonging to Swetambara School.
Rajasthan, 1959.

3010. Sharma, Seema Rani
Jain parampara mein dhyan ka swaroop: Ek sameekshatmak adhyayan (H).
Rohilkhand, 1990.

3011. Sharma, Subodh Chandra
Parshvanath charitam ka sahityik adhyayan (H), (S).
Rohilkhand, 1986.

3012. Shastri, Indira Chandra
Epestomology of the Jain Agams.
BHU, 1952.

3013. Shukla, Virendra Kumar
Trimanikya Dev Suri Virichit Malayai ka sameekshatmak adhyayan (S).
Meerut, 1985.

3014. Sikdar, Jogendra Chandra
Doctrine of matter in Jainism (D. Litt.).
Jabalpur, 1968.

3015. Singh, Indumati
Jainism in Magadh.
Magadh, 1986.

3016. Singh, Krishna Bihari
Value and importance of conduct in Jainism and Buddhism.
Magadh, 1984.

3017. Singh, Narendra Kumar
A critical study of Agana and Gyani Jainism.
Vishwa Bharati, 1986.

3018. Singh, Ramji
The Jain concept of Omniscience.
Bhagalpur, 1966.

3019. Singh, Reeta Kumari
Jain sahitya mein krishna katha ka tulanatmak adhyayan (H), (S).
BHU, 1989.

3020. Sinha, Boshistha Narayan
Treatment of Ahimsa in Jainism.
BHU, 1967.

3021. Sisodia, S.K.
A comparative study of ethical and metaphical srimilarities and differences of main sects of Jainism.
Sukhadia, 1993.

3022. Snehlata
A study of Pramaya parice heads of Prushana Ratnakara.
Delhi, 1978.

3023. Sogani, Kamal Chand
Ethical doctrine of Jainism.
Rajasthan, 1961.

3024. Srinarayan
Jain abhilekhon ka sanskritic adhyayan: prarambh se lagbhag 1200 isvi tak.
BHU, 1990.

3025. Sudhir Kumar
Rise and development of Tarapanth sect.
Sukhadia, 1990.

3026. Sumitrabai, B.N.
A literary and cultural history of the work of

Harivanshapuran of Jainasena.
Mysore, 1987.

3027. Sunil Kumar
A historical study of early Buddhist and Jain monestic order.
Rajasthan, 1986.

3028. Surekha, Srisadhvi
Jain darshan mein samyakalwa ka swaroop (H).
Rajasthan, 1986.

3029. Tatia, Nathumal
Some fundamental problem of Jain philosophy, (D. Litt).
Calcutta, 1951.

3030. Tiwari, Muni Ram
Basubandh aur unki kritiyon (H).
BHU, 1992.

3031. Tripathi, Ranjan
Jain Tarangini: Ek sameekshatmak evam alochnatmak adhyayan (S).
Kanpur, 1987.

3032. Verma, Harendra Prasad
An appraisal of Jainism in modern perspective with special reference to the philosophy of Lord Mahabira.
Bihar, 1978.

3032a. Vijaylakshmi,
The concept of substance in Jain thought.
Jodhpur, 1979.

SIKH PHILOSOPHY

3033. Ashta, Dhawan Pal
Poetry of the Dasam Granth.
Panjab, 1958.

3034. Bath, Sukhwinder Kaur
A philosophical study of Guru Teg Bahadur Vani in the context of Gurumat.
Nanakdeo, 1991.

3035. Bhatia, Satbir Singh
Sikh dharma kee nitika naveen upadan.
Devi Ahilya, 1986.

3036. Barar, Rajinder
Sikh exegetical writing: A study in various traditions.
Punjabi, 1989.

3037. Dhillon, Balwant Singh
Sikh Guru and Mughal state: A study of the political attitude.
Nanakdeo, 1989.

3038. Guinness, Anthea
Textual and themitic study of Guru Arjun's Sukhmani with special reference to Nam and the man of God.
Punjabi, 1989.

3039. Gunwant Kaur
Gurunanak Bani vich adarsh munukhde sankalp (P).
Gurunanak Dev, 1987.

3040. Gupta, Vishesh Kumar
The process of institutionalisation of Sikh Shrines with special reference to prominent Sikh Shrines in Delhi.
Rohilkhand, 1989.

3041. Gurunam Kaur
Reasons and revelations in Sikhism.
Punjabi, 1986.

3042. Gurubachan Kaur
Janamsakhi of Bhai Bala: Authentic text and critical editing.
Gurunanak, 1978.

3043. Gurupreet Kaur
Historical analysis of Sikh rahitnamas,
Gurunanak, 1989.

3044. Jaspal Kaur
Paramperaga janam sakhiyon vich Sikh siddhant vishwas to vichar (P).
Gurunanak, 1992.

3045. Johar, Shemsher Singh
Spread of Sikh religion and culture in Jammu and Kashmir upto 1961.
Jammu, 1985.

3046. Kapoor, Sukhbir Singh
Guru Govind Singh's concept of an ideal man.
Panjab, 1984.

3047. Kulwant Kaur
A critical study of the Bani of Bhagat Ravidas as found in Gurunanak Sahab.
Gurunanak, 1982.

3048. Lahiri, Lajwanti Vadhumak
Concept of man in Sikhism.
Poona, 1984.

3049. Mehrotra, Anita
The native of ethical and spiritual life in Sikhism.
BHU, 1987.

3050. Metharu, Dharam Singh
An analytical study of the social thought of Guru Govind Singh.
Punjabi, 1993.

3051. Mullan, Chareulosmond, M.C.
A survey of the religious belief and practices of the Sikhs in rural Punjab.
Gurunanakdev, 1981.

3052. Raja, Mrigendra Singh
Gururanak's doctrine of name.
Gurunanak, 1981.

3053. Rajinder Kaur
A comparative study of monotheism in semeha and Sikh tradition.
Punjabi, 1990.

3054. Rajinder Kaur
The Sikh conception of Godhood.
Panjab, 1965.

3055. Rajinder Kaur
Guru Govind Singh kee vanika sangeetak mahatva (H).
Delhi, 1991.

3056. Asber, Jasbir Singh
Gian Ratnawali Jonamsakti Sri Guru Nanakdeoji: Editing and texual study.
Gurunanak Dev, 1983.

3057. Sagar, Savinderjit Singh
Historical analysis of Gurunanak Prakash by Santosh Singh.
Gurunanak Dev, 1985.

3058. Satnam Singh
Faith, grace and prayara, Sikh religious thought: An analytic study.
Delhi, 1992.

3059. Sehgal, Manamohan
Philosophical basis of Guru Nanak's Literature.
Panjab, 1962.

3060. Sharma, Vinod Kumar
Satrahavi shatabdi ka ek hastlikhit prati Gurumukhi Sukhmoni shansar namka sanskritic adhyayan (H).
Panjab, 1983.

3061. Singh, Awatar
Ethics of the Sikhs.
Panjab, 1968.

3062. Singh, Baljinder
The life and times of Guru Hargovind.
Punjabi, 1992.

3063. Singh, Balkar
Sikh mysticism: An analytical study in experience and expression.
Punjabi, 1983.

3064. Singh, Dalbir
Sikhism in sixteenth century.
Punjabi, 1983.

3065. Singh, Dhararmjit
Gurunanak ka vishleshnatmak adhyayan samaj ke sandarbh mein (H).
Gurunanak, 1975.

3066. Singh, Gurnak
Twentieth century exgesil of Guru Granth sabib by Sikh scholars: A critical study.
Panjabi, 1993.

3067. Singh, Gurubachan
Granth Sahib mein khari Boli (H).
Osmania, 1990.

3068. Singh Gurusharanjit
Fundamental concerns of Gurunanak Bani.
Gurunanak, 1993.

3069. Singh, Harbansh
The doctrine of Degh-Tegh as a socio-economic ideals in Sikh thought.
Panjab, 1985.

3070. Singh, Harbhajan
Sikh Dharma vich Jyoti da sankalp (P).
Panjab, 1993.

3071. Singh, Hari Mahendra
Sikh dharma mein bhakti kee avadharana: Ek sameekshatmak adhyayan (H).
BHU, 1987.

3072. Singh, Harvinder
Karma and rebirth in Indian religious thought with special reference to Sikhism.
Punjabi, 1990.

3073. Singh, Jasbir
The concept of God in Gurubani.
Gurunanak, 1978.

3074. Singh, Jasmittar
Sikh Rahitanamas: A socio cultural study.
Gurunanak, 1991.

3075. Singh, Kailash Bihari
Nanak Panthi (Sikhatter) Sant parempara (H).
Magadh, 19.

3076. Singh, Kirpal
Gurunanak: A document biography.
Gurunanak, 1981.

3077. Singh, Rattan
Critical study of the puranic composition in the Da Sam Granth.
Panjab, 1962.

3078. Singh, Ravinder
An analytical study of Sikh gestheties.
Punjabi, 1995.

3079. Singh, Santokh
Philosophical foundation of the Sikh value system.
Poona, 1978.

3080. Singh, Sulkhan
Udasis under Sikh rules: 1750-1850.
Gurunanak, 1985.

3081. Singh, Surinder
Dhampad and Guru Nanak Bani: A comparative study.
Gurunanak, 1991.

3082. Singh, Surjeet
Sukhmani Ek alochanatmak adhyayan.
Gurunanak, 1977.

3083. Singh, Taran
Guru Nanak as a poet.
Punjab, 1959.

3084. Singh, Wazir
Philosophy of humanism in Guru Nanak's compositions.
Punjabi, 1970.

3085. Sodhi, Nirmal Singh
Modernisation and the religious practices amongst the Sikhs: A sociological study.
Punjabi, 1981.

3086. Suveet
The Sikh pathway to God realisation with special reference to its stage of spiritual progress.
Punjabi, 1995.

3087. Tarsem Lal
Concept of seva in Gurumat.
Panjab, 1990.

3088. Urminder Kaur
Institutional development of Sikhism: A philosophical perspectives.
Punjabi, 1993.

3089. Usha
The concept of death in Guru Nanak Bani.
Gurunanak, 1982.

ISLAMIC PHILOSOPHY

3090. Abdul Ali
Islam as religion of humanism: A case study. (D. Litt).
Lucknow, 1989.

3091. Abdul Hamid Fazil
A critical study of Sirat of the Prabhat written in Arabic from 1850 to 1970 A.D.
AMU, 1993.

3092. Abdul Razak, P.K.
Modern trends in the interpretations of the Holy Quran.
Calicut, 1993.

3093. Ahmad Mohammed, Husain Al Jarrah
Adwat-al Shartwel Mantiqi at Sharti Fil Guran AL Karim.
Jamia, 1991.

3094. Akhtar Hussain, M.N. Khizar
Sufism in the Deccan early phase.
Marathwada, 1987.

3095. Bhatnagar, Rajindra Swaroop
The philosophy of Sufism in Urdu poetry with special reference to Mixtaqi Dard, Atish and Ghalib.
Allahabad, 1960.

3096. Bhaumik, Ranjit Kumar
Impact of Islamic Art, Culture and Language on the West.
Calcutta, 1992.

3097. Farman Hussain
Qurani akhlaqut ka marooti muteela (H).
AMU, 1986.

3098. Faruqi, Imadual Hasan Azad
The Tanjumanal Quran: A critical analysis of Maulana Abdul Kalam Azad, approach to the understanding of

the Quran.
Jammu, 1980.

3099. Gooshoh, Jalal Soodat
Life and religious work of ulmacqum during third and Forth Century Hijri.
AMU, 1982.

3100. Hasnain, Nazrul
Teaching of Hazrat Ali-Bin Abi Talib in the light of Nahjul Blaghat.
Lucknow, 1989.

3101. Jafri, S. Razia
A detailed study of prominent sects in Islam with special reference to Sharnam.
AMU, 1987.

3102. Jasavatunisa, Begam
A critical study and edition of satwatul Gareeb Wauswatul Areeb.
Osmania, 1991.

3103. Khaki, Ghnai
Quran on the development of social science from early Islamic to the end of Abbaside period.
Kashmir, 1992.

3104. Khan, Abdul Aleem
A critical edition of Nazhat A.F. Tallab Fi manaquip A.L. Ashob.
AMU, 1990.

3105. Khan, Anwar Ali
Religious ideas of Jamaluddin A.L. Afghani.
AMU, 1963.

3106. Khan, Basir Ahmad
Islamic uloom mein Hazi Imdadullah kee khidmat wa asorant.
AMU, 1988.

3107. Khan, Iqtidar Mohammad
Islamic movement in India after 1947.
Jamia, 1993.

3108. Khan, Israr Ahmad
Socio-political and religious implications of the Islamic mission of the prophet Mohammed during his Makkam Phase.
AMU, 1990.

3109. Khan, Khainanisa Sultan
The influence of Suficism on the Deccani literature of Hazrat-Banda Newaz R.
Poona, 1992.

3110. Khan, Mohd Abdul Gaffoor
A critical edition of Khulasat U. Siyari Syed II Busher.
Osmania, 1991.

3111. Khan, Mohd. Abdul Jameel
Life and work of Allama Rasheed Raza with special reference to his commentary of the Quran.
Osmania.

3112. Khan, Mohammad Anwarullah
A critical edition of A.L. Bulzha Fi Tavazim-I-Aimmatin Nahw-I-Wal-Lugah.
Osmania, 1990.

3113. Khan, Mohammad Nooruddin
A study of the basic philosophical concepts in the Literary works of Sir Mohammad Iqbal.
Osmania, 1995.

3114. Khatibi, Mohd. Rehullah
Maulana Jalaluddin Rumi-Aura ka tulsafa, mathnavi Manvwi kee roshni mein.
Jamia, 1995.

3115. Khozair, Mousa Zafar
Tafseer Al Quran BIL Quran Indal Allama: AL-Taba Tabai.
AMU, 1987.

3116. Majumdar, Raina Khatoon
Life and work of Maulana Syed Abdul Hasan Ali Naqwi.
Calcutta, 1991.

3117. Maqsood Ahmad
Contribution of North India to the study of Islamic history from 1890 to 1947 A.D.
Baroda, 1989.

3118. Mohammad, Abdur Rasheed
Islamic views on crime and punishment.
Osmania, 1973.

3119. Mohammad Ali, A.
Dirasalun Muquranatun Li Sahita Hummans Bin Munabbah ma Kutab al abudeesal Ukhra.
Madras, 1992.

3120. Mohammad Hanif
Naqshbandia Muzaddida mazhria system of Sufism.
Agra, 1964.

3121. Mohammad Khalid, S.
Indias contribution to Ha dith literature in Arabic.
Jamia, 1993.

3122. Mohammad, Mabasharuddin
Tareequthul Mohammedia fils seerath Ul-Ahmedia.
Osmania, 1991.

3123. Mohammad, Rup Chand Ali
Concept of Allah and his unity in Islam.
Gauhati, 1993.

3124. Mohammad Saleem
Dir ayal-e-Hadith ka Tafsila Jaizah.
AMU, 1993.

3125. Mohammad Tabar
Bibliometric analysis of the literature in the field of Islamic studies.
Calicut, 1989.

3126. Mohammad Yaqub
Nashl A.L. Tatsir watatwwur ILA earan al salislil hizrah origin of tatsir and its development upto the end of 3rd century Hijri (D. Litt.).
Lucknow, 1990.

3127. Mohammad Yasufuddin
Economic theories of Islam.
Osmania, 1947.

3128. Mohamudul Haque
Mufti Mohammad Abdudu: His life and work.
AMU, 1964.

3129. Naqvi, Mohammad Ghouse
A critical study of Quranic recitation alongwith a critical edition of manuscript entitled Kitab AL Tabseria Fi-AL Qirat AL-Saba by Abu Mohammad Mukki Bin Talib compiled in the year 392 AH died in the year 437 AH.
Osmania, 1981.

3130. Naseen Zehra
Sir William Miyur kee tarakha Islam ke tavqeedi mutalia.
AMU, 1989.

3131. Nasira, Amtul Mazid
Naqush bandi system of Sufism (Mysticism).
Osmania, 1957.

3132. Niazi, Alau-Rehman
Islam kee adarsh uyevasthe ka pratyaya Guriski samajik prasangikata (H).

3133. Noor Ahmed, Babu
Organisation of Islamic Conference objective and structure.
JNU, 1990.

3134. Quzi, Mohammad Rizwanullah.
Maulana Mohammad Anwar Shah Kashmiri: His life and work.
AMU, 1966.

3135. Qusmi, M. Soud Alam
A critical study of the Quranic thought of Shah Walliullah. Delhavi.
AMU, 1992.

3136. Ragheeb Hussain
Sufism in India.
Bihar, 1964.

3137. Rahman, Mohd. Mabhoobur
Muslim religious reform movement in Bengal during the nineteenth century.
AMU, 1995.

3138. Rahman, Syed Ashsanur
Hazrat Ali Ibna Abitalib: His religious and political activities as they are reflected in his sermons.
BHU, 1990.

3139. Razi, Hanifa
Abdullah Ibn Masood and his legal system.
AMU, 1967.

3140. Rizvi, Razia Khatoon
Some biological teaching of the Holi Quran.
AMU, 1986.

3141. Saleha, A.H.S.
Quran ke urdu Tarjume.
Bombay, 1901.

3142. Sayyed, Ahsan
Trends in Islam in Saudi Arabia.
AMU, 1987.

3143. Seorge, Koorichal F.R.
Christian studies of Islam in India.
AMU, 1984.

3144. Shabnam Anjum
Ummahatt—AL Meemi neen ke Maneqib wa Fazil aur unke karama marviyat.
AMU, 1995.

3145. Shore, Syed Hussain Qadri
Gassali: His religious and moral philosophy.
Osmania, 1958.

3146. Shoukat Ali Jeenah
Institutions of marriage and divorce in Islam: An appraisal.
Bombay, 1984.

3147. Siddiqui, M.H.
Islam in the changing world.
Bombay, 1984.

3148. Siddiqui, Mohammad Murtuza
The Qudriyya system of sufism.
Osmania, 1960.

3149. Siddiqui, Zafar Ahmad
Philosophy of Ibn Tufayl.
AMU, 1984.

3150. Sofia, Bano
Maulana Azad's reconstruction of religious thought in Islam.
Osmania, 1977.

3151. Syeda, Firdowsi Khatun
Amriter Sandhana abhisar: Sufibadar aloke darshnik

darshanik vishleshan.
Vishwa Bharati, 1992.

3152. Syed, Faiyaj Haider
The contribution of the Shia blma.
AMU, 1982.

3153. Syed, Moyeenul Hague
Ibanan Nadim on religious sects in ancient India.
Calcutta, 1991.

3154. Syed, N.B.
Quran kee chand Mumtaz Tafseeranka adabi aur Lisani Jaiza.
Bombay, 1986.

3155. Syed, Waheed Akhtar
Khaja Mir Dard's contribution to Sufism.
Osmania, 1961.

3156. Tirmizi, B.A.
Muslim saints of Ahmadabad and Patna.
Gujarat, 1967.

3157. Ummihani, Fakruzzaman
Quran ka Tariq-e-Istidlal (U).
AMU, 1909.

3158. Vazeerunnisa
Hadith literature in India during the tenth century Hijra with special reference to Ali-AL Muttaqui as a traditionist.
Osmania, 1991.

3159. Vendulashy, Chaudri Prabha
Sufivad ke darshanik tatwa aur Bharatiya sanskriti ke aitihas mein unka sthan (H).
Meerut, 1995.

3160. Zia, Rehana
A critical study of Bayannul Quran: The commentary

of the Quran of Maulana Ashraf Ali Thanvi with special reference to exegetical literature in Urdu.
AMU, 1983.

3161. Zaidkhalid, Mohammad Al Zarigut.
Social Justice in Islam.
Jamia, 1988.

CHRISTIAN PHILOSOPHY

3162. John, Joseph Antony
A research on ancient Catholic Churches in Tirunalveli district.
Madurai, 1990.

3163. Justus, M.
History of protestant Christianity in Tinnevelly, 1785 to 1908.
Kerala, 1991.

3164. Selvaraj, Arulanadham G.
Structure, strategies and significance in the Gospel according St John.
Madurai, 1993.

3165. Sutar, Amar Madhur
Christianity in Western Maharashtra in the nineteenth century with special reference to Kolhapur, Satara, and Solapur districts.
Shivaji, 1991.

3166. Varghese, C.J.
Role of the orthodox Syrian Christians Mission in Kerala.
Gauhati, 1980.

SCHOLARS LIST

Singh, M. Kumar, 2622
Singh, Mrityanjay, 2902
Singh, M. Iboton, 2671
Singh, Mrityanjaya N., 639
Singh, Narendra, 1184
Singh, Nagendra, 158
Singh, Nagendra Kr., 3017
Singh, Nathuni, 1185
Singh, Neelam, 1846
Singh, Nibhai, 159
Singh, Padmakar, 1186
Singh, Param Hans., 2101
Singh, Paras Nath, 41
Singh, Pawan Kr., 1187
Singh, P. Suthon, 2412
Singh, Poonam, 1357
Singh, Prabhunath, 1847
Singh, Pramod Kr., 1188
Singh, Pratibha, 1189
Singh, Pratibha, 2413
Singh, Prem, 1190
Singh, Prithpal, 2182
Singh, Priyasen, 2903
Singh, Purnima, 2414
Singh, Pushpa, 2102
Singh, Radhey Syam, 1192
Singh, Radhika Raman, 2672
Singh, Raghav Pratap, 1193
Singh, R. Pratap, 1982
Singh, Rajdeo, 2673
Singh, Rajendra Kumar, 640
Singh, Raj Kumar S., 160
Singh, Rajnath, 1415
Singh, Rajpal, 1194
Singh, Ram, 1195
Singh, Ram Chandra Pd., 2904
Singh, Ramdutt, 2019
Singh, Ramdeo Prasad, 435
Singh, Ramji, 3018
Singh, Ramji, 2674
Singh, Ramkishan, 1848
Singh, R.K., 1191
Singh, Ramlal, 2181
Singh, Ram Nandan, 2905
Singh, Ram Naresh, 2675
Singh, Ram Pratap, 641
Singh, Ramashankar, 436
Singh, Ram Suresh, 2416
Singh, Rama, 2103
Singh, Rameshwar Pd., 1196
Singh, Ramvijay, 1197
Singh, Ranjit, 2676
Singh, Ramvijay, 2906
Singh, Rattan, 3077
Singh, Ravinder, 3078
Singh, Ravindra Nath, 2104
Singh, Reeta Kumari, 3019
Singh, Rudre Narain, 2677
Singh, Sadanand Prasad, 437
Singh, Samev Bahadur, 2419
Singh, Sankata Prasad, 2678
Singh, Santosh, 3079
Singh, Sudarshan, 2105
Singh, S., 2417
Singh, Shashi Devi, 1849
Singh, Sheo Shankar, 2909
Singh, Shashi, 2907
Singh, Sheela, 2908
Singh, Shiv Kumar, 2910
Singh, Soyam L, 438

ABBREVIATIONS

INSTITUTIONS OF HIGHER LEARNING AND RESEARCH

AMU	Aligarh Muslim University.
Agra	Dr. Bhim Rao Ambedkar University, Agra.
Andhra	Andhra University, Waltair.
Annamalai	Annamalai University, Annamalainagar.
Awadh	Dr. Ram Manohar Lohia University, Faizabad.
Awadesh	Awadesh Pratap Singh University, Rewa.
BHU	Banaras Hindu University, Varanasi.
Banasthali	Banasthali Vidyapith.
Bangalore	Bangalore University.
Barkatullah	Barkatullah Vishwavidyalaya, Bhopal.
Baroda	Maharaja Sayajirao University of Baroda, Vadodara.
Berhampur	Berhampur University.
Bharathiar	Barathiar University, Coimbatore.
Bharathidasan	Bharathidasan University, Tiruchirapalli.
Bihar	Babasaheb Bhimrao Ambedkar Bihar University, Muzaffarpur.
Bombay	University of Bombay.

Bundelkhand	University of Bundelkhand, Jhansi.
Burdwan	University of Burdwan.
Calcutta	University of Calcutta.
Calicut	University of Calicut.
Dayanand Ajmer	Dayanand Saraswati University, Ajmer.
Maharishi Dayanand	Maharishi Dayanand University, Rohtak.
Delhi	University of Delhi.
Devi Ahilya	Devi Ahilya Vishwavidyalaya, Indore.
Durgavati	Rani Durgavati Vishwavidyalaya, Jabalpur.
Garhwal	Hemvati Nandan Bahuguna Garhwal University, Srinagar.
Gauhati	Gauhati University, Guwahati.
Ghasidas	Guru Ghasidas University, Bilaspur.
Goa	Goa University.
Gorakhpur	University of Gorakhpur.
Gujarat	Gujarat University, Ahmedabad.
Gurukula	Gurukula Kangri Vishwavidyalaya, Hardwar.
Himachal Pradesh	Himachal Pradesh University, Shimla.
Saugar	Dr. Hari Singh Gour Vishwavidyalaya, Saugar.
Hyderabad	University of Hyderabad.
IIT, Bombay	Indian Institute of Technology, Bombay.
IIT, Delhi	Indian Institute of Technology, Delhi.
IIT, Kanpur	Indian Institute of Technology, Kanpur.
IIT, Kharagpur	Indian Institute of Technology, Kharagpur.
Indore	Devi Ahilya Vishwavidyalays, Indore.
JNU	Jawaharlal Nehru University, New Delhi.

Jadhavpur	Jadhavpur University, Calcutta.
Jagannath	Shri Jagannath Sanskrit Vishwavidyalaya, Puri.
Jamia	Jamia Millia Islamia, New Delhi.
Jammu	University of Jammu.
Jiwaji	Jiwaji University, Gwalior.
Jodhpur	Jai Narayan Vyas University, Jodhpur.
Karnatak	Karnatak University, Dharwad.
Kashi	Mahatma Gandhi Kashi Vidyapith, Varanasi.
Kerala	University of Kerala, Trivandrum.
Kumaun	Kumaun University, Nainital.
Kurukshetra	Kurukshetra University.
Madras	University of Madras.
Madurai	Madurai Kamaraj University.
Magadh	Magadh University, Bodh Gaya.
Mangalore	Mangalore University.
Marathwada	Marathwada University, Aurangabad.
Mithila	Lalit Narayan Mithila University, Darbhanga.
Mysore	University of Mysore.
NBU	North Bengal University, Rajarammohun-pur, Dist. Darjeeling.
NEHU	North Eastern Hill University, Shillong.
Nagarjuna	Nagarjuna University, Nagarjuna Nagar.
Nagpur	Nagpur University.
Nanak	Gurunanak Dev University, Amritsar.
Osmania	Osmania University, Hyderabad.
Panjab	Panjab University, Chandigarh.

Patna	Patna University.
Pondicherry	Pondicherry University.
Pune	University of Poona.
Punjabi	Punjabi University, Patiala.
Ravindra Bharati	Ravindra Bharati University, Calcutta.
Rajasthan	University of Rajasthan.
Rashtriya Sanskrit	Rashtriya Sanskrit Vidyapith, Tirupati.
Ravishankar	Ravishankar University, Raipur.
Rohilkhand	Rohilkhand University, Bareilly.
Sambalpur	Sambalpur University.
Sampurnanand	Sampurnanand Sanskrit Vishwavidyalaya, Varanasi.
Sathya Sai	Shri Sathya Sai Institute of Higher Learning, Anantpur.
Saurashtra	Saurashtra University, Rajkot.
Saugar	Dr. H.S. Gaur Vishwavidyalaya, Saugar.
Shastri Sanskrit	Shri Lal Bahadur Shastri Sanskrit Vidyapith, New Delhi.
Shivaji	Shivaji University, Kolhapur.
Sukhadia	Mohan Lal Sukhadia University, Udaipur.
Utkal	Utkal University, Bhubaneswar.
Venkateshwara	Shri Venkateshwara University, Tirupati.
Vikram	Vikram University, Ujjain.
Visva Bharati	Visva Bharati, Shantiniketan.

ABBREVIATIONS — SUBJECT

B	Bengali
G	Gujarati
H	Hindi
M	Marathi
P	Punjabi
S	Sanskrit
T	Tamil